John Levington

Power with God and with Men

John Levington

Power with God and with Men

ISBN/EAN: 9783337033569

Printed in Europe, USA, Canada, Australia, Japan

Cover: Foto ©Lupo / pixelio.de

More available books at **www.hansebooks.com**

POWER WITH GOD

AND

WITH MEN.

BY

REV. JOHN LEVINGTON.

But ye shall receive power after the Holy Ghost is come upon you.—Acts i, 8.

But the Comforter, the Holy Ghost, whom the Father will send in my name, he shall teach you all things.—John xiv, 26.

And they were all filled with the Holy Ghost, and began to speak, with other tongues, as the Spirit gave them utterance.—Acts ii, 4.

But unto them which are called, both Jews and Greeks, Christ the power of God, and the wisdom of God.—1 Cor. i, 24.

And Jesus came and spake unto them, saying, All power is given unto me in heaven and in earth. Go ye therefore, &c.—Matt. xxviii, 18.

PHILADELPHIA:
METHODIST BOOK ROOM, No. 1018 ARCH STREET.
S. W. THOMAS, Agent.
1868.

CONTENTS.

CHAPTER I.

On power in general. Power can only be discovered in the *phenomena*, or *facts*, resulting therefrom—The existence of the power is as certain as is the existence of the *phenomena* resulting therefrom—In every system there must be a grand central power, or primary cause of motion—The way to discover where and what this power is—Various conjectures as to what the peculiar power of Methodism is, are shown to be unsatisfactory—The advantages of knowing what, and where, this peculiar power is—The advantages of the method here adopted for that purpose—Sources from which facts shall be taken in support of the position—The grand errors which exclude the conditions of this power shall be exposed, . . . 15

CHAPTER II.

Facts of Methodist history down to the conversion of John and Charles Wesley—The poetry of Samuel Wesley and his sons—Mrs. Wesley's Academy—Her method of teaching, and its results—The burning of the Rectory and the narrow escape of John—The three sons sent to higher schools, and John and Charles finally to Oxford—The society at Oxford called the "Holy Club"—The voyage of John and Charles to America, and their labors there—Their return to England—Very interesting particulars—The first and many succeeding interviews with Peter Bohler—A minute account of their convictions and painful struggles; and, finally, of their conversion—The peculiar power is obtained, and begins to manifest itself, ... 22

CONTENTS.

CHAPTER III.

Whitefield's Conversion—His first Sermon and its effects—Providential preparations for the development of the power—Whitefield in America, J. Wesley in Germany, and Charles Wesley in England—They again meet in London, and with about sixty other persons have a Lovefeast, and a baptism of the Spirit—Wonderful developments of the power in London and Bristol—The first Circuit—The first Methodist Church—Numerous incidents, extraordinary and interesting—The new way works so well the old parish plan is abandoned—John Wesley claims the world for his parish—Summing up—The *conditions* of power are specified in nine particulars—The sum; *doctrine, experience,* and *practice.* These particulars are not peculiar to the *minister;* they are essential to the Christian character—An interesting sketch of the life of John Nelson is given in support of the argument. For the same purpose, facts are now adduced from the experience of Luther and the history of his times—Finally, facts are adduced from Apostolic times—Paul's experience is shown to be essentially one with those previously given, ... 64

CHAPTER IV.

Between the position specified, and that of the Pharisee, there is no medium—Pharisees, Sadducees, and Herodians, are presented in Scripture as representative classes of character, and are, as they ever have been, the grand enemies of Christianity—Pharisaism is fully investigated, by reference to Scripture and History—The principle upon which Pharisaism rests, is that of *human merit;* that upon which Christianity rests, is *grace coming through the merit of the atonement*—All who seek at all, rest their expectations upon one of these two principles —*Grace* and *faith* go together, as do merit and works—Pharisaism embraces a great variety of characters, but they all rest upon the same principle, viz: *merit;* hence the appeal is to naked justice: while the Christian rests upon the atonement and expects *all* of *mere grace*—The Pharisee and the Publican are presented as the representatives of the two systems—Salvation by works was, and is, an eternal impossibility—The transition from Pharisaism to Sadducism is easy and frequent, and, to some extent, inevitable—Sadducean history fully examined, and Sadducean character, ancient and modern, carefully delineated; and its evil tendencies exposed—It is not possible for those who think, to rest in Pharisaism; hence, those who think, either fall back upon Bible truth, or pass to Sadducism, and thence to all kinds of skepticism—An interesting account and thrilling description of Herodians, ancient and modern—These three systems concentrated, and formed that horrible thing called Popery—How saved from all these errors, ... 134

CHAPTER V.

The Nature, and Necessity, of Christian Progression.

In support of this proposition the unchangeableness of God, and the essential activity of mind are referred to—*Progression* or *retrogression* inevitable—The word progress furnishes Bunyan with both the title and theme of his remarkable book—This idea runs through all the teachings of the bible—Many authors are quoted in support of this proposition, and many arguments advanced—Many illustrations are given, together with criticisms on the original, ... 175

CHAPTER VI.

Nature of Christian progression—Meaning of the word αρετην, courage. The command and promise of God are essential to Christian courage, and this courage is essential to Christian progression—Interesting examples are given, as Daniel and his three companions; and David slaying Goliath; Luther, also, and many other men of courage are noticed—This courage can only exist in connection with Christian faith—It does not precede, but results from faith—Faith and courage are specially necessary for the work of the minister of Jesus, . . 195

CHAPTER VII.

Add *knowledge*—This is essential to the development of the preceding graces—How these graces mutually increase each other—Luther, Zwingle and others, are produced as examples—Consequences of not adding knowledge. as specified, specially in the case of Ministers, ... 224

CHAPTER VIII.

Add *temperance*. Erroneous views exposed, and the meaning of the word εγκρατεια given—Christian temperance is dwelt upon at great length, and its nature and extent specified—Mr. Wesley's definition and views of temperance—Scripture teachings on this subject—Erroneous views farther exposed—Defects of modern temperance lectures, and temperance movements—It was by not adding temperance that Solomon and multitudes of others were ruined—It was by not adding temperance that the primitive churches were ruined, and the dark ages brought on—The activity essential to the Christian character will lead to ruin if temperance does not keep pace with it, 231

CHAPTER IX.

Add *patience*. This is shown to be absolutely necessary to Christian progress: for, the more Christian activities abound, the more is patience rendered necessary—The peculiar work of patience at different periods in the Christian life—No other grace can take its place and do its work—Sometimes one grace must take the lead, sometimes another—Judgment must lead up first one, and then another, according to circumstances; as an experienced General will lead up to the front first one division, and then another, according to the necessities of the occasion—Meaning of the word υπομενω is given—It always springs from, and is supported by faith, as are all the Christian graces—It is distinguished from stoicism, and from the natural power of endurance as seen in the camel or the ox, . 252

CHAPTER X.

Add *Godliness*. Both action, and inaction, may result either from knowledge or ignorance. Hence, there may be something very like courage, or patience, when there is no Godliness—Godliness results from a knowledge of God, and faith in God—Godliness consists in doing and suffering in the spirit of devotion to God. In other words, doing because God has commanded, or not doing, because he has forbidden—Calmet's definition of Godliness—Godliness in practice, is to imitate God in every thing—Godliness in character, is to be like God —ευσεβεια always, has reference to God—Parkhurst is quoted—

No act can be acceptable to God that is not Godly; various arguments are employed to prove this; also, to show the necessity of adding Godliness just here, ... 263

CHAPTER XI.

Add *brotherly kindness*. Your duty to God will not substitute for your duty to your brother—God will not allow the creature to take his place, nor will he take the place of the creature—Love is varied both by its subject and object—God will not accept your gifts, if you have no gift for your brother—He who loveth God, loveth his brother also—He hates who does not love—Both the *subject* and *object* of this love must be a brother—The difference between kindness and brotherly kindness—A striking illustration—God alone can make a brotherhood, men may assume, or give the name, but they cannot impart what that name imports—Each preceding grace is essential to that which follows—This order must not be broken; to progress, you must make each addition in its place, ... 270

CHAPTER XII.

Add *Love*, which takes a much wider range than brotherly kindness. How Peter was led to make this addition, and how his other graces were increased thereby—Had he not made this addition here, he would have progressed no further, but would have backslidden, as many do just at this point—A striking resemblance between Peter and John Wesley at this point—How they and others continued to be a power, while others ceased to be a power—There is nothing that will substitute for this love—A striking incident in illustration—The addition of love is shown to be absolutely necessary, ... 282

CHAPTER XIII.

All "these things" are to be "in you," and are the fruit of the Spirit—The grand distinction between a Christian and a Pharisee—They are all of grace, yet not without the willing co-operation of the subject—All these things being in you, they are to abound—Between this and retrogression there is no medium—Meaning of the words αργους, and ακαρπους—These things being in you and abounding, you cannot possibly be inactive, and the action is of such a nature that fruitfulness must be the result—This action is irresistible, bidding defiance to every opposing power—Hence all such Christians progress, and are a power—Idleness, inaction, or slothfulness, must result from a want of *faith, courage,* or *love*—Faith, courage, and love are the great moving powers; those who have them are ready for every good work, making tents like Paul; or, like Jesus, preparing a breakfast for the hungry disciples by the sea-shore, when necessary—A country inhabited by such a people must be prosperous—All this is confirmed by the facts of history—A point of great importance—The Apostle connects all with the knowledge of our Lord Jesus Christ—A man may be idle and unfruitful in the knowledge of Plato, Socrates, and other men of fame, but not in the knowledge of our Lord Jesus Christ—To have life and power, we must be connected with Jesus in the way specified by the Apostle, for no other being has either life or power to give to man, ... 293

CHAPTER XIV.

To make the additions here specified, we must give all diligence, "these things" do not come by chance—Having shown the consequences of making these additions; and abounding, we are now shown the awful consequences of not doing so—All this is addressed to them that have obtained Apostolic faith—The distinctive characteristics of those who do, and of those who do not, make these additions—Some thoughts with regard to those who have backslidden as here stated—The infallibility of those who "do these things," 311

CHAPTER XV.

The final result of the progression—An "abundant entrance into the everlasting kingdom of our Lord and Saviour Jesus Christ"—These wonderful words and thoughts could only come to us by inspiration—An attempt to explain the word πλυσιως—The question, shall all who finally reach heaven, have this *abundant* entrance ministered unto them, is examined, and answered in the negative—It is again shown why some are a power, while others are not—Even for the same reason that the glorified shine as stars of different magnitudes —The word of God holds out no encourgement, no reward, to *idleness,* 321

INTRODUCTION.

The author has long been convinced that if we would reason correctly, and order our affairs with discretion, we must make a good use of *facts*. It was by carefully and frequently considering the following facts that he was led to write what is contained in the following pages. *There have been men and churches of power, while other men and churches were powerless; and men and churches who were once a power, have ceased to be a power; and some of the latter have again become a power.* These, we think, are facts which will not be disputed. Meditating upon these facts, and upon the interests involved, he became deeply convinced that a satisfactory solution of these facts would result in much good, especially when he considered the various and dangerous opinions which sometimes are entertained with regard to them. Nor was it long till he became convinced that these interesting phenomena might be satisfactorily accounted for; nor was he less convinced that *Scripture, experience,* and *the facts of history* furnish ample material for this purpose; and it is from these rich mines of *truth* and *fact* that he has gathered material for the purpose here specified.

The power sought is that which in Scripture is called "Power with God and with men," and which, occasionally, we have denominated *the peculiar power.* This Scripture suggests the grand ideas sought. He who would have power with man, *for good*, must first have power with God. It was to this end that God our Saviour became incarnate,—*Emmanuel*, "God with us." To obtain this power with God we must take hold of this Saviour, this *Emmanuel*, by praying faith, as Jacob did. Then, and not till then, will it be true of us, as it was of Jacob,—"As a prince hast thou power with God, and with men, and hast prevailed." This passage is singularly suggestive of the fundamental doctrines of the Christian system, and of the secret of *Christian power.* In this way the perishing sinner becomes a *prince*, has power with God and with men, and prevails. Speaking of wrestling Jacob, Hosea says, "He wept and made supplication unto him." In this way Jacob obtained the power; and who ever obtained it in any other way? Hence the name given to Jacob on this occasion is applied to all the people of God, because *they all wrestle, obtain the power, and prevail in the same way that Jacob did.*

Guided as here stated, the author claims to have shown how this power is *obtained, retained, increased, lost, regained.* The chapters on Christian progression, more especially, show how it is *retained* and *increased.* And as men fail to obtain this power by falling into certain errors, which errors are opposed to the great principles which are essential to this power, he has exposed and refuted those errors, so that all may know and avoid them.

Although the subject here discussed takes a very wide range, and is of the most vital importance, the author has not found it necessary to give prominence to denominational peculiarities; and this fact has not only given him pleasure, but also much hope with regard to the extended usefulness of the book. It will be seen that the facts which were considered necessary for his purpose are taken from the histories of the three great reformations,—viz., those of the first, sixteenth, and eighteenth centuries; by which the men and principles of power are seen to act in places, and times, widely apart. And the principles which are claimed to be essential to this power are found in the different orthodox creeds; hence, if those denominations (the Methodist included) have not the power specified, it is because they do not make a good use of their own principles. It follows, that both the nature of the subject, and the way in which it is discussed, make this a book for all; for while fundamental truths are explained, defended, and enforced, there is nothing, we think, that is at all calculated to give offence to any Christian denomination. True, Pharisaism and kindred errors are exposed and rejected with much earnestness, but surely the advocates of such errors have no claim to orthodoxy; nor dare we either fear or flatter them. Indeed, he is their best friend who deals most faithfully with their errors. It is also true that the author has quoted largely from the history of the reformation in which the Wesleys and Whitefield were prominent actors; but he did so for obvious reasons, one of which is, he is specially anxious to hold his own denomination to first principles. Moreover, he has drawn from other sources a sufficient amount of material to show that the principles and power sought are found in different ages, and in the different orthodox denominations. In this way he has endeavored to hold other denominations, as well as his own, to first principles.

Finally, the author begs to apprise the reader that, in the composition of the following pages, he has made no effort to please a certain taste, by a mere jingle of words. On the contrary, he has simply aimed at expressing useful thoughts, in suitable words. Indeed, he has been careful to avoid what are called big words, and every other thing that seemed calculated to enfeeble the noble language of his fathers. True, in quoting the Scriptures, he has occasionally appealed to the original, but he has done so for reasons which, it is believed, will appear obvious to the thoughtful reader.

And now he commits his little work to the care and disposal of Providence, praying that it may be made a blessing to the children of men, "so long as the moon endureth."

JOHN LEVINGTON.

February 14, 1868.

CHAPTER I.

On power in general. Power can only be discovered in the *phenomena*, or *facts*, resulting therefrom—The existence of the power is as certain as is the existence of the *phenomena* resulting therefrom—In every system there must be a grand central power, or primary cause of motion—The way to discover where and what this power is—Various conjectures as to what the peculiar power of Methodism is, are shown to be unsatisfactory—The advantages of knowing what, and where, this peculiar power is—The advantages of the method here adopted for that purpose—Sources from which facts shall be taken in support of the position—The grand errors which exclude the conditions of this power shall be exposed.

This peculiar power, and the facts resulting therefrom, sustain the relation of cause and effect. Hence the existence of the power is as certain as the existence of the facts. It is not more certain that the motions of the heavenly bodies result from an adequate power, than it is that the facts of Methodist history result from an adequate power. When I turn my eyes to the stellar systems, and behold the velocity with which those huge bodies move, I instantly conclude that there must be a power somewhere, a power adequate to the wonderful phenomena upon which I gaze, and which are evidently so many effects resulting from a given cause. In like manner, when I turn to the facts of Methodist history, I as readily conclude, there must be a power somewhere, a power adequate to the wonderful phenomena which I here behold, and which are as evidently so many effects resulting from an adequate cause. But, as there is something peculiar in the facts of Methodist history, there must also be something peculiar in their cause, for the power, and the facts resulting therefrom, sustain the relation of cause and effect, so that the peculiarity discoverable in the facts must result from a corresponding peculiarity in the cause. The peculiarity of this power, which gives character to the effects resulting therefrom, may consist in the degree of intensity, rather than in an essential difference of nature; but our special object just now is to *discover* this *peculiar power*. And we are the more anxious to do so, first, because we think it is not generally apprehended with much clearness, to say the very least; second, because we think a clear apprehension of this *peculiar power* would lead many more to seek and obtain it. We say the *peculiar power* of Methodism, because, although power may be discovered in all the departments of the system, and in every particular that legitimately belongs to it, it is not in every particular that the *peculiar power* is to be discovered, though it extends to *all*.

In every system there is, and must be, a grand central power, or primary cause of motion. For instance, I look at my watch, and I at once see that the hands move, and at once I am convinced that there is power somewhere; but it is not in the hands, though it extends to them. I now open this wonderful piece of mechanism and I discover the motions of the balance-wheel, but neither is the power in this particular, though it extends to it. I now approach still nearer to the centre, and I discover a number of wheels of different sizes, and all in motion, though their motions vary, some of them moving faster, some slower; but neither is the power in any one of these wheels, though it extends to them all. Thus I continue my advance toward the centre, till, finally, I reach the *mainspring*, and in reaching that, I have reached the power; I know I have, for by stopping this motion I stop all the motions; all the hands and all the wheels at once stand still. Again: See that vast building. As you approach, you discover that a vast amount of machinery is in motion. You enter the building, and you see numerous wheels, drums, shafts, looms, and spindles all in motion; but in none of these is to be found the grand moving power, though it extends to them all. You pass through the vast building from one department to another, and from one shaft to another, but you have not yet found the *peculiar* power. At length you reach a point where are fire, smoke, steam, wheels, shafts, rods, and pins in abundance; but in neither one of these is the grand moving power located. At length you discover a cylinder in which is pent up a certain amount of steam; here is the power; you know this is the power from which the entire machinery has its motion; for if you scatter this pent up steam, all the machinery stands still, though all the other particulars remain as before, only *there is no motion!*

Now turn to that vast system of machinery called

Methodism. It was set in motion in 1738, or, more properly speaking, perhaps, in 1739; and it has been running ever since. Now the power that started, and still runs this machinery, is a *peculiar* power, not absolutely, but in some respects, particularly with regard to *its extraordinary energy, its modes of operating, and its extraordinary results.* Observe there was power before the time here specified, and that power worked a given machinery, and produced corresponding results. But since that time we observe an *extraordinary* power working an *extraordinary* machinery, and, of course, producing *extraordinary* results. These are facts, which, we presume, will not be denied.

Now we wish to know *what* this *peculiar* power is, and *where* it is. The pretended infallible power of the Papal Church has been variously defined and variously located. Just so with regard to the peculiar power of which we speak. Some have attributed the extraordinary results to one thing, some to another. Some have thought that they discovered this *peculiar* power in the adaptation of certain means to the characters of the times, while others have thought that they discovered it in the extraordinary statesmanship and shrewdness of John Wesley. To all these, and many similar conjectures, it is only necessary to give this reply: John Wesley was only one of the agents, in connection with whose labors this power developed itself and produced the results to which we refer. Moreover, John Wesley and his coadjutors have long since passed away, and times have greatly changed, but the *peculiar* power is still working with similar energy, and producing similar results. Indeed, we think we can show that this *peculiar* power is the same, essentially the same, both in energy and results, in every age, and among every people where it is found. Some have supposed that this power is to be found in the doctrines preached. This comes nearer to the point, yet it is not a full answer to the question, for John Wesley and his coadjutors, like the apostles, continually said, "We bring no new commandment unto you." In the Bible and prayer book which were read in the Churches of their fathers every Sabbath, they claim to find every truth that they preached. Nor will it do to tell us that the power which produced these wonderful and glorious results is the power of God; for we know this already—we always knew this; and we know, too, that God's power, like himself, is "the same, yesterday, and to-day and forever;" and so is his wisdom, and so is his goodness. Why, then, was not this power always exerted, as at the time referred to? It will not do to resolve the whole into mystery, nor will it satisfy to refer it to the Divine Sovereignty. We really think that such an answer is no answer at all; indeed, it is worse than none, for it takes all blame from slothful Churches and slothful individuals, and shifts it over upon God Almighty, and it represents him, if we mistake not, as being fitful and capricious in the exercise of his power. But this is contrary to his own account of himself, where he asserts his *immutability*, and where he assures us that on his part "all things are now ready," and that "now is the accepted time, and now is the day of salvation," even when this power does not operate.

Now we not only believe that all the above, and

many other attempts, fail to point out the *peculiar* power from which resulted the great revival of the eighteenth century, but we believe that a proper investigation of the facts of Methodist history will clearly discover the power from which they result; and it is in these facts that we see the revival, as well as the power that produced the revival. This mode of investigation has some peculiar advantages, for the facts themselves are so interesting that they will pay us for all our trouble, if we give them due attention, even though we should fail to discover the *peculiar* power from which they resulted. And if we do succeed, we shall discover, not only the grand cause of the Methodist revival, but also that of all similar revivals; such as the Apostolic, and Lutheran revivals. And we shall see, too, how the revival may be continued or reproduced.

Finally. If we shall succeed in discovering the *peculiar power* that produced such grand results, we shall find it an easy task to discover what is next in importance to this,—viz., the way in which individuals and churches lose the revival spirit, and backslide. I say the latter is next in importance to the former, for when an individual or a church is quickened into life, real, energetic, useful life, the next thing is to continue that life, and thus prevent both individuals and churches from relapsing into their former death, while they retain the name to live. And we may expect just such relapses, so long as the *receipt* or *loss* of this life-giving power is resolved into a deep inexplicable mystery; so long as it is referred to the mere sovereign, or fitful and capricious action of the Almighty. In this way God is blamed for the continued rebellion of the sinner, and for the vile backslidings of individuals, and whole churches. Such views are alike contrary to reason and revelation; and they are, as might be expected, unspeakably ruinous in their tendency. Let us, therefore, earnestly and patiently apply ourselves to the investigation of a subject so interesting, and so important.

The facts which we shall adduce in support of our position, will be taken, principally, from the reformations of the eighteenth, sixteenth, and first centuries,— viz., the Wesleyan, Lutheran, and Apostolic revivals; thereby showing that this peculiar moral power is the same in every age, and among every people. We shall also expose the grand errors which exclude the *conditions* of this power, and thereby render powerless all the systems in which they are found.

CHAPTER II.

Facts of Methodist history down to the conversion of John and Charles Wesley—The poetry of Samuel Wesley and his sons—Mrs. Wesley's Academy—Her method of teaching and its results—The burning of the Rectory and the narrow escape of John—The three sons sent to higher schools, and John and Charles finally to Oxford—The society at Oxford called the "Holy Club"—The voyage of John and Charles to America, and their labors there—Their return to England—Very interesting particulars—The first and many succeeding interviews with Peter Bohler—A minute account of their convictions and painful struggles; and, finally, of their conversion—The peculiar power is obtained, and begins to manifest itself.

WE now turn to the facts of Methodist history to discover that *peculiar* power from which resulted what we see and hear, and what has been matter of glorious experience to millions of precious souls who, with Charles Wesley, have joyfully sung,

"What we have felt and seen,
With confidence we tell;
And publish to the sons of men
The signs infallible."

We commence where Moses commenced, "In the beginning," and will notice the *persons* and the *principles* through which God exerted his power in producing the grand results which shall pass before us in order, and to which, as *facts*, we call attention.

We now repair to the old Rectory at Epworth, in Lincolnshire, England. There we find the good rector, Samuel Wesley, and his wife Susanna, the parents of John and Charles Wesley. The good rector was the author of that beautiful hymn, commencing,

> "Behold the Saviour of mankind
> Nail'd to the shameful tree;
> How vast the love that him inclined
> To bleed and die for thee."

In this fine effusion we see the poet, the theologian, and the Christian. The son to whom this good man gave his own name, not only received the name, but also the poetic genius of the father, as is evident from that fine, pathetic effusion of which he was the author, and of which the following is the first verse:

> "The morning flowers display their sweets,
> And gay their silken leaves unfold,
> As careless of the noontide heats,
> As fearless of the evening cold."

I need not say that John and Charles Wesley were poets, but I may say, that their numerous and exceedingly varied poetic productions contain the strength and elegance of the English language, the heights and depths of Christian theology and Christian experience, and are amongst the richest poetic effusions that ever flowed from the Christian pen. It would be difficult to find any thing in Christian theology, or Christian experience, that is not clearly and forcibly expressed in the hymns of John and Charles Wesley. It is said that the venerable Henry Moor, who was personally acquainted with the Wesleys, remarked on one occasion, that the Wesleyan Hymn-Book was his principal Commentary for many years. We make these remarks that it may be seen how God was already preparing material for the great work whose history we have under review. I believe these hymns, under God, tend to preserve the doctrines and spirit of our holy religion to an extent never fully appreciated. Every feeling that the human soul is the subject of, from the commencement of repentance to the loftiest raptures of the perfect Christian, may find suitable expression in the hymns of the Wesleys. Indeed, they sometimes carry their joyful strains to such an elevation, that they seem, finally, to blend with the rapturous songs that are sung before the throne in heaven; while at other times they flow with a liquid softness, and seem to blend with the very tears of the mourner, or in low and solemn cadence give expression to the most subdued feelings of the adoring soul before the mercy-seat; as in the following lines:

> "The o'erwhelming power of saving grace,
> The sight that veils the seraph's face;
> The speechless awe that dares not move,
> And all the silent heaven of love."

Such hymns flow from, and partake of, that peculiar power of Methodism which we desire to point out.

The mother of these sweet singers, Mrs. Susanna Wesley, was the daughter of the Rev. Dr. Samuel Annesley, whose cousin was the then Earl of Anglesey.

He was an eminent and pious minister of the gospel. Mrs. Wesley told her son John that this good man said, shortly before he died, "that for more than forty years he had no darkness, no fear, no doubt at all of his being 'accepted in the Beloved.'" (Wesley's Works, Vol. III., p. 152, New York edition.) John and Charles Wesley were brought up at the feet of a greater than Gamaliel. Their own mother prepared them for those more elevated studies which they afterwards prosecuted so successfully in the classic halls of Oxford. In a letter to her son John, dated July 24, 1732, and recorded in his Journal, Vol. III., p. 262, she gives us some of the rules which she observed in conducting this holy school in the old Rectory at Epworth. She says, "According to your desire, I have collected the principal rules which I observed in educating my family."   *   *   *   *   *

"Samuel, who was the first child I ever taught, learned the alphabet in a few hours. He was five years old on the tenth of February; the next day he began to learn; and as soon as he knew the letters, began at the first chapter of Genesis. He was taught to spell the first verse, then to read it over and over, till he could read it off-hand without any hesitation; so on to the second, etc., till he took ten verses for a lesson, which he quickly did. Easter fell low that year, and by Whitsuntide he could read a chapter very well; for he read continually."   *   *   *

"The same method was observed with them all. As soon as they knew the letters, they were put first to spell, and read one line, then a verse; never leaving till perfect in their lesson, were it shorter or longer. So one or other continued reading at school-time, without any intermission; and before we left school each child read what he had learned that morning, and ere we parted in the afternoon what they had learned that day. There was no such thing as loud talking, or playing allowed of; but all were kept close to their business, for six hours of school; and it is almost incredible what a child can be taught in a quarter of a year, by a vigorous application, if it have but a tolerable capacity and good health. Every one of the children, Kezzy excepted, could read better in that time, than the most of women can do as long as they live." The dullness of Kezzy she accounts for thus: "None of them were taught to read till five years old, except Kezzy, in whose case I was overruled, and she was more years learning than any of the rest had been months." This, doubtless, is the "dull child" that called forth the following interesting incident. Passing through the school on one occasion, while the patient mother was giving "line upon line, and precept upon precept," Mr. Wesley said, "My dear, why do you sit there hour after hour, telling that dull child the same thing twenty times over." "Because nineteen times are not sufficient," was the prompt reply of the great teacher. The school hours were from nine to twelve and from two to five. The day upon which each succeeding child of her numerous family was received into this sacred school was a marked day, and much to be remembered. Her own account of it must not be withheld. Here it is: "The day before a child began to learn, the house was set in order, every one's work appointed, and a charge given that none should come into the room from nine till twelve, or from two till five; which you know were our school hours. One day was allowed the child wherein to learn its letters; and each of them did in that time know all its letters, great and small, except Molly and Nancy, who were a day and a half before they knew them perfectly."

One more short extract from this interesting letter, and we must leave it; would that every parent might read the whole of it. "For some years we went on very well. Never were children in better order. Never were children better disposed to piety, or in more subjection to their parents, till that fatal dispersion of them into several families, after the fire. In those families they were left at full liberty to converse with servants, which before they had always been restrained from, and to run abroad and play with any children, good or bad. They soon learned to neglect a strict observation of the Sabbath, and got a knowledge of several songs and bad things, which before they had no notion of. That civil behaviour which made them admired, when at home, by all who saw them, was, in a great measure, lost; and a clownish accent, and many rude ways were learned, which were not reformed without some difficulty. When the house was rebuilt, and the children all gathered home, we entered upon a strict reformation; and then was begun the custom of singing Psalms at beginning and leaving school, morning and evening."

The fire mentioned by Mrs. Wesley in the above letter, is that from which little John was so providentially rescued, when about six years old. The deliverance was on this wise:—When the parents and the rest of the family had narrowly escaped, and the little group collected before the burning building, of which the flames had now the complete mastery, little John was missing, but was soon seen standing at an upper window. The house could not be entered, nor could a ladder be obtained in time; but a noble fellow whose body and soul were well adapted to the emergency, quickly placing his back to the wall of the burning building, called upon another man to stand upon his shoulders; the call was promptly obeyed, and the child was taken from the window, immediately after which the roof of the building fell in. When God would save, he has never to go in quest of help to accomplish his purpose! In his life of Wesley, Mr. Watson says, in reference to Mrs. Wesley: "There is a striking passage in one of her private meditations, which contains a reference to this event, and indicates that she considered it as laying her under special obligation 'to be more particularly careful of the soul of a child whom God had so mercifully provided for.'" The memory of this remarkable deliverance is also preserved in one of Mr. Wesley's early portraits, by the representation of a house in flames, with this motto, "Is not this a brand plucked from the burning?"

When John Wesley had reached the age of eight years, his religious character had been so developed, even then, that his father admitted him to the sacrament of the supper. When the three boys, Samuel, John and Charles, had graduated in the Maternal Academy, they were sent to higher seats of learning; but the foundation of their future greatness was unquestionably laid in the Maternal School. Samuel, who was the eldest, was sent to Westminster School, to which, at an after period, Charles was also sent; and in 1714 John was sent to the Charter House. But, observe, they are not yet *born again;* hence we do not yet find that *peculiar power* for which we seek. In due time Samuel is elected to Christ Church, Oxford. He became a ripe scholar, and a fine poet. He finally settled as head master of the Free School at Tiverton, in Devonshire, where he died in 1739, in his 49th year, just as the peculiar power began to be developed. But we return to John and Charles, who, while seasons and years roll on and pass away, continue to prosecute their studies with vigor and success, till they are raised to yet higher seats of learning in the University of Oxford. Here, too, they prosecute their studies, even with increasing vigor and success; but still they are unconverted, and destitute of the peculiar power, though their moral character is more and more developed, but they are not yet "endued with power from on high." Charles, whose moral character seemed to develope more slowly than that of John, now seems to vie with his brother in this particular also, for he seems to have commenced the little Oxford Society, which afterwards was known as "The Holy Club," and which we shall notice in due time. Meantime John became noted for his high and various attainments. "His literary character," says Dr. Whitehead, "was now established in the University; he was acknowledged by all parties to be a man of talents, and an excellent critic in the learned languages. His compositions were distinguished by an elegant simplicity of style, and justness of thought that strongly marked the excellence of his classical taste. His skill in logic, or the art of reasoning, was universally known and admired. The high opinion that was entertained of him in these respects, was soon publicly expressed, by choosing him Greek lecturer and moderator of the classes, on the 7th of November, though he had only been elected Fellow of the College in March. He was little more than twenty-three years of age, and had not proceeded to master of arts." "He took his degree," says Mr. Watson, "in February, 1727; became his father's curate in August of the same year; returned to Oxford in 1728, to obtain priests' orders; and paid another visit to Oxford in 1729, where, during his stay he attended the meetings of a small society formed by his brother Charles, Mr. Morgan and a few others, to assist each other in their studies, and to consult how to emyloy their time to the best advantage. After about a month he returned to Epworth; but upon Dr. Morley, the rector of his college, requiring his residence at the college, he quitted his father's curacy, and in November again settled in Oxford. He now obtained pupils, and became tutor to the college; presided as moderator in the disputations six times a week, and had the chief direction of a religious society. From this time he stood more prominently forward in his religious character, and in his efforts to do good to others; and began more fully to prove that they that will live godly in Christ Jesus must suffer persecution."

Our reformer is now fully employed where he de

lights to be, and where he even now dreams that he shall spend his life, to use his own words,

"Among Academic shades to search for truth."

But God has very different work for him to do, and will lead him by a way which as yet he knows not. Insensibly to himself, his zeal and various other qualifications, make him the centre and soul of the pious nucleus of which his brother was the first centre. Of this interesting little company, Mr. J. Wesley has left on record the following account: (Works, vol. v. p. 246.)

In November, 1729, four young gentlemen of Oxford—Mr. John Wesley, Fellow of Lincoln College; Mr. Charles Wesley, Student of Christ Church; Mr. Morgan, Commoner of Christ Church, and Mr. Kirkham, of Merton College, began to spend some evenings in the week together, in reading, chiefly, the Greek Testament. The next year two or three of Mr. John Wesley's pupils desired the liberty of meeting with them; and afterward one of Mr. Charles Wesley's pupils. It was in 1732, that Mr. Ingham, of Queen's College, and Mr. Broughton, of Exeter, were added to their number. To these, in April, was joined Mr. Clayton, of Brazennose, with two or three of his pupils. About the same time Mr. James Hervey was permitted to meet with them, and in 1735 Mr. Whitefield." * *

"They were all zealous members of the Church of England, not only tenacious of all her doctrines, so far as they knew them, but of all her discipline, to the minutest circumstance."

Here is what is called the first Methodist Society.

But like some other Methodist Societies which we have known, it was destitute of the *peculiar power*, the true power of Methodism. John and Charles Wesley have now everything but this; and they do, it would seem, everything that can be done without it. They visit hospitals, prisons, and the most neglected portions of society. They fast, they pray, they study, they teach, they exhort and they preach. They deprive themselves even of the necessaries of life that they may clothe the naked and feed the hungry. And in these ways they relieve much suffering, and do much good; but, alas! they lack the peculiar power. Hence we do not hear of a single clear conversion. Like many others, they have every qualification, save the *peculiar power*. If classical learning, classical polish, logical argument, various and extensive learning, both literary and scientific; together with incessant labor and self-denial, would do the work, John Wesley would have done it at this time, probably equal to any man of that or any other age. But this work cannot be done without the *peculiar power;* and this the Wesleys have not yet received. Their day of pentecost is not yet come.

Now the classic, and much-loved halls of Oxford, with their precious associations; yea, and old England itself, together with their excellent mother, lately made a widow, brother, sisters, and other friends, are all parted with by the zealous brothers, who are now determined to preach the Gospel in the western world, hoping that they may there have better success than they had in England.

"The holy club" at Oxford, already much diminished under the cruel hand of persecution, is now finally broken up by the departure of the two Wesleys, who, on the 14th of October, 1735, embarked on board the "Simmonds," at Gravesend, for Georgia. They were accompanied by Benjamin Ingham and Charles Delamotte. A single quotation from John Wesley's Journal will suffice to show that these men lived on the great deep, as they had lived at Oxford, a life of incessant toil and self-denial. Having passed through the unavoidable irregularities of embarkation, &c., they now resume the strict Methodistic mode of life:—"We now began to be a little regular. Our common way of living was this:—From four in the morning till five, each of us used private prayer. From five to seven we read the Bible together, carefully comparing it (that we might not lean to our own understanding) with the writings of the earliest ages. At seven we breakfasted. At eight were the public prayers. From nine to twelve I usually learned German, and Mr. Delamotte, Greek. My brother wrote sermons, and Mr. Ingham instructed the children. At twelve we met to give an account to one another of what we had done since our last meeting, and of what we designed to do before our next. About one we dined. The time from dinner to four, we spent in reading to those whom each of us had taken in charge, or in speaking to them severally as need required. At four were the evening prayers; when either the second lesson was explained, (as it always was in the morning,) or the children were catechised and instructed before the congregation. From five to six we again used private prayer. From six to seven I read in our cabin to two or three of the passengers, (of whom there were about eighty English on board,) and each of my brethren to a few more in theirs. At seven I joined with the Germans in their public service, while Mr. Ingham was reading between the decks, to as many as desired to hear. At eight we met again to exhort and instruct one another. Between nine and ten we went to bed, where neither the roaring of the sea, nor the motion of the ship, could take away the refreshing sleep which God gave us." This is what he calls, "A little regular!" Some would think this was regular enough. One may see, however, even here, a development of the rules observed in the maternal academy in the old Rectory at Epworth. Yes, the impressions made by the hand of Susanna Wesley, upon her sons, never left them during their long and useful life. She trained them up in the way they should go, and when they were old they did not depart from it. Yet they are still destitute of the *peculiar power*, like many others, they are Methodists without the true Methodistic power.

Finally, on the 5th of February, 1736, the good ship cast anchor in the destined port, and soon after the Missionaries landed at Savannah, where Mr. Wesley makes the following record in his Journal. "Thursday 5.—Between two and three in the afternoon, God brought us all safe into the Savannah river. We cast anchor near Tybee Island, where the groves of pines, running along the shore, made an agreeable prospect, showing, as it were, the bloom of spring in the depth of winter. Friday 6.—About eight in the morning we first set foot on American ground. It was a small uninhabited island, over against Tybee. Mr. Oglethorp led us to a rising ground, where we all kneeled down to give thanks." Just so it was, that the puritan pilgrims commenced their life and labors upon this continent many years before; nor has God failed to answer the prayers of his servants, either first or last. On the 13th he makes the following record in his Journal: "In the course of reading to-day were these words: 'Thus saith the Lord of hosts, It shall yet come to pass, that there shall come people, and the inhabitants of many cities: and the inhabitants of one city shall go to another, saying, Let us go speedily to pray before the Lord, and to seek the Lord of hosts: I will go also. Yea, many people and strong nations shall come to seek the Lord of hosts in Jerusalem, and to pray before the Lord.'— Zech. viii. 20–22." That was a day of small things; but the great soul of this missionary looked hopefully to the future, though clouds and darkness then rested upon it. And his hopes, as well as the suggestions of the above Scripture, have been gloriously realized; though for the time he and his devoted companions seemed to labor in vain, and spend their strength for naught, for they had not, as yet, the peculiar power; the day of pentecost was not yet come.

The history of the two Wesleys during this period is well known. It is only necessary to say that they labored much, and suffered not a little, and, apparently at least, with very little success. The centre of John's field of labor was Savannah, while that of Charles was Frederica. In July, 1736, Charles was sent to England with despatches from Mr. Oglethorp, and arrived at Deal in December following. The brothers so long united, in childhood and manhood; in studies and travels; by sea and by land; in sufferings and perils, are now for a time separated, and the broad Atlantic rolls between them. But John still seems to say, "None of these things move me, neither count I my life dear unto me so that I might finish my course with joy, and the ministry which I have received of the Lord Jesus, to testify the Gospel of the grace of God." Night and day he toils on, now among the colonists, and then among the Indians; determined, it would seem, to practice and cause all others to practice every thing enjoined in the Bible and in the Prayer-book. But he seems to labor on the rock, and write upon the sand, till finally he brings to a close these unsuccessful labors, and makes the following record in his journal:

"Friday, 16, 1738, I parted with the last of those friends who came with me into America, Mr. Charles Delamotte, from whom I had been but a few days separate since October 14th, 1735." On Sunday, 18th, being quite sick, he says: "yet I had strength enough given to preach once more to this careless people." Again, "Thursday, 22d, I took my leave of America, (though, if it please God, not for ever,) going on board the *Samuel*, Captain Percy." But his personal labors were done in America, God had prepared another field for him; his influence, however, is still felt in America, and in every other country. Again, "Saturday, 24th, we sailed over Charleston bar, and about noon lost sight of land." Being in great heaviness for several days, why he knew not, he says, "I cried earnestly for help, and it pleased God, as in a moment to restore peace to my soul." At another time he says, "Being sorrowful and very heavy, (though I could give no particular reason for it,) and utterly unwilling to speak close to any of my little flock, (about twenty persons,) I was in doubt whether my neglect of them was not one cause of my heaviness. In the evening, therefore, I began instructing the cabin-boy, after which I was much easier." To all who are in similar heaviness, we would earnestly recommend the same remedy; it would, we doubt not, prove as effectual in their case as it did in that of John Wesley. Thus, as hitherto, he continued his labors while the good ship dashed through the billows toward Old England. At one time he tells us, "All in the ship, except the captain and steersman, were present both at the morning and evening service." At another time he says, "I began instructing a negro lad in the principles of Christianity." But he is not satisfied with his labors even yet, hence he says, "I resolved, God being my helper, not only to preach it to all, but to apply the word of God to every single soul in the ship. I no sooner executed this resolution than my spirit revived, so that from this day I had no more of that fearfulness and heaviness which before almost continually weighed me down."

But, still he is destitute of the *peculiar power;* and still he writes bitter things against himself, in a mournful record of which the following is the substance: "By the most infallible proofs, inward feeling," he finds in himself, "unbelief," "pride," "gross irrecollection," and "levity and luxuriancy of spirit," which he says he finds "recurring whenever the pressure is taken off and appearing by my speaking words not tending to edify; but most by my manner of speaking of my enemies." Here he exclaims, "Lord save, or I perish! Save me, 1st. By such faith as implies peace in life and in death. 2d. By such humility as may fill my heart from this hour forever, with a piercing unutterable sense, I have done nothing hitherto, having evidently built without foundation. 3d. By such a recollection as may cry to thee every moment, especially when all is calm; Give me faith or I die; give me a lowly spirit; otherwise let life be a burden to me. 4th. By steadiness, seriousness, or sobriety of spirit, avoiding, as fire, every word that tendeth not to edify, and never speaking of any who oppose me, or sin against God without all my own sins set in array before my face." Soon after he has this reflection, "I reflected much on that vain desire which had pursued me for so many years, of being in solitude, in order to be a Christian. I have now, I thought, solitude enough. But am I, therefore, the nearer being a Christian? Not if Jesus Christ be the model of Christianity. I doubt, indeed, I am much nearer that mystery of Satan, which some writers affect to call by that name. So near that I had probably sunk wholly into it had not the great mercy of God just now thrown me upon reading St. Cyprian's works. O my soul, come not thou into their secret. Stand thou in the good old paths."

Again. Jan. 24, 1738. "We spoke with two ships, outward bound, from whom we had the welcome news, of our wanting but one hundred and sixty leagues of the Land's End. My mind was now full of thought; part of which I write down as follows:—I went to America, to convert the Indians· but O! who shall convert me? Who, what is he that shall deliver me from this evil heart of unbelief? I have a fair summer religion. I can talk well; nay, and believe myself, while no danger is near: but let death look me in the face, and my spirit is troubled. Nor can I say, 'To die is gain!'

> I have a sin of fear, that when I've spun
> My last thread, I shall perish on the shore."

After much more dolorous reflection of this kind, he exclaims, in the most touching language, "O! who shall deliver me from this fear of death? What shall I do? Where shall I fly from it? Shall I fight against it by thinking, or by not thinking of it?"

He has not yet a Christian experience, and he knows it, and acknowledges it. In this he differs from many learned ministers, who are no better than he then was. Alas! alas! many such there are who cannot say, any more than John Wesley could, at that time, "Being justified by faith, we have peace with God, through our Lord Jesus Christ: by whom also we have access by faith into this grace wherein we stand, and rejoice in the hope of the glory of God." Almost in the very words of Scripture, though he does not seem to advert to them, he exclaims, "O wretched man that I am! who shall deliver me from this body of death?" But, thank God he has not fallen into the delusion, the deadly error, of those who teach that such dreadful groans as these belong to the highest Christian experience! If he had, probably Methodism had never known *the peculiar power;* nay, Methodism, so called, in all probability, would never have had an existence.

It was well, therefore, that he passed through such fearful storms as he records in the following extract from his journal of January 13:—"About midnight we were awakened by a confused noise of seas and wind and men's voices, the like to which I had never heard before. The sound of the sea breaking over and against the sides of the ship, I could compare to nothing but large cannon, or American thunder. The rebounding, starting, quivering motion of the ship resembled what is said of earthquakes. The captain was upon deck in an instant. But his men could not hear what he said. It blew a proper hurricane; which, beginning at the south-west, then went west, north-west, north, and, in a quarter of an hour, round by the east to the south-west point again. At the same time the sea running (as they term it) mountain high, and that from many different points at once, the ship would not obey the helm; nor, indeed, could the steersman, through the violent rain see the compass, so he was forced to let her run before the wind, and in half an hour the stress of the storm was over." It was in the midst of this storm that our missionary resolved not only to preach the word of God to all, "but to apply it to every single soul in the ship;" nor did he, like many, resolve in the storm, and forget in the calm; for he says, "I no sooner executed this resolution than my spirit revived; so that from this day I had no more of that fearfulness and heaviness, which before almost continually weighed me down." Thus did God preach to John Wesley by winds and seas, that roared like "American thunder;" as well as by saints and sinners, till he became convinced that he "was building without a foundation," and that he had only "a fair summer religion" that would not bear the test, especially when "death looked him in the face." He resolved, however, not to be satisfied short of that religion described by the Psalmist in these words: "Therefore will not we fear, though the earth be removed, and though the mountains be carried into the midst of the sea; though the waters thereof roar and be troubled; though the mountains shake with the swelling thereof." And we thank God that he so resolved; for in due time he obtained this very religion; and he feared the storms no more, as his after life fully testifies.

The terrible storms have again blown by, and the good ship, which in the kind providence of God so successfully battled them, is now fast approaching the English coast, and the grateful missionary makes the following record in his Journal: "Sunday, January 29, 1738. We saw English land once more; which, about noon, appeared to be the Lizard Point. We ran by it with a fair wind; and at noon, the next day, made the west end of the Isle of Wight." Finally, on the 31st, he says, "Toward evening was a calm; but in the night a strong north wind brought us safe into the Downs. The day before, Mr. Whitfield had sailed out, neither of us then knowing anything of the other. At four in the morning we took boat, and in half an hour landed at Deal; it being Wednesday, February 1."

Once more he treads the shores of his native country, he is again in the land of his birth, the land of his fathers. He is now about 35 years of age. He has been a student, a close student from his childhood.

For many years he has been a preacher of the Gospel. He has preached to the French, the Italians, and the English, in their own tongue, while he was a missionary, and could have preached in Hebrew, Greek, and Latin, had it been necessary. In his journeys seeking the lost sheep in an inhospitable clime, he has slept in the lonely wilderness during the night-watches, when his clothes and his hair were frozen to the earth. He has prosecuted these labors at home and abroad, by sea and by land, with a perseverance seldom equalled, and perhaps never surpassed; but still he confidently avers that he is not yet a Christian, and it is quite certain that he has not *the peculiar power* after which we seek. All his reflections at this time are very interesting, but they cannot be introduced here; some of them, however, are so important in themselves, and so closely connected with the object of our investigation, that we may not wholly pass them by. Vol. iii., p. 56, he says, "It is now two years and almost four months since I left my native country, in order to teach the Georgia Indians the nature of Christianity, but what have I learned myself in the meantime? Why, that I who went to America to convert others, was never myself converted to God." Knowing that this was a startling statement, and that some of his best friends objected to it, he adds, "'I am not mad,' though I thus speak; 'but speak the words of truth and soberness;' if happily some of those who still dream may awake, and see, that as I am so are they." O that the present investigations might, at least in some measure, tend, by the blessing of God, to promote the same important end, the end for which John Wesley recorded his experience. He goes on, "Are they read in philosophy? So was I. In ancient or modern tongues? So was I also. Are they versed in the science of Divinity? I too have studied it many years. Can they talk fluently upon spiritual things? The very same could I do. Are they plenteous in alms? Behold, I gave all my goods to feed the poor. Do they give of their labor as well as of their substance? I have labored more abundantly than they all. Are they willing to suffer for their brethren? I have thrown up my friends, reputation, ease, country; I have put my life in my hand, wandering into strange lands; I have given my body to be devoured by the deep, parched up with heat, consumed by toil and weariness, or whatsoever God should please to bring upon me. But does all this (be it more or less, it matters not,) make me acceptable to God? Does all I ever did or can know, say, give, do, or suffer, justify me in His sight? Yea, or the constant use of all the means of grace, (which, nevertheless, is meet, right, and our bounden duty;) or that I know nothing of myself, that I am, as touching outward moral righteousness, blameless. Or, (to come closer yet,) the having a rational conviction of all the truths of Christianity? Does all this give me a claim to the holy, heavenly, divine character of a Christian? By no means. If the oracles of God are true, if we are still to abide by 'the law and the testimony;' all these things, though, when ennobled by faith in Christ, they are holy, and just, and good, yet without it, are 'dung and dross.'" Again: "Having nothing in or of myself to plead, I have no hope but that of being justified freely 'through the redemption that is in Jesus;' I have no hope but that if I seek I shall find Christ, and 'be found in him, not having mine own righteousness, but that which is through the faith of Christ, the righteousness which is of God by faith.'" A little after he says, "The faith I want is the faith of a son." And again: "I want that faith which St. Paul recommends to all the world, especially in his Epistle to the Romans; the faith which enables every one that hath it to cry out, 'I live not, but Christ liveth in me, and the life which I now live, I live by faith in the Son of God, who loved me, and gave himself for me.' I want that faith which none can have without knowing that he hath it, (though many imagine they have it, who have it not,) for whosoever hath it, is 'freed from sin,' the 'body of sin is destroyed' in him; he is freed from fear, 'having peace with God through Christ, and rejoicing in hope of the glory of God.' And he is freed from doubt, having the love of God shed abroad in his heart by the Holy Ghost which is given unto him, which 'Spirit itself beareth witness with his spirit, that he is a child of God.'"

Now, let it be well observed, that I do not present Mr. Wesley's teachings and views, up to this time, as being all Scriptural, though most of them are pretty near right. My object is to show, from the facts of history, when and how he obtained a knowledge of the great doctrine of justification by faith, and of the kindred doctrine, the direct witness of the Spirit, to show how he and Methodism obtained *the peculiar power*, and to show what that power is.

About this time Mr. Wesley had several conversations with Peter Bohler, Schulius Richter, and Wensel

Neiser, in London, where they had just arrived from Germany. "Finding they had no acquaintance in England," he says, "I offered to procure them a lodging, and did so, near Mr. Hutton's, where I then was. And from this time I did not willingly lose any opportunity of conversing with them, while I stayed in London." The two grand points upon which they principally conversed, were the two kindred doctrines specified above. Upon the same points he had conversed with German Missionaries on his passage to Georgia and in Georgia. By appealing to the standards of the Church of England, to the writings of the Fathers, and especially to the word of God, he became more and more enlightened and confirmed as to the truth and importance of these vital doctrines. It was on the 7th of February, 1738, that he first met with Mr. Bohler to whom he soon became much attached, but much as he loved to converse with this good man, he continued to travel and preach as hitherto. But as we are now fast approaching the important point where the *peculiar power* is to be discovered, we must carefully mark every step, and to that end quote from the journal. On the 17th of February, he makes the following entry:—"I set out for Oxford with Peter Bohler, where we were kindly received by Mr. Sarney, the only one now remaining here, of many who, at our embarking for America, were used to take sweet counsel together and rejoice in bearing the reproach of Christ." Again, on the 18th, he says, "All this time I conversed much with Peter Bohler, but I understood him not; and least of all when he said, *Mi frater, mi frater, excoquenda est ista tua philosophia.* "My brother, my brother, that philosophy of yours must be purged away." John's philosophy and Peter's faith are now fairly at issue; but Peter is unyielding. He is evidently determined that philosophy shall not usurp the place of faith in Christ; nay, nothing will satisfy him short of having it *purged away*; nor can we resist the conviction that there are at this day many ministers who, in this particular at least, stand in need of *purging* much more than did John Wesley. Although Mr. W. records no more than the above, it is evident that his philosophy rather than Peter's faith yielded in this contest. Still, however, he keeps preaching; hence on Sunday the 26th, we find him preaching three times in London. But as he is now fully convinced that he has not justifying faith, he says, Saturday the 4th of March, "Immediately it struck into my mind, leave off preaching. How can you preach to others who have not faith yourself? I asked Bohler whether he thought I ought to leave it off or not. He answered, 'By no means.' I asked, 'But what can I preach?' He said, 'Preach faith *till* you have it; and then, *because* you have it you *will* preach faith." To this advice he at once yields, for he seems to be teachable as a child.

"Accordingly, Monday, 6th, I began to preach this new doctrine, though my soul started back from the work. The first person to whom I offered salvation by faith alone, was a prisoner under sentence of death; his name was Clifford." Observe, he now *began to preach this new doctrine*, justification by faith, and this is *the first person to whom he offered salvation by faith alone*. This deserves special notice, and it is worthy of a passing remark, that his new principle is subjected to a pretty severe test at the commencement, but it is not the first time that it has been thus tested, and that with glorious success, for it saved "the chief of sinners" long before, and we shall see it equally successful pretty soon. In the meantime, he tells us, on the 23d, "The next morning I began the Geeek Testament again, resolving to abide by the 'law and the testimony,' and being confident that God would hereby show me whether this doctrine was of God." On another condemned criminal in "the Castle" at Oxford, he tested his new doctrine. "After preaching," he says, "we prayed with the condemned man, first in several forms of prayer, and then in such words as were given us in that hour. He kneeled down in much heaviness and confusion, having 'no rest in' his 'bones by reason of his sin.' After a space he rose up, and eagerly said, 'I am now ready to die. I know Christ has taken away my sins; and there is no more condemnation for me.' The same composed cheerfulness he showed when he was carried to execution; and in his last moments he was the same, enjoying a perfect peace, in confidence that he was 'accepted in the beloved.'"

His philosophy is now being "purged away," and the teachings of his Greek Testament are taking the place thereof. Here is a triumph by faith in Jesus Christ, that his philosophy never could boast of, and that his logic was equally incapable of. On the first of April we have another very encouraging record; here it is: "Being at Mr. Fox's Society, my heart was so full that I could not confine myself to the forms of prayer which we were accustomed to use there. Neither do I purpose to be confined to them any more; but to pray indifferently, with a form or without, as I may find suitable to particular occasions." It is evident that he is being still further purged, not only from his philosophy, but also from his ritualism and mere formalism; and it is observable, that, just in proportion as human inventions are purged away, Christ and his Gospel take their place; so that we already have some striking indications of the approach of the *peculiar power*. In the name of Jesus he offers pardon to a poor malefactor, and in the same name he offers prayer for him, and his heart is so FULL that he cannot confine himself to the forms of prayer, nor will he do so any more; and the prayer that came from the full heart, instead of coming from the Prayer Book, is answered, and the poor sinner is pardoned, is happy, and dies without fear. It was thus that John Wesley was taught to sing.

"What are our works but sin and death,
 Till thou thy quick'ning spirit breathe?
 Thou giv'st the power thy grace to move;
 O wond'rous grace! O boundless love!

"How can it be, thou heavenly King,
 That thou should'st us to glory bring;
 Make slaves the part'ners of thy throne,
 Deck'd with a never-fading crown?

"Hence our hearts melt, our eyes o'erflow,
 Our words are lost, nor will we know,
 Nor will we think of aught beside, –
 My Lord, my Love, is crucified."

On the 22d of April, Bohler and Wesley are again in close conference, and the latter is now clearly convinced of the *nature* and *fruits* of justifying faith. "But," he says, "I could not understand how this faith should be given in a moment; how a man could *at once* be thus turned from darkness to light, from sin and misery to righteousness and joy in the Holy Ghost. I searched the Scriptures again, touching this very thing, particularly the Acts of the Apostles, but, to my utter astonishment, found scarce any instance there of other than *instantaneous* conversions; scarce any so slow as that of St. Paul, who was three days in the pangs of the new birth. I had but one retreat left, namely, ' *Thus*, I grant God wrought in the first ages of Christianity; but the times are changed. What reason have I to believe that he works in the same manner now?' But on Sunday the 23d, I was beat out of this retreat, too, by the concurring evidence of several living witnesses, who testified that God had thus wrought in themselves, giving them in a moment such a faith in the blood of his Son, as translated them out of darkness into light, out of sin and fear into holiness and happiness. Here ended my disputing. I could now only cry out, ' Lord, help thou my unbelief.' " Bohler and the New Testament are now victorious, and Wesley is completely conquered. Again he proposes " to refrain from teaching others," but Peter will not submit even to this; he says, " Do not hide in the earth the talent God hath given you." This, it will be remembered, is very different teaching from that which the Moravians afterwards taught, and to which Mr. Wesley utterly refused to submit. See Journal, vol. iii., pp. 167, 186, 189, 190, and 337. When the Moravians presented truth to him, after submitting it to the test of his Greek Testament, he embraced it; but when they afterwards introduced error, after submitting it to the same test, he promptly and firmly rejected it. This deserves notice; for it will be seen that not only the Church of England, but the Moravians also, departed from first principles, while Mr. Wesley adhered to them. In compliance with the judicious advice which Mr. Bohler now gave him, he now urged, with increased earnestness, the great truth, justification by faith, and that in private as well as in the public congregation. Hence, on the 25th, he says, "I spoke clearly and fully at Blendon to Mr. Delamotte's family, of the nature and fruits of faith. Mr. Broughton and my brother were there. Mr. Broughton's great objection was, he could never think that I had not faith who had done and suffered such things. My brother was very angry, and told me, I did not know what mischief I had done by talking thus." Had Mr. Wesley, like Mr. Broughton and many others, inferred his justification from what he had done and suffered, the two kindred doctrines of justification by faith, and the *direct* witness of the Spirit, would have been as little known in Methodism, as they are in some other *isms;* or, what is still more likely, Methodism had never existed; or if it had, it would have existed and died, destitute of *the peculiar power*. But, thank God, he did not rest in mere theory and unscriptural inference, as a substitute for experimental religion.

But we will now for a few moments, turn to Charles Wesley, who also, as we have seen, opposes the new doctrine, so called, though it is really as old as the fall of man. Nor will he submit, in this particular, either to his brother or to Peter Bohler. But God takes a somewhat different method with him. He is in his defences at the great seat of learning, Oxford; a kind of head quarters, then, as now, for the army to which he as yet belongs; and like many others, he is surrounded with strong embankments of morality, learning and patronage: so that for the present, even Peter Bohler's artillery seems to make but little impression. Just now he is seized with a violent pleurisy, and John, who is now on his way to see his brother Samuel at Tiverton, receives a message informing him that his brother Charles is dying at Oxford. He hastens thither, and finds him " recovering from his pleurisy, and with him he finds Peter Bohler. But Peter seems to make but little impression upon those strong embankments within which Charles has taken refuge. He recovers from his sickness, and makes his way to London. The hand of God is in this also, for he is more accessible here. His sickness returns, and John is again obliged to suspend his labors, and hasten to London to see him. Of this visit he makes the following record in his Journal:—" May 1. The return of my brother's illness obliged me again to hasten to London. In the evening I found him at James Hutton's, better as to his health than I expected; but strongly averse to what he called 'the new faith.' This evening our little Society began, which afterwards met in Fetter Lane." Here follow the rules which they then fixed upon, ten in all. These rules are very simple, and yet quite sufficient for such persons as were designed to constitute the Society. But here is the point. Rules, or Laws, must be made with reference to bad, as well as good characters. The first rule is this, "That we will meet together once a week to 'confess our faults one to another, and pray one for another, that we may be healed.'" Fifth rule. "That any who desire to be admitted into this Society be asked, What are your reasons for desiring this? Will you be entirely open, using no kind of reserve? Have you any objection to any of our orders?" After two months' trial, if there was no objection, the probationer was admitted into the Society. Every fourth Saturday was to "be observed as a day of general intercession;" and every fourth Sunday evening, from 7 to 10, they were to hold a love-feast. "In obedience to the command of God by St. James, and by the advice of Peter Bohler," these Rules were agreed to; and here these great reformers, simple as children, met for a time, and often had a heaven upon earth, till the rules proved too weak for the devil and his children, who by-and-by crept in among them.

But we must now return to Charles Wesley, who we left at James Hutton's, sick in body, and obstinate enough with regard to what he called "the new faith." This was on the first of May. On the 19th of the same month, John makes the following record in his journal. "Friday 19th. My brother had a second return of his pleurisy. A few of us spent Saturday night in prayer." On the following day, being Whitsunday, the 21st of May, 1738, he says, "I received the surprising news that my brother found rest to his soul. His bodily strength returned also from that hour. Who is so great a God as our God?" From the latter end of February to the 21st of May, he has had little respite from sickness, sometimes apparently at the gate of death. Meantime he is plyed with the great truths which he was so slow to learn, and prayer was continually offered on his behalf, while death looked him in the face, as it did his brother at sea, when the winds and the waves striking the ship roared like "American thunder." Finally, *his* foundation also gave way, and he found that his studies, his learning, his morality, and his preaching, were poor substitutes for the atonement, or for faith in Jesus. At length he cried for mercy, for the alone-sake of Jesus, like any other sinner, and cast himself by faith upon the atonement, and was saved by grace. Or, as he himself expresses it in the following beautiful lines:—

> "Faded my virtuous show,
> My form without the power
> The sin-convincing Spirit blew,
> And blasted every flower.
>
> My mouth was stopp'd, and shame
> Covered my guilty face;
> I fell on the atoning Lamb,
> And I was saved by grace."

Now his *Muse*, as well as his soul, seems to be quickened into glorious life. O how sweetly does he sing, and how vividly and forcibly does he describe both his former and his present state. How sweetly does he now pour out his soul in that beautiful hymn, of which the following are two verses:

"Long my imprisoned spirit lay,
　Fast bound in sin and nature's night;
Thine eye diffused a quick'ning ray;
　I woke; the dungeon flamed with light,
My chains fell off, my heart was free,
I rose went forth, and follow'd thee.

No condemnation now I dread,
　Jesus, with all in him, is mine;
Alive in him, my living head,
　And clothed with righteousness divine;
Bold I approach the eternal throne,
And claim the crown, through Christ, my own.

He is now about thirty years of age; he has been a student from his childhood; he has had many teachers, and now he has fairly entered the school of Christ, at whose feet we now leave him pouring forth his heavenly numbers, while we return to John, whose labors seem to abound yet more and more.

He seems to have adopted Deut. vi. 7 for his model, only he takes the whole human race for his family. His grand topics are, justification by faith, and the knowledge of the fact by the *direct* witness of the Spirit, corroborated by the fruits of the Spirit, *love, peace, hope, joy, and holy living.* These things he teaches "diligently," literally adhering to the above model, for he teaches "by the way," and when he lieth down, and when he riseth up; and wherever he finds an open door he preaches them to the congregation. But, let us turn to his own journal, vol. iii. p. 67 "Sunday 7. I preached at St. Lawrence's in the morning, and afterwards at St. Katharine Cree's. I was enabled to speak strong words at both, and was therefore the less surprised at being informed that I was not to preach any more in either of those churches. Tuesday 9. I preached at Great St. Helen's to a very numerous congregation on, 'He that spared not his own Son, but delivered him up for us all, how shall he not with him also freely give us all things?' My heart was now so enlarged to declare the love of God to all that were oppressed by the devil, that I did not wonder in the least, when I was afterwards told, 'Sir, you must preach here no more.'" On the 10th we find the following entry, "Mr. Stonehouse, vicar of Islington, was convinced of the truth as it is in Jesus. From this time till Saturday 13th, I was sorrowful and very heavy, being neither able to read, nor meditate, nor sing, nor pray, nor do anything. Yet I was a little refreshed by Peter Bohler's letter." Here follows the letter. In it he guards him against "the sin of unbelief," and urges him to "conquer it this very day." He talks sweetly of the love of Jesus, saying, "O how great, how inexpressible, how unexhausted His love!" In view of this love he exhorts, "Delay not, I beseech you, to believe in *your* Jesus Christ." "Surely he is now ready to help; and nothing can offend him but our unbelief." Notwithstanding the awful *solitude, sadness*, and utter *helplessness* of spirit, above described, "being a little refreshed by Peter Bohler's letter," he is up and at it again. Hence on Sunday the 14th, he says, "I preached in the morning at St. Ann's, Aldersgate, and in the afternoon at the Savoy Chapel, free salvation by faith in the blood of Christ. I was quickly apprised that at St. Ann's, likewise, I am to preach no more." On Sunday the 21st, the day on which he received the glad tidings of his brother's salvation, he heard Dr. Heylyn preach in the morning, and afterward assisted him in administering the Sacrament of the Supper; then at three, in the afternoon of the same day, he says, "I preached at St. John's, Wapping, and at St. Bennett's, Paul's Wharf, in the evening. At these churches, likewise, I am to preach no more." What follows is exceedingly touching, especially when his peculiar circumstances are considered. He says, "Monday, Tuesday, and Wednesday, I had continual sorrow and heaviness in my heart."

To the friend to whom he writes "in the broken manner he was able," he says, "I feel what you say, (though not enough,) for I am under the same condemnation. I see that the whole law of God is holy, just and good. I know every thought, every temper of my soul, ought to bear God's image and superscription. But how am I fallen from the glory of God! I feel that 'I am sold under sin.' I know that I too deserve nothing but wrath, being full of all abominations; and having no good thing in me, to atone for them, or to remove the wrath of God. All my words, my righteousness, my prayers, need an atonement for themselves. So that my mouth is stopped; I have nothing to plead. God is holy; I am unholy. God is a consuming fire; I am altogether a sinner, meet to be consumed. Yet I hear a voice (and is it not the voice of God?) saying, 'Believe and thou shalt be saved. He that believeth is passed from death unto life. God so loved the world that he gave his only begotten Son, that whosoever believeth in him should not perish, but have everlasting life.' O let no one deceive us by vain words, as if we had already attained this faith! By its fruits ye shall know. Do we already feel 'peace with God and joy in the Holy Ghost?' Does the Spirit bear witness with our spirit, that we are the children of God?' Alas! with mine he does not; nor, I fear, with yours. O thou Saviour of men, save us from trusting in anything but thee! draw us after thee. Let us be emptied of ourselves, and then fill us with all peace and joy in believing; and let nothing separate us from thy love, in time or in eternity." How clearly he saw himself! How deep his contrition! How comprehensive his prayer! Truly he is now purged of his philosophy; so much so, that Peter Bohler himself, one would think, must be satisfied. The following remarkable lines, in which Charles Wesley described what he passed through before he experienced salvation, as accurately expresses what John now feels:—

> My spirit be alarmed,
> And brought into distress;
> He shook and bound the strong man, arm'd
> In his self-righteousness.
>
> Faded my virtuous show,—
> My form without the power;
> The sin-convincing spirit blew,
> And blasted every flower."

His language, as given in the above letter, shows how terribly he was shaken, and how completely every flower of self-righteousness was blasted. "I feel that I am 'sold under sin.' I know that I deserve nothing but wrath, being full of all abominations; and having no good thing in me, to atone for them, or remove the wrath of God." During the three days here mentioned, he was just where Paul was for the same length of time. Indeed, it is easy to see a very striking resemblance between the case of John Wesley and that of Paul; only John Wesley, I think, was a much more amiable character before his conversion than was Saul of Tarsus; and he certainly might have said, as truly as did Paul, "touching the righteousness which is in the law blameless." But the blessed Jesus stripped them both of their filthy rags, and clothed them with the garments of salvation; but not till they *saw* and *felt*, yea, and *confessed*, both *what* they were, and *where* they were. "I feel that I am sold under sin. I know that I deserve nothing but wrath," is the language of the man for whom the best of parents and the best of earthly schools had done their utmost, and who had done the utmost he could for himself. And now, when the utmost has been done that man can do,—after the effort has continued for about thirty-five years, we find this same John Wesley sinking in utter despair, and exclaiming, "I know that I, TOO, deserve nothing but wrath, being full of all abominations." But just then, the sinking, despairing, helpless spirit says, "I hear a voice, (and is it not the voice of God) saying, 'Believe, and thou shalt be saved.'" O glorious voice! How many, as well as poor Wesley, have heard that same voice when just at the point of despair!

But let us follow him through these painful and mysterious struggles, which terminated on this memorable day, the 24th of May, 1738. He says, "I think it was about five this morning, that I opened my Testament on these words, 2 Peter i. 4, *Ta megisa hemin kai timia epaggelmata dedaretai, ina dia touton genesthe theias koinonoi phuseos:* 'There are given unto us exceeding great and precious promises, even that ye should be partakers of the Divine nature.' Just as I went out, I opened it again on these words, 'Thou art not far from the kingdom of God.' In the afternoon I was asked to go to St. Paul's. The anthem was, 'Out of the deep have I called unto thee, O Lord: Lord, hear my voice; O let thine ears consider well the voice of my complaint.' In the evening I went very unwillingly to a Society, in Aldersgate Street, where one was reading Luther's preface to the epistle to the Romans. About a quarter before nine, while he was describing the change which God works in the heart through faith in Christ, I felt my heart strangely warmed. I felt I did trust in Christ, in Christ alone for salvation: and assurance was given me that he had taken away *my* sins, even *mine*, and saved *me* from the law of sin and death. I began to pray with all my might for those who had in a more especial manner despitefully used me and persecuted me. I then testified openly to all there, what I now felt first in my heart. Thursday 25. The moment I awakened, 'Jesus Master,' was in my heart and in my mouth; and I found all my strength lay in keeping my eye fixed upon him, and my soul waiting on him continually. Being again at St. Paul's in the afternoon, I could taste the good word of God in the anthem, which began, 'My song shall be always of the loving kindness of the Lord: with my mouth will I ever be showing forth thy truth from one generation to another.'"

One cannot but observe how appropriate the anthem

was on the 24th, and again on the 25th. I imagine I see the penitent Wesley, as he bows in that old cathedral, groaning out his deep, dolorous plaint before the mercy seat, and I seem to hear the rich, deep, mellifluous tones of music as they fall in soft cadence upon his ear, and most touchingly express the language of his heart—" O Lord, hear my voice. O let thine ears consider well the voice of my complaint.' And the next day while, as a pardoned sinner, he worships in the same place, the same old organ, with increasing sweetness expresses what was then the very language of his heart. " My song shall be always of the loving kindness of the Lord: with my mouth will I ever be showing forth thy truth from one generation to another." One can hardly refrain from applying to that good old organ on that occasion what is said of the prophets: It spoke as it was moved by the Holy Ghost; for the sentiments uttered in that music, and by the heart and lips of Wesley on that occasion, have proved to be truly prophetic; for Wesley is, and still will be, " Showing forth God's truth from one generation to another;" and his songs, which are still sung by millions, and still will be, are " always of the loving kindness of the Lord." Hear how sweetly he now sings, in the following exquisitely beautiful hymn, 437 —

"Now I have found the ground wherein;
  Sure my soul's anchor may remain;
The wounds of Jesus for my sin,
  Before the world's foundation slain;
Whose mercy shall unshaken stay,
When heaven and earth are fled away.

Father, thine everlasting grace
  Our scanty thought surpasses far;
Thine heart still melts with tenderness;
  Thine arms of love still open are,
Returning sinners to receive,
That mercy they may taste and live

O love, thou bottomless abyss
  My sins are swallowed up in thee;
Covered is my unrighteousness,
  Nor spot of guilt remains on me;
While Jesus' blood, through earth and skies,
Mercy, free, boundless mercy, cries.

By faith I plunge me in this sea,
  Here is my hope, my joy, my rest;
Hither, when hell assails, I flee,
  I look into my Saviour's breast
Away, sad doubt, and anxious fear,
Mercy is all that's written there."

Yes, "sad doubt and anxious fear" are now gone. We no more hear him complain of "continual sorrow and heaviness of heart." From his conversion till he finished his illustrious career, a period of almost 53 years, his soul was kept in peace, notwithstanding the wonderfully varied and trying scenes through which he was almost constantly passing. In the midst of them all he sweetly sang:—

"Though waves and storms go o'er my head,
  Though strength, and health, and friends be gone;
Though joys be withered all, and dead,
  Though every comfort be withdrawn;
On this my steadfast soul relies,—
Father, thy mercy never dies."

Of this state of soul, as all acquainted with him testify, his calm, cheerful, heavenly countenance, was the sure index.

On the Sabbath following this great salvation, he says, "This day I preached in the morning at St. George's, Bloomsbury, on "This is the victory that overcometh the world, even our faith;" and in the afternoon at the Chapel in Long Acre, on God's justifying the ungodly;—the last time (I understand) I am to preach at either. "Not as I will, but as thou wilt."

To this day that Church (with a few honorable exceptions) prefers Ritualism, and other human inventions, to the glorious doctrine of justification by faith; for preaching which, she then closed her doors against John Wesley; nor would he find as much favor within her pale to-day, as do ritualistic and semi-popish doctors.

Now John Wesley has *the peculiar power* for which we have been seeking, and we shall soon see it gloriously developed. But we cannot define, or even think of, power *abstractly*. Power must have something *upon* which to act; and some kind of *machinery*, or *medium through* which to act. The *lever*, the *power*, the *fulcrum*, and the *weight*, must go together to accomplish anything. The grand power, in a measure, is already committed to the Wesley's, but, preparatory to efficient operation there must be a further adjustment of the machinery, and some little hindrances must be cleared out of the way. This also God is now doing. The medium through which this power is to operate, is not *ritualism*, and other *trumpery of human invention*. How it may best operate John Wesley is not yet quite clear.

That he has the power, he knows; and that the Church of his fathers has closed her doors against him, he also knows; and he can, and does say, "Not as I will, but as thou wilt," and God will adjust other matters in due time. A part of the divine arrangement, just at this point, is, that John Wesley shall retire for a short time to Germany. Accordingly, on the 13th of June, 1738, he embarked at London, for the purpose of visiting Germany, to get and do good, and by the blessing of God, these ends were largely accomplished, as his journal shows. But, while God is thus leading his servant about, and more fully preparing him for the great work before him, let us turn to another chosen vessel, who also is to be one of the first depositories of the peculiar power.

CHAPTER III.

Whitefield's Conversion—His first Sermon and its effects—Providential preparations for the development of the power—Whitefield in America, J. Wesley in Germany, and Charles Wesley in England—They again meet in London, and with about 60 other persons have a Lovefeast, and a baptism of the Spirit—Wonderful developments of the power in London and Bristol—The first Circuit—The first Methodist Church—Numerous incidents, extraordinary and interesting—The new way works so well the old parish plan is abandoned—John Wesley claims the world for his parish—Summing up—The conditions of power are specified in nine particulars—The sum; *doctrine*, *experience*, and *practice*. These particulars are not peculiar to the *minister;* they are essential to the Christian character—An interesting sketch of the life of John Nelson is given in support of the argument. For the same purpose facts are now adduced from the experience of Luther and the history of his times—Finally, facts are adduced from Apostolic times—Paul's experience is shown to be essentially one with those previously given.

In the city of Gloucester, in the month of December, 1714, George Whitefield was born. His circumstances in life gave no indications of future greatness. But the child grew, became remarkably serious, and served God according to the light he had. Finally, by a train of remarkable providences, this youth made his way to Oxford, and was entered at Pembroke College when he was about 18 years old. "About a year after," says Mr. Wesley, "he became acquainted with the Methodists, (so called,) whom from that time he loved as his own soul. By them he was convinced that we 'must be born again,' or outward religion would profit us nothing. He joined with them in fasting on Wednesdays and Fridays, in visiting the sick and the prisoners, and in gathering up the very fragments of time that no moment might be lost." * *

"He was soon tried as with fire. Not only was his reputation lost, and himself forsaken by some of his dearest friends: but he was exercised with inward trials, and those of the severest kind. Many nights he lay sleepless upon his bed; many days prostrate upon the ground. But after he had groaned several months under 'the spirit of bondage,' God was pleased to remove the heavy load, by giving him 'the spirit of adoption,' enabling him, through a living faith, to lay hold on the Son of his love. However, it was thought needful, for the recovery of his health, which was much impaired, that he should go into the country. He accordingly went to Gloucester, where God enabled him to awaken several young persons."

Being now urged to enter into holy orders, he finally yielded to the solicitations of the Bishop, and was ordained deacon on Trinity Sunday, 1736. On the next Sunday he preached his first sermon in the Church of St. Mary le cript, Gloucester, to a crowded audience, in the church in which he had been consecrated to God in his infancy. A short extract from his own account of this sermon is worthy of a place here: "Last Sunday, in the afternoon, I preached my first sermon in the Church of St. Mary le cript, where I was baptized, and also first received the Sacrament of the Lord's Supper. Curiosity, as you may easily guess, drew a large congregation together on this occasion. The sight, at first, a little awed me; but I was comforted with the heartfelt sense of the Divine presence, and soon found the unspeakable advantage of having been accustomed to public speaking when a boy at school, and of exhorting the prisoners, and poor people at their private houses, when at the University. By these means I was kept from being daunted overmuch. As I proceeded I perceived the fire kindled, till at last, though so young, and in the midst of a crowd who knew me when in my childish days, I trust I was enabled to speak with some degree of Gospel authority. Some few mocked, but most seemed for the present struck; and I have since learned that a complaint was made to the Bishop that I drove fifteen mad the first sermon. The worthy prelate wished the madness might not be forgotten before next Sunday." This extract I take from the *Christian Guardian* of Dec. 5, 1866. It is only necessary to say that the facts here recorded give striking evidence that Whitefield had already a considerable measure of the *peculiar power!*

The same providence that led the two Wesleys to America, now leads Whitefield to the same field of labor; so that in 1738 we find George Whitefield in America, John Wesley in Germany, and Charles Wesley in England, the latter laboring principally at London and Oxford. In this way God seems to indicate that the world is their parish, as John Wesley afterwards claimed it to be; hence they already *pre-empt* both hemispheres as God's inheritance, and as the future possession of his church. For the development of *the peculiar power*, nothing less than the whole world was sufficient; and it is a fact that from this time the work of culture has been gloriously progressing in the vast desert of the world; so that now it is fast becoming *the garden of the Lord.*

In December of this year, John Wesley and George Whitefield again meet in London. "Hearing that Mr. Whitefield was arrived from Georgia," says Mr. Wesley, "I hastened to London, and on Tuesday, 12, God gave us once more to take sweet counsel together." On the 1st of January, 1739, we once more find John and Charles Wesley, and George Whitefield all together in London; and we shall soon see a grand development of the peculiar power. "Monday, Jan. 1, 1739," says Mr. Wesley, in his Journal, "Messrs. Hall, Kinchin, Ingham, Whitefield, Hutchins, and my brother Charles, were present at our love-feast in Fetter-lane, with about sixty of our brethren. About three in the morning, as we were continuing instant in prayer, the power of God came mightily upon us, insomuch that many cried out for exceeding joy, and many fell to the ground. As soon as we recovered a little from that awe and amazement at the presence of his Majesty, we broke out with one voice, 'We praise thee, O God; we acknowledge thee to be the Lord.'" One might compare this with Acts iv. 31; nor is the history preceding and following in each case, less similar. I think this is the first instance in Methodist history of saints falling down in the meeting under the power of God. We shall soon see sinners fall under the same power, but it is worthy of remark that the saints fell first: this has always been the order, first the saints, then the sinners. A great many forget this order, or would have God to reverse it; nay, they seem to expect it to fall upon the sinner only, and never seem to imagine that they need the baptism at all; whereas the power must always come upon the church before it can come upon the world. It is evident that He who formerly prepared his people at Jerusalem, for the work upon which they were about to enter, is now preparing his servants at London for a similar work. Being thus prepared, these holy men went forth and made full proof of their ministry, first in London, as the Apostles did in Jerusalem, after they were endued with power from on high, as these men now were; and their immense labors, and the results thereof, were alike wonderful. London is stirred now as Jerusalem was of old. Whitefield flies from church to church, and the congregations so increase that no church will hold the multitudes that follow him. This fact first suggested the thought of preaching in the open air. "But," says Mr. Wesley, (Sermon 53, p. 472,) "when he mentioned it to some of his friends, they judged it to be mere madness;" so he did not carry it into execution till he left London. He now flies from London to Bristol, like Paul from Jerusalem to Illyricum, and at Bristol we leave him for the present, and will now turn to the only man living that could compete with him at this time, viz., John Wesley.

We will now follow John a little while, that we may mark the peculiar power in its wonderful developments. "Sunday, 21. We were surprised in the evening, while I was expounding in the Minories. A well-dressed middle-aged woman suddenly cried out as in the agonies of death. She continued so to do for some time, with all the signs of the sharpest anguish of spirit. When she was a little recovered, I desired her to call upon me the next day. She then told me, that about three years before, she was under strong convictions of sin, and such terror of mind that she had no comfort in anything, nor any rest day or night; that she sent for the Minister of her parish, and told him the distress she was in, upon which he told her husband that she was stark mad, and advised him to send for a physician immediately. A physician was sent for accordingly, who ordered her to be blooded, blistered, and so on." Truly the physician, the husband, and the minister of the parish, were "all physicians of no value," and one cannot but pity the poor woman that fell into their hands, especially when it is remembered that she had no better physicians for "about three years." Now, however, she falls into the hands of him who says, the world is his parish, and he directs her to the Great Physician, and she is healed.

Now Mr. Wesley is urged to go to Oxford, and there we find him on March the second. Of this visit he makes the following record:—" A few names I found here also who had not denied the faith, neither been ashamed of their Lord, even in the midst of a perverse generation. And every day we were together we had a convincing proof, such as it had not before entered into our hearts to conceive, that 'He is able to save unto the uttermost all that come to God through Him.' One of the most surprising instances of his power which I ever remember to have seen, was on the Tuesday following, when I visited one who was above measure enraged at this *new way*, and zealous in opposing it. Finding argument to be of no other effect than to inflame her more and more, I broke off the dispute, and desired we might join in prayer, which she so far consented to as to kneel down. In a few minutes she fell into an extreme agony, both of body and soul, and soon after cried out with the utmost earnestness, 'Now I know I am forgiven for Christ's sake.' Many other words she uttered to the same effect, witnessing a hope full of immortality. And from that hour God hath set her face as a flint to declare the faith which before she persecuted." Soon after, he had similar displays of this power in the house of this woman, who now preached to her neighbors as the Samaritan woman had to hers long before. John Wesley, too, is soon in the midst of them, preaching the "new way," and "one who sat at a distance, felt, as it were, the piercing of a sword, and before she could be brought to another house, whither I was going, could not avoid crying out aloud, even in the street. But no sooner had we made our request known to God, than he sent her help from his holy place." Truly the peculiar power is now exerting itself gloriously; but we "shall see greater things than these," for the machinery is not yet in perfect working order, nor are all the hindrances yet taken out of the way: human inventions and divine ordinances are not yet clearly distinguished. But God is leading his servants as they are "able to bear it;" he is leading just as fast as they are able to follow. It is now clearly seen, however, at least by some, that the "new way" is a decided improvement upon the old *practice* of *blood letting* and *blistering!* And it is even preferable to John Wesley's arguments, logical though they were; for they, too, proved a failure, a perfect failure; only tending "to inflame more and more!" But the "new way" worked like a charm, giving "convincing proof, such as it had not before entered into their hearts to conceive, that 'He is able to save unto the uttermost all that come to God through him.'"

But the devil is also working in his way, nor is it a new way, any more than is that in which God is working, though ignorant people call it new, just as they do God's way, though both are old ways, not new. On the 27th, he says, "I was with two persons, who I fear, are properly enthusiasts. For, first, they think to attain the end without the means; which is enthusiasm, properly so called. Again, they think themselves inspired of God, and are not. But false, imaginary inspiration is enthusiasm. That there is only imaginary inspiration appears hence, it contradicts the Law and the Testimony." If such reasoning is lost upon enthusiasts, as it usually is, it may be very useful to those who have not yet fallen into that snare of the devil. It is quite evident, however, that the old enemy could not take John Wesley in that snare, nor was this old deceiver any more successful when he approached him in the shape of a "French prophet." An instance of this kind he mentions on the 28th of this month. "Having been long importuned thereto," he says, "I went about five in the evening, with four or five of my friends, to a house where was one of those commonly called French prophets. After a time she came in. She seemed about four or five and twenty, of an agreeable speech and behavior. She asked why we came. I said, 'to try the spirits whether they be of God.' Presently after she leaned back in her chair, and seemed to have strong workings in her breast, with deep sighings intermixed. Her head, and hands, and by turns every part of her body seemed also to be in a kind of convulsive motion." After a time she began to speak, and quoted scripture largely, and "all," says Mr. Wesley, "as in the person of God." Finally, "two or three of our company were much affected and believed she spoke by the Spirit of God. But this was in no wise clear to me." Here follow his reasons, which like those specified in the case previously mentioned, are conclusive. I have mentioned these cases to show the workings of the devil, and to show how Mr. Wesley foiled all his workings, by Scripture and sound judgment, and also, to show that modern spiritualism has the same devil for its author that those workings had. I wish also to call attention to the fact, that those workings, which he rightly attributed to the Spirit of God, were essentially different from these clumsy imitations by the devil, especially as to the *workings*, the *pretensions* and the *results*. Indeed, it sometimes occurs that when the sinner is coming to Jesus, the last struggles of the devil, before being cast out, sometimes produce effects upon the body similar to those produced on the body of the pretended prophet, and that of the modern spiritualist; but nobody pretends that this is the work of the spirit of God, nor do such persons make any such pretensions as do the pretended prophets; moreover, the result in such cases is the salvation of the individual, who afterward is found humbly seated at the feet of Jesus "clothed and in his right mind;" while spiritualists and false prophets, particularly "mediums," continue to be the subjects of such diabolical influences, from time to time, but converted people never, their characteristics are *sobriety, righteousness,* and *godliness,* "in this present world."

While John Wesley was thus laboring with *prudence, energy,* and *success;* and pushing the battle to the very gate of the enemy, particularly in London and Oxford, Charles was following with cautious step, though with zeal and holy joy. As for Whitefield, he was in Bristol what Philip was in Samaria, in Bristol as in Samaria, "there was great joy;" and there was considerable alarm also, in view of his wonderful movements, and not a little opposition. But the opposition presented to his rapid and powerful movements seemed only to accelerate the motion; for, "finding all the church doors to be closed in Bristol, on Wednesday 21st, at three in the afternoon he went to Kingswood, and preached in the open air to near two thousand people. On Friday he preached there to four or five thousand; and on Sunday to (it was supposed,) ten thousand. The number continually increased all the time he stayed in Bristol; and a flame of holy love was kindled, which will not easily be put out." (Wesley's Sermons vol. 1, p. 472.) Having now discovered the way to outflank the enemy, namely, by taking to the open air when the churches were closed against him, or when they would not contain the vast crowds desiring to hear the word of life, he is determined to attack London again. At the same time, he desires to keep the ground already taken in Bristol and Kingswood, and to have the aggressive march continued. Hence he writes John Wesley with great urgency, to come to Bristol without delay. As John had also out-flanked the enemy, and taken advanced positions of great importance, both in London and Oxford, he hesitated to leave London at present; and his brother Charles and others decidedly objected. But after consultation and prayer, they all decided to allow their leader to depart, and Mr. Wesley himself, at length recognized the call as the call of God. Accordingly, he left London, and on Saturday, 31st March, reached Bristol, and was soon in consultation with Whitefield, who, of course, told him what great things God had been doing; and leaving this important charge in the hands of his friend, Mr. Whitefield departed for London.

Following these great reformers in their wonderful career, one is forcibly reminded of Luther and Melancthon, nor are the workings of Providence very dissimilar in each case. The same Providence that guided and defended the German reformers, now guides and defends these English reformers.

But let us hear Mr. Wesley's reflections when commencing "this new period" of his life.

[March, 1739.] "Saturday 31. In the evening I met Mr. Whitefield. I could scarce reconcile myself at first to this strange way of preaching in the fields, of which he set me an example on Sunday; having been all my life (till very lately) so tenacious of every point relating to decency and order, that I should have thought the saving of souls almost a sin, if it had not been done in a church," that is, a certain building consecrated by a bishop! "Till very lately," his conversion, and still more lately, the baptism which he experienced in the love-feast in Fetter-lane, on the night of the first of January last, are the events here referred to, as also the teachings of the Holy Spirit, which he readily received after experiencing his regenerating and sanctifying influences on the occasion here specified. And now being pretty well freed from the trammels of human invention, and from the prejudices that they had produced, as also from all the slow and cumbersome ceremonies of "Church order" and "Church officers," the *peculiar power* will have a chance to operate *unrestrained;* and we may expect to see glorious doings. To this end let us follow our reformer in his onward march. On Monday, the second of April, with the example of Whitefield before him, and the example of our blessed Lord in the sermon on the mount, which he had been expounding the previous day, he says, "At four in the afternoon, I submitted to be more vile, and proclaimed in the highways the glad tidings of salvation, speaking from a little eminence in a ground adjoining to the city, to about three thousand people." His text on this occasion was, "The Spirit of the Lord is upon me, &c., Luke iv., 18-19. On Wednesday, the 4th, he says, "At Baptist Mills, (a sort of suburb or village about half a mile from Bristol,) I offered the grace of God to about fifteen hundred persons from these words, 'I will heal their backslidings, I will love them freely.'" On the evening of each day it was his custom to hold private, or, at least, less public meetings; at which he made it his special business to care for those who had been either wounded, or wounded and healed in the open-air services. Hence on the evening of the second he held a meeting in Baldwin street, and on the evening of the fourth, at Baptist Mills, it would seem. He says, "three women agreed to meet together weekly with the same intention as those at London, viz: To confess their faults one to another, and pray one for another, that they may be healed. At eight, four young men agreed to meet in pursuance of the same design." This *nucleus* appears to have been formed in a different place, probably in Bristol, for he is flying from place to place almost night and day. On the 5th, he is "in Castle street," on the 6th, "in Glouster-lane," on the 7th, Saturday, "at Weaver's Hill," where he "declared that Gospel to all, which is 'the power of God unto salvation to every one that believeth.'" Well, this is pretty fair for the first week after fairly breaking loose; and now comes the first Sabbath upon which he adopted "this strange way of preaching in the fields."

Of this Sabbath's work he has left us the following record: "Sunday 8th. At seven in the morning I preached to about a thousand persons at Bristol, and afterward to about fifteen hundred on the top of Hannam Mount, Kingswood. I called to them in the words of the evangelical prophet, 'Ho! every one that thirsteth, come ye to the waters; come and buy wine and milk, without money and without price.' About five thousand were at Rose Green, in the afternoon, (on the other side of Kingswood,) among whom I stood and cried in the name of the Lord, 'If any man thirst, let him come unto me and drink. He that believeth on me, as the Scripture hath said, out of his belly shall flow rivers of living water.'" It will be seen, Wesley is now fairly broken loose, and that "this strange way" works just as well in his hands as it did in the hands of Whitefield. On this holy Sabbath he proclaimed the "glad tidings" in Bristol, Kingswood, and Rose Green, to some seven or eight thousand. The reader is requested carefully to mark the facts, for in them we shall soon see wonderful displays of the peculiar power. Light bodies may be quickly put to the highest speed, but heavy bodies move slow at first. On the 10th he is invited to go to Bath, where he offers to about 1000 "the free grace of God to 'heal their backslidings.'" And next morning he preached to over two thousand in the same place; and in the afternoon to about the same number at Baptist Mills, from, "Christ made of God unto us wisdom, and righteousness, and sanctification, and redemption." "Saturday 14th," he says, "I preached at the poor house; three or four hundred were within, and more than twice that number without, to whom I explained those comfortable words, 'when they had nothing to pay, he frankly forgave them both.' Sunday 15th, I explained at seven, to five or six thousand persons, the story of the Pharisee and the Publican. About three thousand were present at Hannam Mount. I preached at New Gate after dinner to a crowded congregation. Between five and six we went to Rose Green: it rained hard at Bristol, but not a drop fell on us, while I declared to about five thousand, 'Christ, our wisdom, and righteousness, and sanctification, and redemption.' I concluded the day by showing at the Society in Baldwin-street, that 'his blood cleanseth us from all sin.'" On this day he preached five times, and three of his congregations amounted to about thirteen or fourteen thousand; how many were in the other two congregations we are not told. This was pretty good for one Sabbath, but the highest momentum and velocity of these movements is not yet reached. On Tuesday the 17th, while preaching in a house in Black-lane, the floor gave way under the weight of the congregation, the principal prop falling down with a "great noise," apparently indicating the wonderful yielding of *false props* that was about to take place; but the courageous preacher and the anxious hearers continued till the service was closed. On the same evening, while expounding the fourth chapter of the Acts, in Baldwin-street, the *peculiar power* operated gloriously. Having expounded, Mr. Wesley says, "We then called upon God to confirm his word. Immediately one cried out aloud, with the utmost vehemence, even as in the agonies of death. But we continued in prayer till 'a new song was put in her mouth, a thanksgiving to our God.' Soon after, two other persons (well-known in this place as laboring to live in all good conscience toward all men) were seized with strong pain, and constrained to 'roar for the disquietness of their heart.' But it was not long before they likewise burst forth in praise to God their Saviour." Soon after another "called upon God as out of the belly of hell, and in a short time he also was overwhelmed with joy and love, knowing that God had healed his backslidings. So many living witnesses hath God given that his hand is still 'stretched out to heal,' and that 'signs and wonders are even now wrought by his holy child Jesus.'" On the 18th he received several into society, one of them a Quaker, who had been baptized the day before. One was scarcely able to speak or look up," being still in very great distress. But, he says, "we poured out our complaint before God" till "she felt in herself that 'being justified by faith she had peace with God through our Lord Jesus Christ.'" On the 21st, he says, "At Weaver's Hall a young man was suddenly seized with a violent trembling all over, and in a few minutes sunk down to the ground. But we ceased not calling upon God, till he raised him up full of 'peace and joy in the Holy Ghost.'" "On Easter day," he says, "it being a thorough rain, I could only preach at Newgate in the morning, and two in the afternoon; in a house near Hannam Mount at eleven, and in one near Rose Green at five. At the Society in the evening, many were cut to the heart, and many comforted." "It being a thorough rain," this is all he could do this day, that is, preach *five* times, and "many were cut to the heart and many comforted!"

He still desires to preach in the churches, probably from a desire to reach a class that he was not likely to reach in the open air. Hence, being repeatedly urged to go to Pensford, about five miles from Bristol, he "sent to the minister to ask leave to preach in the church," but having waited some time, and having received no answer, he took the field at Pensford also, where on the 23d he preached from, "If any man thirst let him come unto me and drink." At four in the afternoon, he "preached in a convenient place near Bristol to about three thousand." On Tuesday morning, " he preached at Bath to about a thousand. And at four in the afternoon to the poor colliers, at a place about the middle of Kingswood, called Two-Mile-Hill. In the evening at Baldwin street, a young man, after a sharp, though short agony, both of body and mind, found his soul filled with peace, knowing in whom he had believed." On the 25th, he says, "while I was preaching at Newgate, on these words, 'He that believeth hath everlasting life,' I was insensibly led, without any previous design, to declare strongly and explicitly, that God willeth 'all men to be thus saved;' and to pray, that 'if this were not the truth of God, he would not suffer the blind to go out of the way; but if it were, he would bear witness to his word.' Immediately one, and another, and another, sunk to the earth; they dropped on every side as if thunder-struck. One of them cried aloud. We besought God in her behalf, and he turned her heaviness into joy. A second being in the same agony, we called upon God for her also; and he spoke peace to her soul. In the evening I was again pressed in spirit to declare, that 'Christ gave himself a ransom for all.' And almost before we called upon him to set to his seal, he answered. One was so wounded by the sword of the spirit, that you would have imagined she could not live a moment. But immediately his abundant kindness was showed, and she loudly sang of his righteousness. Friday 26. All Newgate rang with the cries of those whom the word of God cut to the heart, two of whom were in a moment filled with joy, to the astonishment of those who beheld them." On Sunday, the 28th, he commenced the day in Bristol by preaching to about four thousand. "At that hour," he says, "it was that one who had long continued in sin, from a despair of finding mercy, received a clear sense of God's pardoning love, and power to sin no more." Being invited to supply the place of a minister, who was sick, at Clifton, about a mile from Bristol, he preached there twice, and officiated at a burial service. Between these services he preached near Hannam Mount to about three thousand. From Clifton he went to Rose Green, and preached to about seven thousand. From Rose Green he went to Gloucester-lane Society, and, finally, he held a love-feast in Baldwin street. Hence, he had eight services this day, including the burial service. Upon this he has simply this comment, " O how has God renewed my strength, who used ten years ago to be so faint and weary with preaching *twice* in one day!" It should be observed that Mr. Wesley is always careful to give God credit for all blessing, both temporal and spiritual. Those who are ever and anon elevating natural laws into the place of Deity, would do well to learn a lesson from him in this particular also. The love-feast here mentioned is the first that ever was held in Bristol, and it was held in the sacred place where the *peculiar power* was first witnessed in its extraordinary operations, convincing and converting sinners; and it came in answer to the special prayer, that God would "confirm his word." He preached in faith, and prayed in faith, and the result was as here stated.

The extraordinary effects produced upon sinners gave great offence to some. One of these was a physician, who thought it was fraud. But when he saw one he had known for many years, and who was wonderfully affected while Mr. Wesley was preaching at Newgate, " he could hardly believe his own eyes and ears. He went and stood close to her, and observed every symptom, till great drops of sweat ran down her face, and all her bones shook. He then knew not what to think, being clearly convinced it was not fraud, nor yet any natural disorder. But when her soul and body were healed in a moment, he acknowledged the finger of God. Tuesday, May the first, many were offended again, and, indeed, much more than before, for at Baldwin street, my voice could scarce be heard amidst the groanings of some, and the cries of others calling aloud to 'Him that is mighty to save.' I desired all that were sincere of heart, to beseech with me the Prince exalted for us, that he would 'proclaim deliverance to the captives.' And he soon showed that he heard our voice. Many of those who had been long in darkness saw the dawn of a great light, and ten persons, I afterward found, then began to say in faith, 'My Lord and my God.' A Quaker who stood by was not a little displeased, at the dissimulation of those creatures, and was biting his lips and knitting his brows, when he dropped down as if thunderstruck. The agony he was in was even terrible to behold. We besought God not to lay folly to his charge, and he soon lifted up his head and cried aloud. ' Now I know thou art a prophet of the Lord.' " Being still at Newgate on the Second of May, where the work is still going on gloriously, he says, " I was desired to step into a house, to see a letter wrote against me, as a 'deceiver of the people' by teaching that 'God willeth all men to be saved.' One who had long asserted the contrary was there, when a young woman came in all in tears, and in deep anguish of spirit. She said she had been reasoning with herself, how these things could be, till she was perplexed more and more; and she now found that the spirit of God was departed from her. We began to pray, and she cried out, 'He is come! He is come! I again rejoice in God my Saviour.' Just as we rose from giving thanks, another person reeled four or five steps, and then dropped down. We prayed with her, and left her strongly convinced of sin, and earnestly groaning for deliverance." The case of "J——n H——n," as it occurred at Baldwin street the previous night, is worthy of notice. "He was (I understood,) a man of regular life and conversation, one who constantly attended the public prayers and sacrament, and was zealous for the church, and against dissenters of every denomination. Being informed that the people fell into strange fits at the societies, he came to see and judge for himself. But he was less satisfied than before, insomuch that he went about to his acquaintances, one after another, till one in the morning, and labored above measure to convince them that it was a delusion of the devil. We were going home when one met us in the street and informed us, that J——n H. was fallen raving mad. It seems that he had sat down to dinner, but had a mind to end a sermon he had borrowed on Salvation by Faith. In reading the last page he changed color, fell off his chair, and began screaming terribly, and beating himself against the ground. The neighbors were alarmed and flocked together to the house. Between one and two I came in, and found him on the floor, the room being full of people, whom his wife would have kept out; but he cried aloud, 'No, let them all come, let all the world see the just judgment of God.' Two or three men were holding him as well as they could. He immediately fixed his eyes on *me*, and stretching out his hand, cried, 'Ay, this is he who I said was a deceiver of the people, but God has overtaken me. I said it was all a delusion, but this is no delusion.' He then roared out, 'O thou devil! Thou cursed devil! Yea thou legion of devils! Thou canst not stay. Christ will cast thee out. I know his work is begun. Tear me to pieces if thou wilt, but thou canst not hurt me.' He then beat himself against the ground again, his breast heaving at the same time, as in the pangs of death, and great drops of sweat trickling down his face. We all took ourselves to prayer. His pangs ceased, and both his body and soul were set at liberty." In Luke ix. 42, a similar case is recorded. "And as he was yet coming, the devil threw him down and *tare him*. And Jesus rebuked the unclean spirit, and healed the child, and delivered him again to his father." To all who are not infidels, this text will be a satisfactory explanation of the above and similar cases recorded by Mr. Wesley and others. It was to " cast out devils and heal the sick," that Jesus sent out his servants; and for this very purpose it was that they received the peculiar power of which we speak; not to advocate certain creeds and perform certain ceremonies; any ignoramus or imposter could do this, but none but such as have the peculiar power can " cast out devils and heal the sick," the sin-sick soul. That God gives this power, and that he gives it for this very purpose is the unmistakable declaration of his own word. See Luke ix. 1, 2. Mark iii. 13, and vii. 7. Also Matt. x. 1. Bodily sickness was also healed as a sign of the healing of the soul. And in the above, and many other cases stated by Mr. Wesley, both body and soul were healed in an instant. As to who they are to whom Jesus entrusts this power, or through whom he exerts it, we shall see pretty soon; in the meantime we will follow our great reformer a little farther before we sum up; for we desire to give such an array of facts as shall be overwhelming—yea, irresistible.

Though we must pass over much of the journal that is very interesting, we will not omit the following, on p. 131, Vol. III: "I was preparing to set out for Pensford, having now had leave to preach in the church, when I received the following note: 'Sir, our minister having been informed you are beside yourself, does, not care you should preach in any of his churches.' I went, however, and on Priest Down, about half a mile from Pensford, preached Christ our 'Wisdom, righteousness, sanctification, and redemption.'" Thus he gave the people of Pensford a good chance to judge whether he was "beside himself." We think that it is not often that *crazy* men display as good judgment as John Wesley displayed on this occasion, and on many other similar occasions. "I went to Bath," he continues, "but was not suffered to be in the meadow where I was before, which occasioned the offer of a much more convenient place, where I preached Christ to about a thousand souls." The 9th of May, 1739, is a memorable day, because on that day the first movement was made to build the first Methodist church, or "room," as he called it, that ever was built upon the earth. Little did Mr. Wesley, or any other man, then know that Methodist churches would soon dot the face of the earth all over. Such, however, is the fact. But let us hear Mr. Wesley's own record of this interesting event. "Wednesday, 9th, we took possession of a piece of ground near St. James' church-yard, in the Horse-Fair, where it was designed to build a room, large enough to contain both the societies of Nicholas and Baldwin street, and such of their acquaintance as might desire to be present with them at such times as the Scripture was expounded. And on Saturday, 12th, the first stone was laid, with the voice of praise and thanksgiving." * * * * "Money, it is true, I had not, nor any human prospect or probability of procuring it; but I knew 'the earth is the Lord's, and the fullness thereof;' and in His name set out, nothing doubting." Some would consider this to be rather a singular provision for building a church! but the sequel shows that it proved quite sufficient. Having laid the foundation of the material temple, he proceeds with the spiritual temple thus: "In the evening while I was declaring that Jesus Christ had given himself a ransom for all, three persons, almost at once, sunk down as dead, having all their sins set in array before them. But in a short time they were raised up, and knew 'that the Lamb of God that taketh away the sin of the world,' had taken away their sins." He now tells us what his "ordinary employment" was about this time, specifying when and where he held each meeting; but for the sake of brevity we have counted, and will simply give the round sum of each day's work, viz: On Sunday he preached *five* times, and on every other day *three* times, the last meeting usually long, often continuing to a very late hour—sometimes till morning—not being able to dismiss; such was the intensity of the religious feeling. This is what he calls his "ordinary employment." Some would consider it extraordinary; indeed, some said he was "beside himself!"

Occasionally he selected a subject that fell with unpleasing weight upon objectors and persecutors. The following is an instance: At Newgate, on the 16th, his text was John vii. 7, with which he connected the 12th verse. A sermon preached by John Wesley from these verses must have been as scathing to some of his countrymen, as was Stephen's sermon to his countrymen just before they stoned him to death; and the sequel seems to favor such an opinion, for the result is thus recorded in his journal: "After sermon, I was informed that the sheriffs had ordered I should preach here, for the future, but once a week." On this order he has simply this reflection, "Yea, and this is once too often 'if he deceiveth the people,' but if otherwise why not once a day?" From this *keen*, and yet just, rebuke one can easily imagine how he wielded his sharp sword when preaching from the above text. Even the *timidity* of his persecutors, as seen in their going so far, and yet no farther, only exposed them still more to the keen edge of the sword that he wielded. His coolness, his clear, penetrating thought, his classical polish, and his *acute* logic, only tended to make his sharp reproofs still sharper, especially when he chose to use a little well-timed wit, which he frequently did with fine effect.

While the work was thus gloriously progressing, and signs and wonders were being wrought in the name of Jesus, Mr. Wesley was called upon to answer numerous enquiries and objections, both verbal and written, regarding the extraordinary exercises of some. After stating at some length his answers to such enquiries and objections, which are very judicious, he says, "To-day, Monday, 21st, our Lord answered for himself. For while I was enforcing these words, 'Be still and know that I am God,' he began to make bare his arm, not in a close room, neither in private, but in the open air, and before more than two thousand witnesses. One, and another, and another, was struck to the earth, exceedingly trembling at the presence of his power. Others cried with a loud and bitter cry, 'What must we do to be saved?' And in less than an hour seven persons, wholly unknown to me till that time, were rejoicing and singing, and with all their might giving thanks to the God of their salvation. In the evening I was interrupted at Nicholas street, almost as soon as I had begun to speak, by the cries of one who was 'pricked to the heart,' and strongly groaned for pardon and peace. Yet I went on to declare what God had already done in proof of that important truth, that he is 'not willing *any* should perish, but that all should come to repentance.' Another person dropped down close to one who was a strong asserter of the contrary doctrine. While he stood astonished at the sight, a little boy near him was seized in the same manner. A young man who stood up behind, fixed his eyes on him, and sank down himself as one dead, but soon began to roar out, and beat himself against the ground so that six men could scarcely hold him. His name was Thomas Maxfield. Except J——n H——n, I never saw one so torn of the evil one. Meantime many others began to cry out to the 'Saviour of all,' that he would come and help them, insomuch that all the house (and, indeed all the street for some space) was in an uproar. But we continued in prayer, and before ten, the greater part found rest to their souls." One being seized by conviction, "ran out of the society with all haste that she might not expose herself. But the hand of God followed her still; so that after going a few steps she was forced to be carried home, and when there, grew worse and worse; she was in a violent agony when we came. We called upon God and her soul found rest. About twelve, I was greatly importuned to go and visit one more person. She had only one struggle after we came, and was then filled with peace and joy. I think, twenty-nine in all had their heaviness turned into joy this day." We may set this down as a pretty good day's work, ending sometime after midnight, I know not how long, only it was about midnight that he was sent for to see this last person. But he is not laid up the next day; on the contrary, we find him still urging on with unfaltering step, doing what he calls his "ordinary work," preaching to about a thousand in Bath, among whom were "several gay things," which, with others, he tried to alarm from the text, "Awake, thou that sleepest," &c. "One came in deep despair, but after an hour spent in prayer, went away in peace." His keen eye observing every movement, he is always prepared with "a portion in due season." Hence he says, "Having observed in many a zeal which did not suit with the sweetness and gentleness of love, I preached at Rose Green, on those words, 'Ye know not what manner of spirit ye are of; for the Son of man is not come to destroy men's lives, but to save them.' At the society in the evening, eleven were deeply convinced of sin, and soon after comforted." It will be observed that the grain cut down in the fields during the day, is carefully gatherd and secured every evening. This work was done " in the societies." To all who labor in the same vineyard we will only say, " go thou and do likewise."

"Monday, 28. I began preaching at Weaver's Hall, at eleven in the forenoon, where two persons were enabled to cry out in faith, ' My Lord and my God,' as were seven during the sermon in the afternoon, before several thousand witnesses, and ten in the evening at Baldwin-street, of whom two were children." On Sunday, June 3rd, he preached to about six thousand persons in the morning. At Hannam Mount he preached in the forenoon; in the afternoon he preached at Rose Green to, he thinks, " eight or nine thousand." " In the evening," he says, " not being permitted to meet in Baldwin-street, we met in the shell of our new society room. The Scripture which came in course to be explained, was, 'Marvel not if the world hate you.' We sung,

> 'Arm of the Lord awake, awake;
> Thine own immortal strength put on,
> With terror clothed, hell's kingdom shake,
> And cast thy foes with fury down.' "

This is the first Methodist Church that ever was

built. "The first stone was laid" on the 13th of May, 1739, and the first sermon was preached in it on the 3rd of June following, from these words: "Marvel not if the world hate you." Then as though they would hurl defiance at the world, and at every other opposing power, they sang as above. Charles Wesley is the author of this bold and spirited effusion. Hence we learn that, even at this early period, the Methodists were singing his hymns in their public worship; nor have they lacked a sufficient variety for every occasion, however peculiar, from then till now. "Not being permitted to meet in Baldwin-Street," they were glad to crowd into "the shell" of their new building, which the zeal of these young converts, and that of their spiritual father had hurried up in so short a time. And joyfully did they worship in "the shell" of that humble structure, for God was with them, as Mr. Wesley testifies in these words, "'And God, even our own God,' gave us his blessing." One may observe, that as they were driven from the churches of their fathers, and even from meadows, fields, and streets; yea, and even from *commons*, God always opened some other place for them, and marvellously overruled these painful circumstances and cruel persecutions, to call out their energies, and hurry forward new churches; and thus forward his own gracious purposes, in separating them from what would only have entangled his servants in their glorious work of founding a system that was to fill the whole earth; though neither its friends nor its enemies ever dreamt of such a thing. It was this that led John Wesley to sing so sweetly of God's providence; take a verse as an instance:

> "Leave to his sov'reign sway
>   To choose and to command:
> So shalt thou wond'ring own his way,
>   How wise, how strong his hand
> Far, far above thy thought
>   His counsel shall appear,
> When fully he the work hath wrought
>   That caused thy needless fear."

Observing the same providence, Charles sang as sweetly as his brother, and much more abundantly. Take a single verse in proof of this also:

> "When passing through the watery deep,
>   I ask in faith thy promised aid;
> The waves an awful distance keep,
>   And shrink from my devoted head:
> Fearless, their violence I dare;
> They cannot harm, for God is there."

While Mr. Wesley's enemies are determined to drive him from open-air preaching as well as from the churches of his fathers, he is equally determined that they shall not. In proof of this we give the following quotations: after which we will sum up, and point out the peculiar power, whose wonderful developments we have been witnessing. "Monday, June 4.—Many came to me and earnestly advised me not to preach abroad in the afternoon, because there was a combination of several persons who threatened terrible things. This report being spread abroad, brought many thither of the better sort of people, (so called,) and added I believe, more than a thousand to the ordinary congregation. The Scripture to which, not my choice, but the providence of God, directed me, was, 'Fear not thou, for I am with thee; be not dismayed, for I am thy God. I will strengthen thee; yea, I will uphold thee with the right hand of my righteousness.' The power of God came with his word; so that none scoffed, or interrupted, or opened his mouth." Thus *faith, grace* and *providence*, again triumph.

The next day, however, Tuesday, the fifth, his enemies are permitted to go a little further, but it is only that their disposition and folly may be further manifested. The following interesting scene, in which the noted functionary, Beau Nash, is the principal actor, is presented in all its vividness, in the following extract, which I take from Mr. Wesley's Journal, vol. iii. p. 136. "There was great expectation at Bath of what a noted man was to do there; and I was much intreated not to preach, because no one knew what might happen. By this report I also gained a much larger audience, among whom were many of the rich and great. I told them plainly, the Scripture had concluded them all under sin,—high and low, rich and poor, one with another. Many of them seemed to be a little surprised, and were sinking apace into seriousness, when their champion appeared, and coming close to me, asked by what authority I did these things. I replied 'By the authority of Jesus Christ, conveyed to me by the (now) Archbishop of Canterbury, when he laid his hands upon me, and said, 'Take thou authority to preach the Gospel.' He said, 'This is contrary to act of Parliament: this is a conventicle.' I answered, 'Sir, the conventicles mentioned in the act (as the preamble shows) are seditious meetings; but this is not such; here is no shadow of sedition; therefore, it is not contrary to that act.' He replied, 'I say it is: and, beside, your preaching frightens people out of their wits.' 'Sir, did you ever hear me preach?' 'No.' 'How, then, can you judge of what you never heard?' 'Sir, by common report.' 'Common report is not enough. Give me leave, sir, to ask, Is not your name Nash?' 'My name is Nash.' 'Sir, I dare not judge of you by common report: I think it not enough to judge by.' Here he paused a while, and, having recovered himself, said, 'I desire to know what this people comes here for:' upon which one replied, 'Sir, leave him to me: let an old woman answer him. You, Mr. Nash, take care of your body; we take care of our souls; and for the food of our souls we come here.' He replied not a word, but went away. As I returned, the street was full of people, hurrying to and fro, and speaking great words. But when any of them asked, 'which is he?' and I replied, 'I am he,' they were immediately silent. Several ladies following me into Mr. Merchant's house; the servant told me there were some wanted to speak to me. I went to them, and said, 'I believe, ladies, the maid mistook; you only wanted to look at me.' I added, 'I do not expect that the rich and great should want either to speak with me, or to hear me; for I speak the plain truth, a thing you hear little of, and do not desire to hear.' A few more words passed between us, and I retired."

On the 7th of June we find him preaching on Priest Down, from "What must I do to be saved?" "In the midst of the prayer after sermon, two men," he says, "began singing a ballad. After a few mild words, (for I saw they were angry,) used without effect, we all began singing a psalm, which put them utterly to silence. We then poured out our souls in prayer for them, and they appeared altogether confounded." Neither the praying, nor the "mild words," even of a Wesley, could silence two ballad singers; but the singing of fifty or a hundred young converts, could, and did silence them; and this being done, the conquerors "poured our their souls in prayer" for the conquered; the result was, they were "altogether confounded;" and well they might be, for this was a mode of warfare that they neither understood nor expected! They were "outflanked!"

That John Wesley and his noble coadjutors, now have "power with God and with men," is as certain as are the profoundly interesting facts that have passed under review; nor is it less evident, that he was destitute of this power previous to the period which we have specified. To establish these two grand points, it will be remembered, is the end for which we have adduced the facts.

On the 11th, he says, "I received a pressing letter from London, (as I had several others before,) to come thither as soon as possible, our brethren in Fetter-lane being in perfect confusion for want of my presence and advice. I therefore preached in the afternoon, on these words: 'I take you to record this day, that I am pure from the blood of all men; for I have not shunned to declare unto you all the counsel of God.' After sermon I commended them to the grace of God, in whom they had believed. Surely God hath yet a work to do in this place. I have not found such love, no, not in England; nor so childlike, artless, teachable a temper, as he hath given to this people. Yet, during this whole time, I had many thoughts concerning the unusual manner of my ministering among them. But after frequently laying it before the Lord, and calmly weighing whatever objections I heard against it, I could not but adhere to what I had written to a friend, who had freely spoken his sentiments concerning it. An extract of that letter I here subjoin, that the matter may be placed in a clear light." And for the same reason, viz: "that the matter may be placed in a clear light," we will now give the substance of this remarkable and very important letter:

"Dear Sir,—The best return I can make for the kind freedom you use, is to use the same to you. O may God whom we serve sanctify it to us both, and teach us the whole truth as it is in Jesus!

"You say you cannot reconcile some parts of my behaviour with the character I have long sustained. No, nor ever will. Therefore I have disclaimed that character on every possible occasion. I told all on our ship, all at Savannah, all at Frederica, and that over and over, in express terms, 'I am not a Christian; I only follow after; if happily I may attain it.' When they urged my works and self-denial, I answered short, 'Though I give all my goods to feed the poor, and my body to be burned, and have not charity, I am nothing.' If they added, 'Nay, but you could not preach as you do, if you were not a Christian;' I again confronted them with St. Paul: 'Though I speak with the tongues of men and of angels and have not charity, I am nothing.' * * * * If you ask on what principle, then, I acted? it was this: a desire to be a Christian, and a conviction that whatever I judge conducive thereto, that I am bound to do." To the advice to "settle in college," or "to accept of a cure of souls," he gives a reply as clear and as conclusive. To the objection that he entered "other men's parishes, to sing psalms and pray, and expound the Scriptures, to Christians who were not of his charge," he replies thus:

"Permit me to speak plainly. If by Catholic principles you mean any other than Scriptural, they weigh nothing with me: I allow no other rule, whether of faith or practice, than the Holy Scriptures: but on Scriptural principles, I do not think it hard to justify whatever I do. God, in Scripture, commands me, according to my power, to instruct the ignorant, reform the wicked, confirm the virtuous. Man forbids me to do this in another's parish; that is, in effect, to do it at all; seeing I have now no parish of my own, nor probably ever shall. Whom, then, shall I hear, God, or man? 'If it be just to obey man rather than God judge you. A dispensation of the Gospel is committed unto me; and woe is me, if I preach not the Gospel.' But where shall I preach it upon the principles you mention? Why, not in Europe, Asia, Africa, or America; not in any of the Christian parts, at least, of the inhabitable earth. For all these are, after a sort, divided into parishes. If it be said, 'Go back, then, to the heathens from whence you came:' nay, but neither could I now (on your principles) preach to them; for all the heathens in Georgia belong to the parish either of Savannah or Frederica." "On Catholic principles" Mr. Wesley's friend could not justify his (Mr. Wesley's) conduct, when *he sung psalms and expounded the Scriptures in other men's parishes!* But in his *laconic* and forcible manner he disposes of "Catholic principles" by simply substituting "Scriptural principles" for what his friend called "Catholic principles." In this way Mr. Wesley did not think it hard to justify whatever he did. And as to the parish question, that is disposed of thus: "Suffer me now to tell you my principles in this matter. I look upon all the world as my parish; thus far I mean, that, in whatever part of it I am, I judge it meet, right, and my bounden duty to declare, unto all that are willing to hear, the glad tidings of salvation. This is the work which I know God has called me to, and sure I am that his blessing attends it." It will be seen that what he here urges in his own defence contains the substance of what he ever after recognized as "marks" of a call to the ministry, and they are still the "marks" which our Church requires in all whom she receives into that holy office—the *Divine call*, the *Christian experience*, the *gifts*, and the *fruits*. (See Discipline, p. 60.) Mr. Wesley now returns the kindness of his friend by the following faithful admonitions and warning: "If you ask how can this be? 'How can one do good, of whom *men say all manner of evil?*' I will put you in mind, (though you once knew this, yea, and much established me in that great truth,) the more evil men say of me for my Lord's sake, the more good will he do by me. That it is for his sake, I know, and He knoweth, and the event agreeth thereto; for He mightily confirms the words I speak, by the Holy Ghost given unto those who hear them. O, my friend, my heart is moved toward you

I fear you have herein 'made shipwreck of the faith.' I fear, 'Satan transformed into an angel of light,' hath assaulted you and prevailed also. I fear, that offspring of hell, worldly or mystic prudence, has drawn you away from the simplicity of the gospel. How else could you ever conceive that the being reviled and 'hated of all men,' should make us less fit for our Master's service? How else could you ever think of saving yourself and them that hear you, without being 'the filth and off-scouring of the world?' To this hour this Scripture is true; and I therein rejoice, yea, and will rejoice. Blessed be God, I enjoy the reproach of Christ."

It will be seen, that the position here taken by Mr. Wesley, especially with regard to the *parish question*, is precisely the same as that which Rev. Mr. Tyng and others, after so long a time, find it necessary for them to take. We are glad that they at length recognize the correctness of Mr. Wesley's position. "Better late than never."

From the very interesting historic facts which have passed under review, we learn the following particulars, viz: Bristol, with its surrounding towns and country for about five miles, formed the first methodist Circuit in the world. John Wesley was the preacher in charge, and God Almighty made the appointment. The Circuit was thoroughly worked, and the *Itinerant plan* thoroughly tested by this first Itinerant preacher. He preached three times every week-day, and five times on the Sabbath, at least this was his "ordinary work." His place of worship, for the most part, was the open air, on the hill-top, on the common, in the meadow, or in the streets and lanes. The meadow, it should be observed, was considered too good for this Itinerant and his followers; hence they were indulged with that delightful place only a few times, and then excluded, as they had been from the churches. In addition to these public labors, this preacher had to meet the societies, made up of young converts; this he did usually at night, it not being convenient to preach in the open air during the night season. In this, as in other things, he observed great economy. He also went from house to house—and that by night and by day—praying with penitents, especially with those who were "grievously vexed with a devil." In dealing with this old enemy, however, he had a short and easy method: while others were blistering, blooding, &c., &c., he simply fell upon his knees and applied to the Saviour whom he preached, imploring help; nor did he cry in vain, for the salvation was alike instant and glorious. In addition to all this, he had to answer questions and meet objections which came thick and fast from near and from far, and which furnished a large amount of work for his mind, his tongue, and his pen. But this, also, God overruled for good, for these answers form a most interesting part of his journal, and in them may be found an answer to almost every question, and every objection, that is started at the present day. He who had his first "parish" in Savannah, now claims the world for his "parish," and will "allow no other rule, whether of faith or practice, than the Holy Scriptures." Finding that the "circuit plan" works so much better than did the *old parish plan*, he tells his friend that he has "now no parish," in that sense, "nor probably ever shall." *The new circuit* works so well that the *old parish* evidently has no longer any attraction for him. And we may safely say that all who have Wesley's spirit, feel as he did, in this particular also! Our observation is, that none go back to the *old parish* till they loose the power (if ever they had it) that drove Wesley out of *the old parish* and placed him on *the circuit*. Without this power the circuit would work even worse than the old parish, but with it *the circuit plan* works like a charm. To discover this power was the object of our search; and we think we are now prepared to point it out, with unmistakable clearness, and specify *the particulars that are essential to its development.*

In the history which has passed under review, we have two classes of facts. The first class, which extends to May, 1738, demonstrates the *absence* of this power. The second class, which extends from that period, as clearly demonstrates the *presence* of this power. Up to the period specified, these men had not the peculiar power of which we speak; from that period they had it. The conclusion in each case is as certain as are the facts adduced in its favor. Now, what had these men at, and from that period, which they had not before? This is the momentous question. For it is evident that the principles then acquired must be *the elements of power, or the medium through which the power operates.* In other words, the *conditions* of power. This will become evident in the highest degree, if we can show, as we believe we can, that this power is always found where these elements are, and never where they are not. What then, are the principles which

9*

these reformers acquired at the period referred to, and which they had not before?

I answer:—First—*They obtained a clear knowledge of the two essential and kindred principles, viz: justification by faith alone, and regeneration by the Holy Spirit.* Second—*They sought and obtained these two great blessings, with the direct witness of the Spirit.* Third—*They sought and obtained that peculiar qualification for the work of the ministry, viz: the baptism of the Holy Ghost;* they were "endued with power from on high." Fourth—*Being assured that God had called them to the work of the ministry, they unreservedly offered themselves to him for this very purpose, and wholly gave themselves up to the guidance of his providence, regardless of all consequences.* If it be said, that they had previously done what is specified in the fourth place, I answer this was not possible before they had this *salvation*, and the *faith* which is the condition thereof; nor could they, before this, have *that love* which is essential to every offering, and to every work. Fifth—They now went forth and preached *justification by faith alone, and regeneration by the Spirit alone.* Sixth—They preached that *the knowledge of justification is given to the party justified by the direct witness of the Spirit.* Seventh—*All this they corroborated by their own experience—Their unmistakable consciousness.* Eighth—*This testimony was corroborated by a uniformly good judgment and holy life.* Ninth—*This salvation they offered alike to all, without any distinction.*

Now, I aver that every thing comprehended in the above nine specifications was obtained or done at the period marked in the historic record, and not before.

If it be said that they preached salvation to all before this period; I am so far from admitting this, that I do not believe that, in the proper sense of the word, they preached salvation at all! How could they, when they were ignorant of its essential elements, as well as of the condition upon which it is obtained? Hence it is that I make this knowledge the first specification in the list of principles obtained. John Wesley first obtained this knowledge, but Charles, for a time, still persisted in pronouncing the whole a *new doctrine.* That they should be thus ignorant, one may well wonder, and they afterward wondered themselves. Hence, Charles says, speaking of the Church generally, "I marvel that we were so soon removed unto another Gospel. Who would believe that our Church had been founded on this important article of justification by faith alone. I am astonished I should ever think this a new doctrine, especially while our articles and homilies stand unrepealed, and the key of knowledge is yet not taken away." But while people wonder at the ignorance of John and Charles Wesley, I beg to call attention to what is still more wonderful, viz: the fact, that to this day there are thousands in the pulpits of the different churches, who are no farther forward now than the Wesleys were in the early part of the year 1738, and many not half so far! True, they can talk about certain truths, and so did the poor creature upon which Balaam rode, and probably it talked better than some poor creatures talk in the pulpit, for it did not read its talk from a manuscript, nor did it say anything but what was true, and what is also of great importance, it talked to the point, kept to its text, and gave over when it had done! But that creature, like many creatures in the pulpit, could not preach experimental religion; neither could John and Charles Wesley till they had a Christian experience, nor can any man! And they are many, alas! very many, who occupy both the pulpits and the pews of our churches, who have not a Christian experience: and these too will talk about power as they do about other things, not knowing what they talk about.

I do not say that any one of the above principles is the power of which I speak, nor do I believe that all of them put together are that power; but I claim that they are *essential to that power.* For where these principles are not, the power is not, and it is always present where they are. These principles and the peculiar power go together, and are inseparable. I do not say that the possession of these elements to the extent that the Wesleys had them, is essential to the very existence of this power. But I do say that a deficiency in the elements will result in a deficiency in the power. For instance, a man that is wholly given up to the guidance of divine providence, will be a greater power than one who is not. Nor do I say that there is no power in these elements, considered in themselves. On the contrary, I think the relation of a clear religious experience is, in itself, very forcible, and so is the clear announcement of Scripture truth, particularly the fundamental doctrines here specified: but this peculiar power is not *natural,* but *divine; it is the power of the Spirit,* and it is exerted *through the agent in whom the above principles meet; and according to the degree in which they meet in him.* Nor will anything prevent the successful operations of such power, but *resistance on the part of those for whose salvation the power is exerted.* Where the word of God is preached and the power of the Spirit does not accompany it, or accompanying it, fails to produce the desired result, the cause is to be found in the preacher, or in the hearers, or in both; for the Holy Spirit is always infinitely disposed to exert his power for the salvation of souls. The *absence* and *variations* of the Spirit's power are not caused by changes in the Divine mind, but by the *moral obstructions* which are presented either by those *through* whom he would exert his power, or by those *upon* whom he would exert his power. The power and goodness of the Holy Spirit were the same before the conversion of Whitefield and the Wesleys, that they were afterward—the very same, but those men were not the same before and after their conversion. No, after they were converted and qualified for the ministry, as stated above, they were " vessels unto honor, sanctified and meet for the Master's use, and prepared unto every good work." Before this time they were not. Hence God *could*, and did, use them now as he *did not*, and *could not* before. If any are startled by this statement, I will ask such this question: Do you believe that God could use an ignorant sinner in the work of the ministry just as well as he could Whitefield and the Wesleys, when they had all the qualifications specified above? If you say no, you grant all I claim. And if you say yes, I join issue with you and do not hesitate to say no. In my judgment you might just as well say that God could convert all men at any time, if he were so disposed, whether they would or not, as say that he can make the same use of a sinner that he can of a saint; for if there is no moral obstruction in the one case, neither is there in the other. Moreover, such a conclusion would attach all blame to the Almighty, and none to sinners, whether in the pulpit, the pew, or the world! I wish, to the very utmost of my power, to expose and condemn this most pernicious and wicked practice, and brand it, if possible, with the ever-during infamy which it so justly deserves.

Idle and useless professors, like other sinners, would have us believe that they are useless simply because God does not see fit to give them the power. And they would have us believe that they are very pious in all this; they are "waiting God's time;" they are simply "submitting to his sovereign will." No, my friend, nothing of the sort; you are simply *resisting* his sovereign will, and this is the sole reason why he does not, and can not, either use you, or save you. He tells you most distinctly, "I would, and ye would not." "Ye will not come to me that ye might have life." "Ye stiffnecked, and uncircumcised in heart and ears, ye do always *resist* the Holy Ghost." These are the reasons why you have neither life nor power. Only come to God as Whitefield and the Wesleys did, and he will put you upon the wheel, as he did them, and make you "vessels unto honor, sanctified and meet for the master's use, and prepared unto every good work." As to the sphere in which it may please God to use you, we have nothing to say; God will mark that out for you as seemeth him good, and lead and defend you in it, if you will give yourself up to the guidance of his providence. All we claim is, that you will be *a power*, whatever be your sphere. No man can unite in himself the nine elements specified above, and not be a power. *The Master will always use the vessel that is sanctified and meet for his use. And, observe, every element here specified, should enter into the character and life of every Christian, however humble his sphere of action.* The only *seeming* exception to this statement is the call to the regular work of the ministry. But this is really no exception, inasmuch as it merely regards the *sphere* in which the elements of power are to be exercised. For instance, Carvosso, the Cornish class-leader, was called to a given *sphere*, and obeyed the call; and in that sphere he was a man of power, and developed all the above elements of power as really as did John Wesley in his sphere of action. He preached the doctrine of justification by faith, corroborating it by his own happy experience, just as did Whitefield and the Wesleys, and that with similar success, though moving in a very humble sphere; so humble, that he, like many in similar circumstances, would have lived and died in obscurity, had it not been that he became conspicuous by the refulgent light that he shed upon his benighted neighbors, by his holy and useful life. Yes, all these elements of power met in Carvosso, as really as in John Wesley. The machinery and location were different, but the power was the same. The power that works a grist-mill, and that which drives the huge steamboat across the vast Atlantic, are essentially one. The machinery is a little varied to adapt the power to the different circumstances, that is all. And the difference between Carvosso and Wesley was similar. The engine in the country grist-mill would not supply the place of that in the Atlantic steamer, neither would

Carvosso supply the place of John Wesley, or George Whitefield, but the machinery and the power in the two former cases, and the elements and the power in the two latter, are *essentially the same;* NOR CAN YOU HAVE THE POWER WITHOUT THE ELEMENTS, NOR THE ELEMENTS WITHOUT THE POWER. I have used the word *elements,* because I could not think of another word that would comprehend and express, with less ambiguity, all the nine particulars specified. Any other word that is supposed to be more suitable, may be used, provided no one of the nine specifications is either excluded or altered.

The nine specifications, however, may be comprehended in three terms, viz: these, *Doctrine, Experience,* and *Practice,* the two latter flowing from the former, invariably so, as the word of God and Christian consciousness do most clearly testify: "Believe on the Lord Jesus Christ and thou shalt be saved." "He that believeth hath the witness in himself." "Being justified by faith, we have peace with God through our Lord Jesus Christ, by whom also we have access by faith into this grace wherein we stand, and rejoice in hope of the glory of God." The same truth is thus expressed in the Assembly's Catechism:—"The blessings which do in this life accompany or flow from justification, adoption, and sanctification, are assurance of God's love, peace of conscience, joy in the Holy Ghost." "We are his workmanship, created in Christ Jesus unto good works, which God hath before ordained that we should walk in them." "He that abideth in me, and I in him, the same bringeth forth much fruit, for separate from me ye can do nothing." "But ye shall receive power after that the Holy Ghost is come upon you." "I can do all things through Christ that strengtheneth me." Such is the *connection* and *order* of the *doctrines*, the *experience*, the *practice*, and the *power*. Not only are the principles here specified essentially connected, *but they are connected in this order*. The *experience*, the *practice*, and the *power*, follow faith, never go before, for "he that believeth not shall be damned."

I have not specified as necessary to this peculiar power the doctrine of *entire* satisfaction. First, because I do not find it in the facts of history which have passed under review, though I do find the power. Second, because I believe this power is both *retained* and *increased* by going on to this state of perfection; and, observe, here too we find the very same *connection* and *order* of *doctrine, experience, practice,* and *power*. "For whosoever hath, to him shall be given, and he shall have more abundance; but whosoever hath not, from him shall be taken away even that which he hath." It will be seen that these principles being *connected* in this *order*, exclude alike, *pharisaism, antinomianism,* and *latitudinarianism,* and as sure as this *connection* and *order* are not adhered to, one or other of these errors will creep in. As to the limited sanctification, I have not made that one of the specifications, because all who are justified are *thus* sanctified, and because it is necessarily included and implied in the specifications given.

Being convinced that the peculiar power and the principles above specified are inseparable, so much so, that no man or Church can have the principles without the power, or the power without the principles, we may well be permitted to dwell upon the subject a little longer, and bring forward two or three additional witnesses in support of our position.

Our next witness is John Nelson. We bring him forward, not only for the purpose above specified, but also, to show that every man, whether learned or unlearned, may, and should have the principles and, consequently, the power, for the principles may be viewed as the conditions of the power.

John Nelson was, I think, the first lay preacher raised up to bear witness to this power, in connection with Mr. Wesley. He heard Mr. Wesley preach his first sermon in Upper Moorfields on Sunday the 17th of June, 1739, from "Ho, every man that thristeth come ye to the waters," &c. His simple, unaffected account of himself, is alike touching and instructive. In his journal, p. 12, he says, "I went from church to church, but found no ease: one minister at St. Paul's preached about man doing his duty to God and his neighbor; and when such came to lie upon a death-bed, what joy they would have in their own breast by looking back on their well-spent life. But that sermon had like to have destroyed my soul, for I looked back, and could not see one day in all my life wherein I had not left undone something which I ought to have done, and wherein I had not done many things wrong; that I was so far from having a well-spent life to reflect upon, that I saw, if one day well-spent would save my soul, I must be damned for ever. After that I heard another sermon, wherein the preacher summed up all the Christian duties, but he said, man, since the fall, could not perfectly fulfil the will of his Maker; but God required him to do all he could and Christ would make out the rest, but if man did not do all he could, he must unavoidably perish. Then I thought, not only I, but every soul must be damned. Therefore I concluded that none could be saved but little children. I thought I would try others, and went to hear Dissenters of divers denominations, but to no purpose. Then I went to the Romans, but was soon surfeited with their ways of worship. Then I went to the Quakers, and prayed that God would not suffer the blind to go out of the way, but join me to the people that worshipped him in spirit and in truth; I cared not what they were called, nor what I suffered upon earth, so that my soul might be saved at last. I believe I heard them every Sunday for three months. What made me continue so long was, almost at my first going, one spoke something that nearly suited the state of my soul, but showed no remedy. I had now tried all but the Jews, and I thought it was to no purpose to go to them, so I thought I would go to church, and read and pray, whether I perished or not. But I was amazed when I came to join in the morning prayers, to see that I had mocked my Maker all my days by praying for things I did not expect, or desire. In the Spring [1739] Mr. Whitefield came into Moorfields, and I went to hear him; he was to me like a man that could play well upon an instrument, for his preaching was pleasant to me and I loved the man; so that if any one offered to disturb him, I was ready to fight for him." * * * "But sometimes as I was reading, I thought, if none are Christians but such as St. John and St. Paul describe,

I do not know one person that is a Christian, either in town or country. As for me, I am no more a Christian than is a devil, and my hope of ever being one is very small."

Thus he continued to wander about, still becoming more and more miserable. Nor did sleep afford him much relief, for he says, "In this struggle I had but little sleep; if I slept four hours out of twenty-four, I thought it was a great deal; sometimes I started as if I was falling into some horrible place, at other times I dreamed that I was fighting with Satan, and when I awoke I was sweating, and as fatigued as if I had really been fighting. In all this time I did not open my mind to any person, either by word or by letter, but I was like a wandering bird cast out of the nest till Mr. John Wesley came to preach his first sermon in Moorfields. O, that was a blessed morning to my soul! As soon as he got upon the stand he stroked back his hair and turned his face to where I stood, and, I thought, fixed his eyes on me; his countenance struck me with such an awful dread, before I heard him speak, that it made my heart beat like the pendulum of a clock, and when he did speak I thought his whole discourse was aimed at me. When he had done, I said, This man can tell the secrets of my heart; but he hath not left me there, for he hath showed me the remedy, even the blood of Jesus. Then was my soul filled with consolation through hope, that God for Christ's sake would save me; neither did I doubt in such a manner any more, till within twenty-four hours of the time when the Lord wrote pardon on my heart, though it was a little after midsummer that I heard him, and it was three weeks after Michaelmas before I found the true peace of God." This painful struggle continued till about the middle of October. Meantime, he says, " All my acquaintances set upon me to persuade me not to go too far in religion lest it should unfit me for my business, and so bring poverty and distress upon my family; and they said they wished I had never heard Mr. Wesley, for they were afraid it would be the ruin of me. I told them I had reason to bless God that ever he was born, for by hearing him I was sensible that my business in this world was to get well out of it; and as for my trade, health, wisdom, and all things in the world, they were no blessing to me any farther than as so many instruments to help me by the grace of God to work out my salvation. Then they said they were sorry for me, and should be glad to knock Mr. Wesley's brains out, for he would be the ruin of many families if he was allowed to live and go on as he did. Some of them said they would not hear him preach for fifty pounds." Shortly before he found salvation his distresses was great, so that he could neither rest, eat, nor sleep. But hear him: "When I went back to my lodging at noon, dinner was ready, and the gentlewoman said, ' Come, sit down, you have need of your dinner, for you have eaten nothing to-day;' but when I looked on the meat I said, 'Shall such a wretch as I devour the good creatures of God in the state I am now in? No, I deserve to be thrust into hell.' I then went into my chamber, shut the door, and fell down on my knees, crying, 'Lord save or I perish.' When I had prayed till I could pray no more, I got up and walked to and

fro, being resolved I would neither eat nor drink till I
had found the kingdom of God. I fell down to prayer
again, but found no relief; got up and walked again;
then tears began to flow from my eyes like great drops
of rain, and I fell on my knees a third time; but now
I was as dumb as a beast, and could not put up one
petition if it would have saved my soul. I kneeled
before the Lord sometime, and saw myself a criminal
before the judge; then I said, 'Lord, thy will be done,
damn or save.' That moment Jesus Christ was as
evidently set before the eye of my mind, as crucified
for my sins, as if I had seen him with my bodily eyes;
and in that instant my heart was set at liberty from
guilt and tormenting fear, and filled with a calm and
serene peace. I could then say, without any dread or
fear, 'Thou art my Lord and my God.' Now did I
begin to sing that part of the twelfth chapter of
Isaiah, 'O Lord, I will praise thee; though thou wast
angry with me, thine anger is turned away from me,
and thou comfortest me; behold, God is my salvation,
I will trust and not be afraid, for the LORD JEHO-
VAH is my strength and my song, he also is become
my salvation.' My heart was filled with love to God
and every soul of man, and next to my wife and
children, my mother, brethren and sisters, my greatest
enemies had an interest in my prayers, and I cried,
'O Lord, give me to see my desire on them; let them
experience thy redeeming love.' That evening, under
Mr. Wesley's sermon, I could do nothing but weep,
and love, and praise God for sending his servant into
fields to show me the way of salvation. All the day
I neither ate nor drank anything, for before I found

peace to my soul the hand of God was so heavy upon me, that I refused to eat; and after I had found peace I was so filled with the manna of redeeming love that I had no need of the bread that perisheth for that season."

His host and hostess, with whom he had long been a lodger, now became alarmed, and told him he must seek for lodging elsewhere, for he made so much fuss about religion, and prayed so much, they feared some mischief would happen! Accordingly, on Wednesday night he came to take away his few articles of clothing. While he was fixing up his little bundle, the good old man said to his wife, "Suppose John should be right, and we wrong, it would be a sad thing to turn him out of doors." This thought wrought a marvellous change in the mind of the woman, as well as in that of the man; hence, when John had pronounced his blessings upon them, and was about to start, the woman went between him and the door, and said, "You shall not go out of this house to night." To this unexpected opposition, John replied, "What, will you neither let me go nor stay?" She replied, "My husband is not willing you should go; for he saith, if God hath done anything more for you than for us, he would have you show us how we may find the same mercy." "So I sat down with them," says John, "and told them of God's dealing with my soul, and prayed with them; soon after which they both went to hear Mr. Wesley preach, when the woman was made partaker of the same grace; and I hope to meet them both in heaven." On the following Saturday, John had another trial; the "chief foreman" said to him. "John Nelson, you must look after such and such men to-morrow; there is a piece of work to be done with all speed, for the lord of the exchequer will be here on a particular day, by which time it must be completed." "Sir," replied John, "you have forgotten yourself; to-morrow is the Sabbath." "He said he knew that as well as me, but the King's business required haste, and it was common to work on Sunday for his majesty. I told him I would not work upon the Sabbath for any man in England, except it was to quench fire, or something that required the same immediate help." After reasoning with John to no purpose, the foreman told him he should lose his business. To this the young convert replied, "I cannot help it, though it may be ten pounds out of my way to be turned out of my work at this time of the year, I will not wilfully offend God; for I would much rather want bread, nay, I would much rather see my wife and children beg their bread barefooted to heaven, than ride in a coach to hell." The foreman now told Mr. Nelson that he would soon be "as mad as Whitefield," and added, "What hast thou done, that thou needest make so much ado about salvation! I always took thee to be as honest a man as any I have in the work, and could have trusted thee with five hundred pounds." "So you might," replied Mr. Nelson, "and not have lost one penny by me." But when Nelson undertook to show him that he deserved hell notwithstanding, he replied, "I have a worse opinion of thee now than ever." To this Mr. N. promptly replied, "Master, I have the odds of you, for I have a much worse opinion of myself than you can have." In the evening, the foreman asked Nelson if he were still obstinate, to which the latter replied, "I am determined not to break the Sabbath, for I will run the hazard of wanting bread here, rather than run the hazard of wanting water hereafter." In this interesting dialogue, the foreman gave his last reply in these words, "Wesley has made a fool of thee, and thou wilt beggar thy family." The next day the young convert had a glorious Sabbath, as might be expected. He says, "God blessed my soul wonderfully, both under the word and at the sacrament." On Monday morning Mr. Nelson went to the exchequer to take away his tools, but God had given the foreman another mind, so that he would not allow Mr. Nelson to leave, but gave him the superintendence of a part of the work, "neither had he set any man to work on the Sabbath, as he had said he would." If this good man had defiled his conscience by yielding to these temptations, he would have been as powerless as other men. But he did not, hence he not only retained the power he had, but had it greatly increased; and God made his power felt, so that the foreman respected the law of the Sabbath, and all the men were permitted to rest on the Lord's day.

With remarkable zeal and self-denial this young convert continued to labor for both worlds, though he says, "I had never spoken with Mr. Wesley in my life, nor conversed with any experienced man about religion. I longed to find one to talk with, but I sought in vain, for I could find none." Again, speaking of the first winter after his conversion, he says, "All that hard winter I still fasted from Thursday night till Saturday morning, and gave to the poor the meat that I saved by fasting, spending my time in praying and reading the

Scriptures." A little more than a year after his conversion, he had an interview with Mr. Wesley. The following is the record which he makes of this interesting event:—"I was at St Paul's, where Mr. John Wesley also was, and I contrived to walk with him after sacrament, for I had often wished I could speak with him; therefore I seized this opportunity; so we continued in discourse all the way from St. Paul's, to the farther end of Upper Moorfields, and it was a blessed conference to me. When parting, he took hold of my hand, and looking me full in the face, bid me take care I did not quench the spirit."

In December, 1740, he had a remarkable conviction that he must return to his home, in Birstal, Yorkshire. He did so, and soon told his experience to his friends. "But," he says, "they begged I would not tell any that my sins were forgiven, for no one would believe me, and they should be ashamed to show their face in the street. I should not be ashamed," he replied, "to tell what God had done for my soul, if I could speak loud enough for all the world to hear me at once." His mother told him his "head was turned," to which he replied, "Yes, and my heart too, I thank the Lord!" As he continued to reprove, rebuke, and exhort, his wife "desired that he would leave off abusing his neighbors, or go back to London." But he did neither, for he continued to "abuse his neighbors" by reproving them and telling them his experience. He now went to a meeting where he says, "One read in an old book for nearly an hour, then sang a hymn, and read a form of prayer. I told them that way would never convert sinners, and began to relate some of my experience; several were struck with convictions while I was speaking, and some soon bore witness to the same grace that God showed me. In a little time all I said was noised abroad, and people of all denominations came to dispute with me. As soon as I came home from work, my house was filled with people, which made my wife uneasy, for she could do no work, and did not yet believe that what I said was true.

"Generally, when I came in and sat down, some one would ask me a question, and others would begin to dispute with me, while others stood to hear. When any one began to cavil, I commonly asked what *Church* they belonged to, and if they said the Church of England, then I replied, Do you know your sins forgiven? Several said, 'No, nor never expect to know that in this world.' Then I said, You are no member of the Church of England, if you have not a full trust and confidence that God, for Christ's sake, hath forgiven you. Read the homilies of the Church, and you will see what I say is true. I used to have the Bible and Common Prayer Book by me, and I showed them the articles of the Church, saying, You deny inspiration, and the Church you profess to belong to says, '*Before the grace of Christ, and the inspiration of his Spirit, no good works can be done.*' When any said they were of the Church of Scotland, I asked them if they did not know their sins forgiven. They told me they did not; nay, further, they thought it presumption for any one to pretend to know it, or to expect such high attainments as I spoke of; and they told me I was a Papist, or I would not talk as I did." To this he replied, "I think you neither know what a Papist or a Presbyterian is, for your own lips declare that you are no members of the Church of Scotland; that Church disowns you, for none are allowed members thereof but those who are effectually called; and they that are effectually called, do in this life partake of *justification, adoption* and *sanctification*. And the same Church saith, that *justification* is an act of God's free grace, wherein he pardoneth all our sins; *adoption* is an act of God's free grace, by which we are received into the number, and have a right to all the privileges of God's sons; and that *sanctification* is a work of God's free grace, whereby we are renewed in the whole man, after the image of God, and all that are so effectually called, do enjoy an assurance of God's love, peace of conscience, and joy in the Holy Ghost. And I pray you what have I said more? By your talking, you are the sons of Rome, and enemies to the true Protestant religion. Let me beg you to go home, and read the Assembly's Catechism, and come and talk with me again. Several of them did so, and came with tears in their eyes, and are now witnesses that God hath power on earth to forgive sins."

Soon, two of his brothers, his wife, his mother, his aunt, two of his cousins, and many of his neighbors were converted. Soon the house became too small for the crowds that waited upon him when he returned from his daily employment, as a stonecutter; and he too had to take to the open air. The writer has been in that good old house, and marked with interest the old door yard in which the honest stonemason preached the Gospel so successfully to his neighbors. His labors and wonderful success as recorded in his interesting journal, from which I have quoted the above are well known. We have quoted sufficient to establish our position, viz: that John Nelson, like the Wesleys and Whitefield, was powerless for good up to the period marked in history: from that period he was a power, as really and truly, as were the noted characters previously presented, though he had neither the learning nor the formal ordination which they had. They were powerless *with* these two particulars; he was a power *without* them! He *obtained* the power, and *retained* it in precisely the same way that they obtained and retained it. And he united in himself all the nine particulars which we have discovered in the Wesleys and Whitefield, connected with this power. The principles and the power always go together; are never found separate. You cannot find a man, or a church, possessing the one and not the other. Hence we conclude that the principles are the *conditions* of the power. And as every man may and should have the principles, every man may and should have the power. The whole is necessary to the full development of the Christian character.

In further support of our position, we will now glance very briefly at the history of Luther and that of the Apostles.

It is well known that, at the beginning of the sixteenth century, not only the heathen world, but also the nominally Christian world, was wrapped in darkness of unparalleled density, only mitigated by a few rays of light that still lingered in the valleys of the Alps, among the ancient Waldenses. But these good people were so shut in on every side by the

Pope and the devil, that no one seemed capable of passing beyond the valleys to carry the torch of revelation to the benighted and perishing world outside.

Now, I simply propose to show, that God came to the *rescue*, and that he enlightened and saved in precisely the same way that he did at the beginning of the eighteenth century.

Martin Luther was the son of a miner, in Mansfeld, a little town in Saxony. His thoughtful father soon discovered in the mind of young Luther a remarkable activity, and put forth noble efforts to give him a liberal education. He is finally sent to the University of Erfurt. Here, like the Wesleys, he became distinguished by his close application to his studies, and by his literary acquirements. But the religious tendency of his mind led him, contrary to the wishes of his father, to seek for help in the Convent of the Hermits of St. Augustine. This event took place on the 17th of August, 1505, when he had reached the age of twenty-one years and nine months.

In the hope of obtaining peace to his troubled soul, and of reaching heaven at last, he now prosecutes with intense ardor the pharisaic and superstitious work assigned him, to that end, in the Convent. But God, who always helps the sincere, though erring seeker, did not fail to help this poor monk in his superstitious, though honest efforts. Hence, "He found," says D'Aubigne, " in the convent, a Bible fastened to its place by a chain, and returned constantly to the perusal of this enfettered Bible. He little understood the meaning of the word; but it was, nevertheless, his most pleasing study. He was sometimes in the habit of passing a whole day contemplating the subject of a single passage." But although the Pharisee is still determined to save himself in his own way, the light of revelation begins to penetrate his dark mind, and lead him to doubt the possibility of his doing so. Hence he is at length led to exclaim, "I see myself to be, in the sight of God, a great sinner, and I do not believe it possible for me to appease his wrath by any merits of my own."

But this Pharisee, like the Wesleys long after, still persevered in his efforts " to establish his own righteousness." Hence, at an after period he says, "I have tormented myself even unto death, in order to procure for my troubled heart and agonized conscience peace with God; but, surrounded with horrible darkness, I nowhere found that peace." Again, when at the point of despair, he says, "Immediately I would run to a thousand shifts to appease the accusations of my heart. I made confession of my sins every day; but that brought me no relief. Then, overwhelmed with sorrow, I harassed my soul by the multitude of my thoughts. Look here! I would cry to myself, behold you are still as envious as ever, as impatient, as passionate!
* * * * * It has then been of no use to me, unhappy being that I am, to have entered in communion with this holy order." The following, from D'Aubigne, is very affecting:—" The young monk, like a shadow, paced along the lengthened corridors of the cloister, making their vaults ring with the sounds of his groaning. His body wasted away, his strength forsook him, and he sometimes remained in a condition resembling the state of death. On one

occasion, his spirits crushed with care, he shut himself up in his cell, and, for many days and nights, forbade the approach of any one within its door. One of his friends, Lucas Edenberger, distressed with the conduct of the unhappy monk, and having some presentiment of the state of his mind, took with him certain young boys accustomed to sing in the choir, and went to knock at the door of his cell. But no one either opened the door or answered to the call thus made. The worthy Edenberger, still more alarmed, broke open the door. Luther lay extended on the floor, deprived of his senses, and without exhibiting any symptoms of life. His friend strove in vain to bring back the use of his faculties. Then the boys began to sing a sweet hymn. Their sweet voices acted as a charm upon the deadened feelings of the poor monk, for whom music had always possessed a singular pleasure. By degrees he recovered his strength, his senses and his life."

These are but a few of the terrible struggles through which this poor pharisaic monk passed in his efforts to reach heaven by "climbing up some other way;" but they are sufficient to enable us to appreciate the following reflections, which he made after he had experienced redemption in the blood of Jesus. Writing to the duke Gregory of Saxony, he says, "Truly I have been a pious monk, and have fulfilled the regulations of my order more rigidly than I would wish to express. If ever a monk had been able to enter the gates of heaven by means of his monkish observances, most assuredly I should have gained an entrance therein. A fact which can be proved by the whole of the religious fraternity with whom I was acquainted. Had my monastic life continued much longer, I would have suffered the death of martyrdom, on account of my watchings, prayings, readings, and other labor."

But he who sent Annanias to the penitent Saul, another pharisee, now sends Staupitz to the pharisaic, but now self-despairing Luther, to point him to "the Lamb of God that taketh away the sins of the world." "Wherefore" said the venerable Staupitz, "do you torment yourself with all these vain speculations and high thoughts? * * * * * Look to the sufferings of Jesus Christ, to the blood he has shed for you; it is in these things the grace of God will appear to you. In place of making yourself a martyr on account of your faults, throw yourself into the arms of the Redeemer. Trust you in him, in the uprightness of his life, in the expiation of his death." Having received the truth from the chained Bible in the Convent, and then from the lips of Staupitz, the Holy Spirit now speaks that same truth to Luther, first at Wirtemberg, then at Bologna; and, finally at Rome, while the poor monk was still striving to "climb up some other way," while he was literally climbing up what were called "Pilot's Stairs." The words which were mysteriously spoken to his inmost soul, were, "the just shall live by faith." Thus were his filthy rags of pharisaic and monkish righteousness swept away, and the miserable sinner was saved by grace through faith, and the monk, now transformed into a Christian, forsook Rome and pharisaism at the same time, and having consecrated himself to his God and Saviour, and being now in possession of the peculiar power, he becomes the great reformer of the sixteenth century!

To establish our position beyond the possibility of mistake, we may be permitted to give a few additional quotations. We cannot deny ourselves the pleasure of giving D'Aubigne's reflections upon this important event. "The same effectual weapon that had been wielded by the apostles, was now at last drawn forth in its original brightness, from the armory of the mighty God. At the instant when Luther rose from his knees in Rome, awakened and called to reason by the same words which Paul had addressed fifteen hundred years before to the inhabitants of the same metropolis, the truth, until then mournfully bound and kept captured, was also relieved from bondage, never again to suffer imprisonment." But, as our historian observes, we must here listen to Luther's own words:—"although I was a holy and irreproachable monk, my conscience was nevertheless filled with trouble and despair. I could not suffer this expression, the righteousness of God. I did not love this just and holy God who punished sinners. I was affected against him with secret rage; I hated him, because that, not content with alarming us with the terrors of the law, and the miseries of this life, we poor creatures already lost in original sin, he still augmented our torments by the revelations of the Gospel. * * * But, when through the Spirit of God, I was made to comprehend these words, when I learned how the justification of the sinner proceeded from the pure mercy of the Lord by means of faith * * * then I found my nature refreshed like a new man; I entered, as it were, at an open door into the very Paradise of God." "I see," said he on another occasion, "that the devil attacks without ceasing this fundamental article by means of his doctrines, and that he cannot, in respect of it, either leave off or take any rest. Very well, for myself Dr. Martin Luther, an unworthy evangelist of our Lord, Jesus Christ, I confess this article, that *faith alone justifies in the sight of God, without works;* and I declare that the emperor of the Romans, the emperor of the Turks, the emperor of the Tartars, the emperor of the Persians, the Pope, all the cardinals, the bishops, priests, monks, nuns, kings, princes, everybody else, with all devils, must allow it to continue upright, and admit that it shall forever endure." After continuing to pour out his fervent spirit for some time, in language similar to the above, and asserting that this doctrine "is found in the true and holy gospel," and that Jesus Christ is the only Saviour, he adds, "And if it is he alone who can take away sin, it cannot be us who do so with our works." But good works follow redemption, as the fruit is seen upon the tree. This is our doctrine, it is the doctrine of the Holy Spirit, received and taught by all holy Christians. We hold it in the name of God. Amen." It is quite clear that this man believes what he says; yea, and that he knows it by happy and unmistakable experience. Upon another occasion, he said, "In my heart reigns single, and ought to reign there alone, faith in my Lord Jesus Christ, who only is the beginning, the middle, and the end of all the thoughts which occupy my mind night and day." This language is worthy of a Christian reformer, and should be the language of all who name the name of Christ.

It was some of these fervent and truly evangelic utterances, that reached the heart of John Wesley in a house in Aldersgate street, in London, more than two hundred years afterward, and led to the reformation of the eighteenth century.

The above quotations are from D'Aubigne's History of the Reformation. On looking over Luther's sermons, I find similar sentiments, uttered with similar fervor, and they are in every sermon, no matter what his text is. In his sermon on Gal. iv. 1—7, he says, "Neither is it a controversy among the godly, that man is not justified by works, but righteousness must come from some other source than from his works." Again, "There are two sorts of works; those before justification, and those after it; these last are good works, indeed, but the former only appear to be good." Of the latter, he says, "These are not the works of nature, but of grace." Again, "He that studieth to fulfil the law without faith, continues a persecutor both of faith and the law, until he come to himself, and cease to trust in his own works; he then gives glory to God, who justifies the ungodly, and acknowledgeth himself to be nothing, and sighs for the grace of God, of which he knows that he hath need. Faith and grace now fill his empty mind, and satisfy his hunger, then follow works which are truly good." And these works, he says, are "of the spirit of faith and grace." In his sermon on Luke, chap. vi. 36–42, he says, "We should place our trust and confidence in God alone for whatsoever things we need, for we enjoy no blessing, either temporal or spiritual, that does not proceed from his bounteous grace and goodness. But there are some who place confidence in themselves, and in other men; who rest upon their traditions, and put their trust in things that some great man hath invented. Of such God speaketh in Jer. ii. 13: 'For my people have committed two great evils; they have forsaken me, the fountain of living water, and have hewn them out cisterns, broken cisterns, that can hold no water.' In the same manner, the papists of the present time, forsaking the way of life, which is faith in Christ, look for salvation through their own works, such as their fastings and formal prayers, and the celebration of masses which they have instituted. This religion of rites and forms, though it may appear to them a living fountain, is nevertheless a broken cistern, capable of holding no water." When his text is the first commandment, he preaches the same doctrine. He shows that "idolatry reigns in the bosom of every man, until he is freely healed by the faith which is in Jesus Christ." Being thus saved, he says, "nothing remains with you but Jesus, Jesus alone; Jesus proving sufficient to gratify every longing of your soul. No longer hoping for any assistance from any creature, you look exclusively to Christ, from whom you hope to receive all, and whom you love more than all beside. Now Jesus is the only true God. When you possess him for your God, you no longer possess any other gods." Such is Luther's method of curing all idolators. And just such is the cure which the apostle John offers in the following words, having, like Luther, preached Jesus, he adds, "This is the true God, and eternal life. Little children, keep yourselves from Idols. Amen." Nor is there any other cure for idolatry. Where this doctrine is received idolatry cannot exist; where it is not received, and preached, idolatry will exist and reign, either in a ritualistic, or some other form. Truly, it is with a poor grace that a Church professes the doctrines of the Reformation, and yet returns to ritualism, and covers herself with the trappings of popish superstition and idolatry. The Church that does not hold and preach the great doctrine of justification by faith alone, must, to be consistent, reject both Protestantism and the Bible; for, all that is vital in the Bible, all that is vital in Protestantism, is essentially connected with this doctrine. Hence, it is not possible for any Church or individual to have the power of which we speak till this doctrine is embraced.

It will be seen by all who examine the historic facts here given, that Martin Luther united in himself all the nine principles which we have specified as the *conditions* of this power; and from the time he did so, he was a power, while before that time he was utterly helpless. In short, both before and after, he was, in every essential particular, like the men previously mentioned.

With the history of the apostles, and the reformation of their times, all are, or should be, familiar. Hence it is only necessary to challenge a comparison of the historic records of the New Testament with those here given. We are confident that every intelligent person who will be at the trouble of doing so, will discover a perfect harmony between the two records, and that the principles and the power here specified, and exhibited in the facts of history, are found in every truly Christian man, and in every truly

Christian Church. The principles and the power always go together; they are never found separate; they are as inseparable as are matter and figure.

To present this subject with the utmost clearness, even to those who are too indolent to make a more lengthened comparison, we will glance at the case of St. Paul.

He tells us that he was "a Pharisee, the son of a Pharisee." He says, "after the straitest sect of our religion, I lived a Pharisee." And, like Luther, he tells his Pharisaic brethren that they could "testify" to the truth of this statement. "if they would." See Acts xxiii. 6, and xxvi. 5. Again, "If any other man thinketh that he hath whereof he might trust in the flesh, I more: circumcised the eighth day, of the stock of Israel, of the tribe of Benjamin, an Hebrew of the Hebrews; as touching the law, a Pharisee, concerning zeal, persecuting the Church, touching the righteousness which is in the law, blameless. But what things were gain to me, those I counted loss for Christ. Yea, doubtless, and I count all things but loss for the excellency of the knowledge of Christ Jesus my Lord; for whom I have suffered the loss of all things, and do count them but dung that I may win Christ, and be found in him, not having mine own righteousness, which is of the law, but that which is through the faith of Christ, the righteousness which is of God by faith; that I may know him, and the power of his resurrection, and the fellowship of his sufferings, being made conformable unto his death, if by any means I might attain unto the resurrection of the dead." Phil. iii. 4, 11. In his epistle to the Galatians chap. i. 13,

16, he says, "For ye have heard of my conversation in time past, in the Jews' religion, how that beyond measure I persecuted the Church of God, and wasted it; and profited in the Jews' religion above many my equals in mine own nation, being more exceeding zealous of the traditions of my fathers. But when it pleased God, who separated me from my mother's womb, and called me by his grace, to reveal his son in me, that I might preach him among the heathen, immediately I conferred not with flesh and blood." Now, let no one glance hastily at these quotations, as though everybody understood and believed them already. Examine them carefully and you will see that Paul's record of himself is essentially one with that of Luther,. the Wesleys, Whitefield, and John Nelson. The same *doctrine*, the same *experience*, the same *consecration*, the same *practice*, and the same *power*. Before justification by faith, Paul was as powerless as was Luther the pharisaic monk, but as soon as he is *justified by faith alone*, he is a power and becomes one of those who "turn the world upside down;" being determined "to know nothing among men save Jesus Christ and him crucified," he wields a power that is felt by all worlds. He who before "made havock of the Church, and wasted it," now makes havoc alike of gentile philosophy and pharisaic traditions, exclaiming, "Where is the wise? Where is the scribe? Where is the disputer of this world? Hath not God made foolish the wisdom of this world? For after that in the wisdom of God the world by wisdom knew not God, it pleased God by the foolishness of preaching to save them that believe. For the

Jews require a sign, and the Greeks seek after wisdom, but we preach Christ crucified, unto the Jews a stumbling-block, and unto the Greeks foolishness; but unto them which are called both Jews and Greeks, Christ the power of God and the wisdom of God." Now, anticipating the contemptuous and contemptible objections of proud pharisees, and proud philosophers, he exclaims, "I am not ashamed of the Gospel of Christ: for it is the power of God unto salvation to every one that believeth, to the Jew first, and also to the Greek. For therein is the righteousness of God revealed from faith to faith; as it is written, The just shall live by faith."

It is worthy of notice, that Paul and Luther look out upon the world and with similar zeal and courage, hurl defiance at all the enemies of Christ and the Gospel. In conclusion, we simply call attention to the *oneness* of the *men*, the *principles*, and the *power*, that God employed in the reformations of the first, six- and the eighteenth centuries.

CHAPTER IV.

Between the position specified, and that of the Pharisee, there is no medium—Pharisees, Sadducees, and Herodians, are presented in Scripture as representative classes of character, and are, as they ever have been, the grand enemies of Christianity—Pharisaism is fully investigated, by reference to Scripture and History—The principle upon which Pharisaism rests, is that of *human merit;* that upon which Christianity rests, is *grace coming through the merit of the atonement*—All who seek at all, rest their expectations upon one of these two principles—*Grace* and *faith* go together, as do merit and works—Pharisaism embraces a great variety of characters, but they all rest upon the same principle, viz: *merit;* hence the appeal is to naked justice: while the Christian rests upon the atonement and expects *all* of *mere grace*—The Pharisee and the Publican are presented as the representatives of the two systems—Salvation by works, was, and is, an eternal impossibility—The transition from Pharisaism to Sadducism is easy and frequent, and, to some extent, inevitable—Sadducean history fully examined, and Sadducean character, ancient and modern, carefully delineated; and its evil tendencies exposed—It is not possible for those who think, to rest in Pharisaism; hence, those who think, either fall back upon Bible truth, or pass to Sadducism, and thence to all kinds of skepticism—An interesting account and thrilling description of Herodians, ancient and modern—These three systems concentrated, and formed that horrible thing called Popery—How saved from all these errors.

PHARISAISM.

BUT suppose you have not the power of which we have been speaking, because you have not the principles which are essential to its existence, what then? Why, just this; at the very best you are a Pharisee; for between the position here specified, and that of the Pharisee, there is no medium. Of course we do not here include the state of the penitent, which is a *transition* state. Nor do we include the case of the heathen; we do not think that their case belongs to the subject under discussion: but having discovered and developed moral power, and the principles essential thereto, we now purpose to point out the grand principles of error which are essentially opposed thereto; so much so, that both cannot exist in the same mind at the same time; either must exclude the other. We believe that all in Christendom who have not embraced the principles and power which we have specified, are either *Pharisees, Sadducees,* or *Herodians.* These are the grand enemies of Christianity. Hence, we purpose to expose these grand errors, to the end they may be dispossessed of the ground which they now occupy, so that the principles and power of which we speak may take their place. This has been, still is, and ever will be, the great work of the Christian reformer. So long as it is even *tacitly* admitted, that men may be destitute of the principles and power specified, and yet be Christians, it is in vain that we look for Christian reformation. It was not thus that the reformations of the first, sixteenth and eighteenth centuries were produced, as may be clearly seen by reference to the historic facts which we have adduced. And it was for this purpose that we adduced them.

The Pharisees, the Sadducees, and the Herodians are presented to us in the New Testament as the great enemies of Jesus, his teachings, and his followers; sometimes separately, and sometimes combinedly. For a time our blessed Lord was popular with the masses of the people; "The common people heard him gladly," till they were perverted and moved to opposition by the leaders of these classes. We believe that these three classes are presented to us in Scripture as representative characters, and that they still exist, and are still the grand enemies of Jesus, his teachings, and his followers. And as we purpose to show that all in Christendom who do not embrace, theoretically and experimentally, the grand doctrine of justification by faith, belong to one or other of these three classes, it will be necessary to point out the distinguishing characteristics and principles of each sect. It is cause of thankfulness that the New Testament furnishes ample material for this purpose, and, by the way, this fact marks the importance of the subject; God has set a mark upon them as he did on Cain, the first Pharisee.

Of the better class of Pharisees, Paul gives us the following comprehensive and lucid description: "For I bear them record that they have a zeal for God, but not according to knowledge. For they, being ignorant of God's righteousness, and going about to establish their own righteousness, have not submitted themselves to the righteousness of God." In his epistle to the Phil. Chap. iii., he tells us what he means by the "righteousness of God," as distinguished from that of a Pharisee. Having given us his own character and experience as a Pharisee specifying the things in which he gloried, he says, "But what things were gain to me, those I counted loss for Christ, yea, doubtless, and I count all things but loss for the excellency of the knowledge of Christ Jesus my Lord, for whom I have suffered the loss of all things, and do count them but dung that I may win Christ, and be found in him, not having mine own righteousness, which is of the law, but that which is through the faith of Christ, the righteousness which is of God by faith." Again, Rom. iv. 3–5, " For what saith the Scripture? Abraham believed God, and it was counted unto him for righteousness. Now to him that worketh is the reward not reckoned of grace, but of debt. But to him that worketh not, but believeth on him that justifieth the ungodly, his faith is counted for righteousness." Let it be well observed, that according to this teaching, *grace, faith* and *righteousness* go together, and that the Pharisee by "going about to establish his own righteousness" by his works, thereby excludes *faith* and *grace*, and thus renders righteousness impossible, for "by the deeds of the law shall no flesh living be justified." It follows that the Pharisaic method presents an absolute antagonism to the economy of grace, for " to him that worketh is the reward not reckoned of grace, but of debt," and this excludes the very idea of grace! If what I receive is the mere payment of a debt for work done, I receive it not of grace, but of naked justice. Hence, the Apostle says, "it is of faith, that it might be by grace." Nor is there any medium between Paul's position and that of the Pharisee. This is asserted by him in his epistle to the Romans, Chap. xi. 6. "And if by grace, then is it no more of works, otherwise grace is no more grace. But if it be of works, then it is no more grace; otherwise, work is no more work. If it is by *grace*, it is not by *works*, and if it is by *works*, it is not by *grace*. These two principles are absolutely opposed, the one to the other, so much so that either one absolutely excludes the other; and, observe, every one who seeks righteousness at all, must seek it in one of these two ways; there is absolutely no medium; we are shut up to this alternative; we must seek by faith or by works. Hence, we repeat, between the Christian and the Pharisee there is no medium; these two classes comprehend all in Christendom who are not Sadducees, or Herodians, and these two last classes cannot be said to seek at all, as we shall show; they have got away beyond the region where seekers live; they cannot be classed either with Christians, Pharisees, or heathens.

Seeing pharisaic righteousness is the only substitute for God's righteousness, and seeing all who do not seek *by grace through faith* are "going about to establish their own righteousness," if they seek at all, we will quote another passage of holy writ to show with the utmost clearness how a Pharisee *goes about to establish his own righteousness*. We think our blessed Lord has given us the clearest possible view of this whole subject in the following narrative or parable, and his comment upon it. This parable is in the 18th chapter of Luke, and reads thus:—"And he spake this parable unto certain who trusted in themselves that they were righteous, [margin, as being righteous,] and despised others: two men went up into the temple to pray, the one a Pharisee, and the other a publican. The Pharisee stood and prayed thus with himself: God, I thank thee that I am not as other men *are*, extortioners, unjust, adulterers, or even as this publican. I fast twice in the week; I give tithes of all that I possess. And the publican standing afar off, would not lift up so much as his eyes to heaven, but smote upon his breast, saying, God be merciful to me a sinner. I tell you, this man went down to his house justified, *rather* than the other, for every one that exalteth himself shall be abased, and he that humbleth himself shall be exalted." We doubt whether it is possible to have a more striking test of the two principles, salvation by *grace*, and salvation by *works*, than that here given. God being the judge, the one is a perfect failure, and the other a perfect success; though on the one hand, the pharisaic system is represented by one of the best pharisees that can be produced; while on the other hand, God's plan of salvation is tested by a publican, a more than ordinary sinner, acknowledged to be such, both by himself and all others. The Pharisee pleads the best works that a Pharisee can offer, but he is rejected, he remains unpardoned, unsaved, a pharisaic sinner in the sight of God, though a saint in his own estimation; while the other makes no mention of his righteousness, honestly denies that he has any, acknowledges that he is a sinner, and as such, simply *cries for mercy*. The result is, God forgives; he saves the penitent, praying sinner, just as he saved the Wesleys, Whitefield, Nelson, Luther, Paul; and the publican goes "down to his house justified," exclaiming, doubtless, " O to grace how great a debtor." While the Pharisee goes away, still making mention of his own righteousness, and still determined to purchase heaven by offering his *mint*, his *anise*, and his *cummin*, instead of the atonement of Christ. And, - by the way, this is the true idea of pharisaism; it offers to eternal justice, "mint, anise and cummin," or ritualistic trumpery, instead of the atonement of Jesus Christ. And, observe, *this is true of all who are seeking, but not seeking justification by faith alone.* To ALL such the language of the Psalmist is entirely applicable, "Ye fools, when will ye be wise?"

But let us examine the character and principles of this Pharisee still more minutely; this is the more necessary as he is a representative character. This is evident from the fact that this parable is addressed to ALL "who trust in themselves that they are righteous, and despise others," as all Pharisees do, and this man is given as a living specimen of all such. He "went up into the temple to pray," but he evidently did not know the meaning of the word *pray,* for he never offered up a single petition. How could he, seeing he "trusted in himself" as being righteous already? Like the Laodiceans he considered himself "rich and increased in goods and had need of nothing," while, like them, he knew not that he was "wretched, and miserable, and poor, and blind, and naked." "The Pharisee stood and prayed thus with himself," yes, just THUS, "God, I thank thee that I am not as other men." Mark, a Pharisee is always comparing himself with others, and, of course, he always brings himself off first best, as in this case. Dr. Adam Clark, in his comment on this text gives a remarkable instance, as illustrative of the fact here stated :—"Rabbi Simeon, the son of Jochai, said, if there were only thirty righteous persons in the world, I and my son should make two of them; but if there were but twenty, I and my son would be of the number; and if there were but ten, I and my son would be of the number; and if there were but five, I and my son would be of the five; and if there were but two, I and my son would be those two: and if there were but one, myself should be that one." "This," adds the doctor, "is a genuine specimen of pharisaic pride." No marvel that such a man "prayed thus with himself, God, I thank thee." Like Cain, and all other Deists, he could bring a thank-offering but no *sacrifice*, no *atonement for sin*, for he did not believe he had any sin that rendered an atonement necessary; hence, we are told *that he exalted himself, and trusted in himself that he was righteous*. The sum of his righteousness, as stated by himself, was this: he was free from certain outward sins; he attended the public ordinances, after the Pharisaic fashion, of course; he fasted twice in the week, and he paid tithes of all that he possessed. Of course it will not be supposed that all Pharisees go this far; this is given as the very best specimen, of the best righteousness that the best Pharisee can offer; it is all that this Pharisee claimed, and with it he was entirely satisfied. It must be observed, too, that all the righteousness here specified, is merely outward; inward religion, holiness of heart, is not so much as thought of, nor is there the slightest reference to pardon or to the work, or witness of the Spirit; though all these have a prominent place in the promises and prayers of the Old Testament Scripture, so that this Pharisee was without excuse, and so are all Pharisees. But the fact is, natural powers and natural laws, are entirely competent to produce Pharisaic righteousness, hence the supernatural is neither sought nor desired; a Pharisee feels entirely competent to do his own work, which is merely outward, and, at best, the merest semblance of God's righteousness leaving the heart unchanged and corrupt. It is of this, the best class of Pharisees, that our Lord says, "Now do ye Pharisees make clean the outside of the cup and platter, but your inward part is full of ravening and wickedness." Hence he solemnly declares, "That except your righteousness shall exceed the righteousness of the Scribes and Pharisees, ye shall in no case enter into the kingdom of heaven." This is final. He that hath an ear let him hear! And, mark well, no righteousness of fallen man is any better, or any other, than that of the Pharisee, except "the righteousness of God, which is by faith of Jesus Christ, unto all and upon all that believe." Justification, regeneration, sanctification, adoption, assurance, love, peace, joy, all follow faith in Jesus Christ, and cannot go before, for faith is the *condition* of this salvation, every part of which is the work of the eternal Spirit, coming to us, and working in us, for the sake of what Christ has done and suffered.

Such is the righteousness of God, and such is the way in which it is obtained. Therefore between this doctrine and Pharisaism there is no medium. All who do not seek this righteousness, in this way, are Pharisees if they seek at all. In the matter of salvation we are shut up to one of two principles, *merit* or *grace*, and equally shut up to one of two conditions *faith* or *works*. Works imply *merit*, faith implies *grace*. And either principle excludes the other. Hence Paul says, "If by grace, then is it no more of works: but if it be of works, then is it no more of grace."

And as salvation by works is impossible, the apostle says, "It is of *faith*, that it might be by *grace*." Again, Eph. ii. 5, "By grace are ye saved." And yet, again, verse 8, "For by grace are ye saved, through faith, and that not of yourselves: *it is* the gift of God: not of works, lest any man should boast. For we are his workmanship, created in Christ Jesus unto good works, which God hath before ordained that we should walk in them." The fact is, justification or pardon by works, implies a positive contradiction; for work implies *merit*, and *merit* excludes the very idea of pardon. Hence Universalists, very consistently with their principle, which is, that we all suffer in this life according to the extent of our sins, say there can be no such thing as pardon. Very true, if your principle is true. But, remember, your principle is not true, if Scripture teaching is true; for, according to that teaching, *it is by grace we are saved through faith.*" The whole "is the gift of God," faith the *condition*. "Not of works, lest any man should boast." It will be well, too, for Universalists to remember, that they are of the sect of the Pharisees, and so are all others who seek salvation in any other way than "by grace through faith," for, I repeat it, between this doctrine and Pharisaism there is no medium. Men may call themselves what they please, but if they seek or expect salvation at all, their whole religious system must rest upon one of these two principles, salvation by *grace* through *faith;* or salvation by *merit*, through *works*. If they consistently act out the former principle, they are Christians; if the latter, they are Pharisees, and as such, "shall in no case enter into the kingdom of heaven." "The mouth of the Lord hath spoken it."

It is only by examining these principles, *merit* and *grace, faith* and *works,* that we can form anything like a just conception of the number, the vast number of Pharisees. If you are a Christian, and would test this matter more fully, just do the following: Converse closely with the first non-professor you meet. He has not sought and obtained pardon by faith in Jesus; to this religion he makes no pretensions. Yet he expects to go to heaven when he dies. Why? Examine closely, and you will probably find that his expectation rests upon something like this: "He is not as other men are." He is free from certain outward sins; he does many good things, and, perhaps, he goes to Church; and if he does not, it is because he despises those who do, and considers himself much better than most of them. Now, compare this with the statements of the Pharisee as given above, and you will find it substantially the same. *Hence he is a Pharisee.* Let any one who is comparatively moral, but who has not experienced what is specified, Rom. v. 1, 2, examine himself closely, and he will find, I doubt not, that his hopes of heaven rest on substantially the same basis. Hence, you, too, are a Pharisee. No doubt you take into account the fact, that God is good, hence you are saved, simply because God is good and you are not very bad. You forget that it is the *ungodly,* the *sinner,* that God saves *by grace through faith.* Moreover, if the simple fact that God is good, saves you, it will, of course, save all; so that your Pharisaism runs in the direction of Universalism. You forget, too, that although God is good, he says, "he that believeth not shall be damned." "He that believeth on the Son hath everlasting life; and he that believeth not the Son, shall not see life; but the wrath of God abideth on him." Hence it is evident that the mere fact that God is good, does not save sinners from suffering, either here or hereafter. Examine still more carefully and you will probably discover as did Luther when he was a Pharisaic monk, that you consider all this unjust; that you secretly hate this God; and, remember, there is no other God: this is the only true God; and this is the only true religion; and this is the only way in which this true religion can be obtained. So that after all, if the Bible is true, *you are without hope and without God in the world.* Moreover, if, as you think, it would be unjust for God to shut out of heaven such amiable persons, as you think yourself and other Pharisees are, you thereby think that he is bound in *justice* to receive you all into heaven; so that, after all, you expect heaven on the principle of *naked justice*, and that without justification, regeneration, adoption, or sanctification; for to these blessings you make no pretensions, and probably you consider them all hypocrites who do. Hence you are just where Saul was when he was a Pharisee and the son of a Pharisee. So true it is that there is no medium between Pharisaism and the doctrine of justification by faith alone; for the *dogma* of justification by faith and works unitedly, is absurd, contradictory and impossible.

Pharisaism embraces an almost endless variety of character, from the comparatively amiable man presented by our blessed Lord in the above parable, to the infamous Simon, the sorcerer, who thought that the gift of God might be purchased with money; together with the still more infamous Tetzel, who peddled "indulgences," that is, taught the people that the pardon of sin committed, and to be committed, may be purchased with money, and he, claiming to be the salesman, received all the money he could obtain from such as were foolish enough to believe him. Thus while the ancient Pharisees offered tithes of their mint, anise and cummin, Tetzel was shrewd enough to claim more valuable considerations for so rich a boon, but the principle in each case was precisely the same. The fact is, the whole system of Popery is neither more nor less than Pharisaism carried out to its worst consequences. Luther commenced to reform himself, and then to reform Popery, by attempting to correct, first one thing, and then another. But God taught him that neither himself nor the Church could be reformed in this way. He taught him what was not only a shorter way, but the only way, even justification by faith; and that the Bible is the only rule, and the all-sufficient rule, both of our faith and conduct. These two principles, when faithfully applied, and as far as applied, destroy Popery, root and branch. Nor can any system of error be destroyed in any other way. It is not possible to effect a moral reformation in any other way. By one of these principles, the great upas-tree, upon which grow traditions, and all other human inventions, is cut down at a stroke; while, by the other, the sinner himself is slain, his mouth is stopped, so that he can no longer utter the language of the self-righteous Pharisee; he can only say, and he does say, "Jesus, thou son of David, have mercy upon me;" to which cry he soon hears the glorious response, "Believe on the Lord Jesus Christ and thou shalt be saved." Being assisted by the Holy Spirit, whom he asks and receives for the sake of Christ, he does believe, he is saved, and goes on his way rejoicing.

The fact is, salvation by works always was, and eternally will be, an absolute impossibility. Some people loosely talk about unfallen Adam, and unfallen angels being saved by works. I beg to say that the word *soterion*, salvation, can never, with propriety, be applied to any unfallen and holy being. It is applicable only to fallen beings whose recovery is still possible.

Let this suffice for the Pharisees. We will now turn to the Sadducees.

SADDUCISM.

As there is no medium between *grace* and *merit*, it follows that those who depart from the doctrine of justification by *grace* through *faith*, pass to Pharisaism at the first step, though they may not be aware of it. But as this ground is not tenable, and will not bear the test of calm reflection, and close scrutiny, especially when moved thereto by the force of Gospel truth applied by the Holy Spirit, those who occupy it become dissatisfied and unsettled, and if they do not return to the fundamental principle of justification by faith, they pass on to Sadducism; that is they become skeptical; in other words, they try to disbelieve certain fundamental principles of the Christian system, especially those which trouble them most. As the transition from Pharisaism to Sadducism is so easy, and, under some circumstances, inevitable, we find these two classes of character in close proximity, and sometimes commingling together in the same churches: yea, and occupying the same pulpits and the same pews. In support of these views, and to obtain a correct knowledge of Sadducism, we will now glance at the principles and character of the ancient Sadducees, as presented in the New Testament.

Matt. iii. 7. "But when he saw many of the Pharisees and Sadducees come to his baptism, he said unto them, O generation of vipers, who hath warned you to flee from the wrath to come? Bring forth therefore fruits meet for repentance." Mark! Here we find them together, and both classes commingling with the true seekers and worshippers. Here is a lesson for those who are engaged in religious revivals; look out for a union of Pharisees and Sadducees on such occasions.

And mark well how this intrepid and faithful preacher addressed them. His keen eye discriminated, and his eloquent lips pronounce truth and reproof equally appropriate. These hypocritical Pharisees and Sadducees are denominated a "generation of vipers," and are threatened with "wrath to come." This is just what the Sadducee did not believe, and what the self-righteous Pharisee did not fear. Hence such preaching is the most appropriate for such characters; people need to hear what they do not believe, more than what they do, but a coward can preach the latter, while it requires a hero to preach the former. Matt. xvi. 1, "The Pharisees also with the Sadducees came, and tempting desired him that he would show them a sign from heaven." Here we find the Pharisees and the Sadducees again together, and so much alike, that it would be difficult to distinguish them; they are alike unbelieving, and alike hypocritical: hence Jesus pronounces them all "hypocrites," and "a wicked and adulterous generation;" and refusing to give them "a sign," save that of "Jonas the prophet," "he left them and departed." Then to his disciples he said, "Take heed and beware of the leaven of the Pharisees and of the Sadducees." At the 12th verse this "leaven" is called "the doctrine of the Pharisees and of the Sadducees," thus marking the *oneness* of the two parties, and showing that they were both poisoned by the same *leaven*, and that this leaven is so poisonous that the disciples had need to "beware of it." And the disciples of Jesus still need to beware of this deadly poison, for just as soon as you depart from the doctrine of justification by *grace*, through faith, you are on Pharisaic ground, and on the high road to Sadducism, and absolutely destitute of the peculiar power. Hence the necessity of the present investigation. But, let us follow these Sadducees still further for the purpose already specified.

The Pharisees, Sadducees, and Herodians, have such an affinity for each other, that we cannot do justice to our subject or obtain a full and clear view of either class by confining our investigations to one class at a time. We must take them up as they are presented in Scripture, sometimes separately, and sometimes unitedly. In Matt. xxii. we find all the three classes attacking Jesus, sometimes separately, and sometimes unitedly. At verse 15 we read, "Then went the Pharisees and took counsel how they might entangle him in his talk. And they sent unto him their disciples, with the Herodians, saying, Master, we know that thou art true, and teachest the way of God in truth, neither carest thou for any *man;* for thou regardest not the person of men. Tell us therefore, what thinkest thou? Is it lawful to give tribute unto Cesar or not?" The wicked and hypocritical Pharisees having consulted how they might "entangle" Jesus, concluded that they would succeed better in political than in theological questions, and knowing that the Herodians were expert in such matters, they called them to their assistance, and promptly did the Herodians obey the call, and with an ability worthy of thorough politicians, they propounded their ensnaring question. "But Jesus perceiving their wickedness, said, why tempt ye me, ye hypocrites?" Observing with what wisdom he foiled them in their wicked purpose, and exposed their hypocrisy, "they marvelled, and left him, and went their way." They simply recognized our blessed Lord as being too shrewd for them, in this instance, hoping, doubtless, to outwit him at some future time; for, like most politicians, they had no idea of anything superior to successful political strategy; in their thinking they never rose high enough to embrace a purely theological or religious idea; all their questions were "highly political."

Jesus having repulsed the first and third divisions of this great antichristian army, the second division is at once advanced into line of battle, hence at verse 28 we read, "The same day came to him the Sadducees, which say there is no resurrection, and asked him saying," &c., &c. "Jesus answered and said unto them, ye do err, not knowing the Scriptures, nor the power of God." Having exposed their ignorance, and the weakness of their attempt to turn Scripture teaching into ridicule, he no longer acts on the defensive merely, but proceeds to refute their grand principle, viz: that there is neither angel, spirit nor resurrection. To this end he quotes from Moses, whom they profess to believe, and who represents God as saying, "I am the God of Abraham, and the God of Isaac, and the God of Jacob. God is not the God of the dead, but of the living." The Sadducees were now silenced and routed. And although it does not appear that they were benefitted at all, the listening multitude were; for it is said "when the multitudes heard *this*, they were astonished at his doctrine." " But when the Pharisees heard that he had put the Sadducees to silence, they were gathered together. Then one of them, a lawyer, asked, tempting him, and saying, which is the great commandment in the law? Jesus said unto him, Thou shalt love the Lord thy God with all thy heart, and with all thy soul, and with all thy mind. This is the first and great commandment. And the second is like unto it, Thou shalt love thy neighbor as thyself. On these two commandments hang all the law and the prophets." Having answered all the questions and refuted all the objections of his three grand opponents, the *Pharisee*, the *Sadducee*, and the *Herodian*, Jesus asked the former a question, "Saying, what think ye of Christ? Whose son is he? They say unto him, the son of David. He saith unto them, How then doth David in spirit call him Lord, saying, The LORD said unto my Lord, sit thou on my right hand, till I make thine enemies thy footstool? If David then call him Lord, how is he his son? And no man was able to answer him a word, neither durst any man, from that day forth, ask him any more questions." Thus did Jesus turn to flight, in one day, these three grand armies of the aliens. The principles defended and established by our blessed Lord and by his forerunner, John the Baptist, and rejected, directly or impliedly, by these three sects, demand the most serious attention. We will simply specify them. *The inspiration of the Scriptures; the person, character and work of Christ; the doctrine of the Trinity; the nature of true religion; the existence of angels, and of human spirits after death; the resurrection of the human body; and wrath to come.* Now, let it be distinctly observed, that these are the doctrines which are still denied, directly or impliedly, by all who do not embrace the doctrine of justification by faith; and it is not embraced by Sadducees, Pharisees, or Herodians. Other doctrines they may deny, but these are specially objectionable to them. The Pharisees may not *directly* deny all these doctrines, but they positively deny some of them, and do not properly believe any of them. At best they have unbelief enough to render their salvation impossible, while they persist in it; enough to render a union with Sadducees and Herodians easy here, and certain hereafter. Of course, under certain circumstances they will fight with these their near neighbors, but under others they will readily unite with them, as all history shows; though all these doctrines are denied by the Sadducees. And as for the Herodians they are so earthly-minded that their thoughts do not rise high enough, even to enter into a controversy about them. Moreover, as political flatterers and office seekers, it would not comport with their selfish interests to assert or deny any of them, unless it should seem that by doing so they would promote their political interests; for all their movements are "highly political!" as we shall show in due time.

Meantime, let us dwell a little longer upon the character and doings of the Sadducees. In Acts, iv. 1–8, we read, "And as they spake unto the people, the priests, and the captain of the temple, and the Sadducees came upon them, being grieved that they taught the people, and preached through Jesus the resurrection from the dead. And they laid hands on them, and put them in hold unto the next day; for it was now eventide." Again, the Apostles having wrought some of the most wonderful miracles, in consequence of which the work of God was progressing gloriously, we are told, Chap. v., 17–20, "Then the high priest rose up, and all they that were with him, (which is the sect of the Sadducees,) and were filled with indignation, and laid their hands on the apostles, and put them in the common prison. But the angel of the Lord by night opened the prison doors, and brought them forth, and said, "Go stand and speak in the temple to the people all the words of this life." But neither the preaching nor the miracles had any influence upon the Sadducees, save to develop their hatred of the holy teachers, and of that which they taught. It is necessary to observe this that we may appreciate the truth here contended for, and dread the errors here opposed. For whoever rejects the doctrine of justification by faith, is on the high road to all the hopelessness and ruin of these Pharisees and Sadducees! Nor will anything short of the principles and power for which we contend, fortify us against the soul-destroying principles, and the incessant and deadily opposition of Pharisees and Sadducees. The voice of God to all is, "Save yourselves from this untoward generation," for, remember, these characters now, as of old time, are in the pulpits and pews of God's temple. That they filled the highest offices in the Jewish Church and nation is quite certain, the Sadducees as well as the Pharisees. Indeed, the Sadducees seem to have gained the ascendancy, both in the church and nation. Calmet, in his Dictionary, says, "They held the chief offices in the nation, and many of the priests were Sadducees." Again, he says, "John Hircanus, high priest of the nation, separated himself in a signal manner from the sect of the Pharisees, and went over to that of the Sadducees. It is said, also, that he strictly commanded all Jews, on pain of death, to receive the maxims of this sect. Aristobulus and Alexander Jannaeus, son of Hircanus, continued to favor the Sadducees, and Abraham Vendior, Cabbaly, and Maimonides, assure us, that under these princes they possessed all the offices of the Sanhedrim, and that there remained in the party of the Pharisees, only Simon, son of Secre. Caiphas, who condemned our Saviour, was a Sadducee, as was Ananias the younger, who put to death James, brother of our Lord." Learned men are very much perplexed in attempting to account for this, seeing "the Sadducees say there is no resurrection, neither angel nor spirit, but the Pharisees confess both." Acts, xxiii. 8. They are at a loss to know how they could profess a belief in the Scriptures; how they could hold offices in the church, while these were their sentiments. They also find it difficult to account for the fact that the Pharisees and Sadducees commingled together in the same Church, while holding such opposite views. And conceiving the thing to be impossible, some learned men have even attempted to show that the Sadducees did not hold the opinions attributed to them in the Scriptures. But even though they should succeed in this attempt, what will they do with the fact that the same *phenomena* exists in the professedly Christian church at the present day? Are there not multitudes of Pharisees and Sadducees in the Church of England? Yes, verily, so much so that the Sadducees threaten to gain the ascendancy, even over the Pharisees, numerous and influential as they are. Nor is it much better, if any, in a large proportion of professedly protestant Germany. Has not *rationalism*, or, more properly speaking, Sadducism, already gained the ascendancy? And as for the Church of Rome, it would be difficult to find one within her pale, from the Pope down, that is not a Sadducee or a Pharisee. And as to the people called Adventists, or no-soulites, they unblushingly preach the very same tenets attributed to the ancient Sadducees. The Universalists and Swedenborgians occupy about the same ground, together with spiritualists, and a whole host of phrenological and other lecturers. To these must be added Deists, Unitarians, and all the various tribes of Arians. Nor does the evil stop here. If we turn to what are called orthodox churches, we shall find multitudes of Pharisees, and not a few Sadducees; persons who do not believe that there is a hell of fire, where the unsaved shall eternally suffer; do not believe in the existence of the devil and his angels; do not believe in the resurrection of the human body, any more than did the ancient Sadducees. Yet all these profess to believe the Scriptures, yea, and preach too, and that to crowded and highly delighted audiences. These are all Pharisees or Sadducees, as are all others who do not hold the doctrine of *salvation by grace through faith.* And as to Pharisees and Sadducees complacently mingling with each other, most of them do so now as formerly, when they find it necessary to oppose a revival of genuine religion. At other times they will quarrel as formerly, especially when the Pharisees become very zealous in support of their traditions and ritualistic nonsense, for a Sadducee is not inclined to lay much stress upon any religious opinions. This is the necessary tendency of his system of *unbelief.* Both Sadducees and Pharisees, however, dread an attack from a genuine gospel minister, and were it not that they are afraid of provoking some Luther to make such an attack upon them, they would manifest their hatred to gospel truth and gospel Christians more than they do. Indeed it has become a part of their strategy to censure with great severity all who attempt to expose their errors; to do so is represented as *prima facie* evidence of a return to the dark days of illiberality and bigotry. And they are not a few who in this way are frighted into silence, so that in many places Pharisaism and Sadducism gain the ascendant, and then they become as intolerant as in the days of old. But no reformer or faithful minister ever remained silent with regard to the religious errors of his times. Every faithful minister understands the following words and acts accordingly, "Every plant which my heavenly father hath not planted, shall be rooted up." He knows that the plants of truth and grace cannot grow where such plants are permitted to grow. Hence, like his Master, he proceeds to root them up, by showing that they are poisonous plants, and that "the enemy that sowed them is the devil." And all who engage in this work of rooting up, will surely bring upon themselves the wrath of Pharisees and Sadducees, and they will as surely be annoyed by weak disciples, who will say to them, as certain disciples said to Jesus, " Knowest thou that the Pharisees were offended after they heard this saying?" but let all such faithful men reply in the words of their Master, and steadily proceed with their work of rooting up; it will pay in the end; yea, and bring peace too.

The reason why Pharisaism tends to Sadducism, and why there is an affinity between these two sects, may, I think, be easily accounted for in this way. Pharisaism commences by substituting human opinion or invention for Divine revelation. This leads to the substitution of human merit for that of the atonement, to salvation by works, instead of salvation by grace through faith. This view is fully supported by the word of God, and by matter of fact. An appeal to matter of fact will show that this is precisely the way in which Pharisaism has been propagated, and the word of God is distinct and unmistakable on the subject. Hear what Jesus said to the Pharisees of his day, when the Pharisees were bold enough to reprove Jesus and his disciples for not adhering to their traditions, saying, "Why do thy disciples transgress the tradition of the elders? for they wash not their hands when they eat bread;" Jesus "answered and said unto them, why do ye also transgress the commandment of God by your tradition?" Observe, *tradition* and *transgression*, go together, and are inseparable! After specifying some of the commandments which were transgressed in this way, our blessed Lord adds, "thus have ye made the commandment of God of none effect by your tradition." Now, when human *invention*, human *merit*, and *authority*, are thus substituted for Divine *teaching*, Divine *grace*, and Divine *authority*, the cable is slipped, and the bark is afloat, without compass, rudder, or commander, and without special Divine interposition, will surely be lost. It is not possible for a thinking man to rest in Pharisaism; a careful examination of Pharisaic principles will drive him back to orthodoxy, or forward to Sadducism. It is not possible for any thinking man to believe that Pharisaic righteousness will merit heaven, or qualify for it; nor is it possible for such to believe that a holy and just God will send him to a hell of quenchless fire merely because he is not a Pharisee. Hence, I repeat, when Pharisees *think*, they will either fall back upon Bible truth, or go on to Sadducism, and thence, it may be, to down-right Atheism. But, only let a man see, from God's own word, that God is good to all, that Jesus died for all, that there is salvation in no other, that this salvation, consequently, is by *grace* through *faith*, the gift of a merciful God through the atonement of Christ, that by the deeds of the law no flesh living shall be justified, that in this way God is just, while he justifies the ungodly that believe in Jesus; that being thus justified he has peace with God through our Lord Jesus Christ, and rejoices in hope of the glory of God. Let him see that there is no other way in which fallen man can be saved, that is, made holy and happy, and finally glorified, and that, consequently, if he rejects this gracious offer of salvation, for he cannot be forced, "there remaineth, therefore, no more sacrifice for sin, but a certain fearful looking for of judgment and fiery indignation, which shall devour the adversaries." Let him see all this, I say, from God's own word, and instead of flying from Pharisaism to what is no better, Sadducism, he will fly to Jesus, and find redemption in his blood. And instead of being a self-righteous Pharisee, or a cavilling Sadducee, he will be a happy Christian, preaching the faith he once destroyed, and counting all things but loss for the excellency of the knowledge of Christ Jesus his Lord, for whom he is now willing to suffer the loss of all things, and count them but dung that he may win Christ.

Pharisaism is the source of, and leads to, all error; and the doctrine of justification by faith strikes at the root of, and is the only sure cure for all error, and all evil. "This is the victory that overcometh the world, even our faith."

THE HERODIANS.

In the New Testament this sect is presented to our notice in connection with the Pharisees and the Sadducees. And though they appear as a distinct sect, they are, nevertheless, strangely connected with the other sects, and seem to be an integral part both of the Church and Nation of the Jews. They seem to be the most undefinable beings that are presented to our notice either in sacred or profane history. Hence commentators and others are puzzled in their attempts to define the character and fix the position of this anomalous sect. We think, however, that a somewhat definite and satisfactory judgment may be reached with regard to them; and as we believe them to be one of the representative classes of exceptional character, we will make the attempt. And to this end we will now give a brief exhibit of what sacred and other writers say concerning them.

The first place we meet with them in the New Testament is in Matt. xxii. And here we find them united with the Pharisees and Sadducees in an attempt to "entangle" our blessed Lord. To this end they propose in a very subtile manner this political question: "Is it lawful to give tribute unto Cæsar, or not?" But "Jesus perceived their wickedness, and said, Why tempt ye me, ye hypocrites?" How our blessed Lord exposed, confounded, and caused them to retire in confusion, is well known. In Mark xii. 13, we have the same or a similar record of these Herodians. In his third chapter, also, this Evangelist gives us the following, at verse 6. "And the Pharisees went forth, and straightway took counsel with the Herodians against him, how they might destroy him."

By these inspired records the following particulars are clearly established. First, the Herodians were "wicked," and they were "hypocritical," so wicked that they were always ready to "entangle" and "destroy" "the Lord of life and glory;" so hypocritical, that while this was their object, they pretended to act for the good of the Church and State. Second, when the Pharisees would accomplish their worst purposes against Jesus, they consulted and employed the wicked and hypocritical Herodians, who, to accomplish their own wicked and selfish ends, were always ready to offer their service. Hence, third, while they maintain a kind of distinct organization, we, nevertheless, find them connected with Church and State parties, whether Pharisees or Sadducees. But, fourth, although they were ready to unite with, or be employed by any party, if they thought their selfish ends would thereby be promoted, they were, nevertheless, strangely *non-committal.* They were not religious enough to profess Pharisaism, nor honest enough to profess Sadducism; because, fifth, all their movements were "highly political." Hence, they were ready to sell themselves to any party or to perpetrate any crime, if thereby they might promote their political and selfish purposes. The object of their worship was the reigning prince, whether Herod, Caligula, or Cæsar. His dictum was with them "the higher law." To afford additional proof of all that we have here said, we may now glance at what has been said of these bad men by uninspired writers.

In Colmet's Dictionary, under the article Herodians, we have the following.—"Dr. Prideaux judges that their doctrines were reducible to two heads: 1. a belief that the dominion of the Romans over the Jews was just, and that it was their duty to submit to it; 2. that in the present circumstances they might with a good conscience follow many heathen modes and usages. It is certain these were Herod's principles, who pleaded the necessity of the times, for doing many things contrary to the maxims of the Jewish religion." Dr. Adam Clark, when speaking of Herod and the Herodians, in his comment on Matt. xvi., says, "He built temples, set up images, and joined in heathen worship, though he professed the Jewish religion; and this was in opposition to all the law and the prophets. From this we may learn that the *Herodians* were such as, first, held it lawful to transfer the divine government to a heathen ruler; and secondly, to conform occasionally, to heathenish rites in their religious worship. In short, they appear to have been persons who *trimmed* between God and the world—who endeavored to reconcile his service with that of mammon —and who were religious just as far as it tended to secure their secular interests. It is probable that this sect was at last so blended with, that it became lost in, the sect of the Sadducees; for the persons who are called Herodians, Mark viii. 15, are styled *Sadducees* in verse 6 of this chapter."

In support of these inspired and uninspired sketches of Herodian character, we might quote Josephus and other writers, but we judge it unnecessary; the delineation of character being already sufficiently clear and full, and sufficiently authenticated. We will now group together the more striking features of their character, that the whole may be seen at a glance; then we shall be prepared for the application.

They were so *carnal* and *selfish* that their sole object of pursuit was their own temporal interest. Hence, to this end, they were ready to lay anything and everything, under contribution, whether sacred or profane.

It is this fact that rendered their character so undefinable, especially when viewed at a distance. But the more prominent actors in this class of character, having turned their attention, more especially to politics, their more distinguishing characteristic was that of the office-seeking politicians. Hence, most of their movements were "highly political," they were, as Dr. Doddredge observes, "complaisant courtiers." The object of their worship was the reigning prince, whether Jew or Gentile it mattered not; his views were theirs; and with him they were ready to "swing round the entire circle" at any time; whether the circle comprehended Judaism or heathenism. For the same reason they were ready to flatter, or unite with any party, whether Pharisees, Sadducees, Essenes—or even Fenians, if such creatures then existed. For the same reason, "they held it lawful," as Dr. Clark observes, "to transfer the divine government to a heathen ruler," whose *ipse dixit,* in their view, was "the higher law." Hence, as the doctor further observes, "they were religious just as far as it tended to promote their secular interest." It follows, that they were just what the unerring Judge says they were, WICKED HYPOCRITES. Finally, the *affinity*, if not the *oneness*, of Pharisaism, Sadducism, and Herodianism, is such, that our blessed Lord comprehends the whole in the *same* term and in the same warning—" And he charged them saying, Take heed, beware of the leaven of the Pharisees, and the leaven of Herod." Mark viii. 15. This selfish and hypocritical leaven corrupts and assimilates all in whom it finds a lodgment; therefore "Take heed," says Jesus, "beware of the leaven of the

Pharisees and of the Herodians." Pharisees, Sadducees, and Herodians are so numerous and so deceitful, and their leaven has such an affinity to fallen humanity, that even the disciples of Jesus are in danger of being infected by this terrible plague. Hence Jesus addresses this warning to his disciples, his immediate followers. O how much danger there is of "having men's persons in admiration because of advantage." None are free from this *leaven*, this *virus*, but those who have *a pure heart, a single eye.* And none have this but those who are "justified by faith," "born of the Spirit," "created anew in Christ Jesus unto good works, which God hath before ordained that we should walk in them." These only have the mind that was in Jesus; the mind of him who "went about doing good;" who, "though he was rich, for our sakes became poor, that we through his poverty might be rich." None but these know that great truth and practice it—"It is more blessed to give than to receive." All others are carnal and selfish—are Pharisees, Sadducees, or Herodians. For if they give anything, *they give it to purchase the favor of God or the favor of Herod.* And if they give nothing, it is because they are Sadducees, and "neither fear God nor regard man." And as all are Pharisees, Sadducees, or Herodians, who are not justified by faith, it follows that none but those who are justified by faith have the peculiar, the moral power, of which we have been writing. Pharisees, Sadducees and Herodians, are alike destitute of moral power. They are not "vessels of honor, sanctified and meet for the master's use." They have not a pure heart, a single eye; they are carnal and selfish: and no power in the universe can make them otherwise, but the power that regenerates, that creates anew in Christ Jesus. And, observe, it is only the penitent, believing soul that is thus renewed! None are regenerated, sanctified, and constitute the temple of God but those who are justified; and none are justified but those who believe—"For by grace are ye saved, through faith; and that not of yourselves; it is the gift of God; not of works, lest any man should boast." Thus again our principle is established.

Those who will carefully examine the character of the ancient Herodians, as above delineated, will not need to be told that this class of character still is, and ever has been very numerous. O how many are there who adopt, vary, modify, and change, both their political and religious principles, just as their temporal interests may seem to demand: and all such are Herodians, if not Sadducees also; for the transition from one of these classes to the other, is so easy, that it is constantly going on: and Pharisaism is the great *depot* from which both these classes receive their supplies, while Pharisaism itself is the first-born son of fallen Adam! Now, I must repeat, once more, the doctrine of justification by faith, and that alone, is the grand remedy for all these deadly errors: there is not another! No preaching that does not clearly develop and faithfully apply this great doctrine, this fundamental principle, will ever raise the people above mere heathen morality. All other preaching is a mere daubing with untempered mortar: it may cleanse the outside of the cup and platter; it may whitewash the sepulchre; but it leaves untouched the corruption within. Where this doctrine is not preached, the doctrine of the fall, the doctrine of man's total depravity and utter helplessness, is not preached. Where this doctrine is not preached, Pharisaism, Sadducism, Herodianism, Arianism, Socinianism, Unitarianism, Universalism, Adventism, Spiritualism, Swedenborgianism, Antinomianism, Nestorianism, Sabellianism, Eutychianism, Pelagianism, Manichianism, Fatalism, Materialism, Mysticism, Fanaticism, Stoicism, and every other pernicious *ism*, may be expected to abound, just as circumstances, and the whims and ignorance of men may suggest. And the preacher that is not in favor of these *isms*, but does not preach the doctrine of justification by faith, may declaim against them all, with the eloquence of a Demosthenes, the philosophy of a Plato, and the logical acumen of an Aristotle, but he will not prevail. Yea, Pharisaism, which is the source of all the *isms*, will grow and prevail right in his church, and Pharisees will sit undisturbed around his desk, regardless of all he can say; unless he clearly and faithfully develops and applies the great doctrine of justification by faith alone! *He is a power, and he only, who enjoys and preaches* SALVATION BY FAITH. The Scriptures which we have quoted, the historic facts which we have adduced, and the Christian experience to which we have appealed, all go to establish this great truth. No man can point to a single moral reform that did not result from the preaching of this doctrine. No man can point to a living church at this day, in which this doctrine is not preached. Nor do I hesitate to say, that a careful investigation will discover the fact that every church is alive or dead, just in proportion as this doctrine is, or is not, clearly and faithfully preached. Nor can you find under the whole heaven, a man or church possessing moral power, only in so far as that man or church has experienced, and still holds and propagates, the glorious doctrine of SALVATION BY GRACE THROUGH FAITH. With this doctrine the whole Christian system stands or falls. Reject this doctrine and you cannot consistently hold any other doctrine in the system. Hold this doctrine, and to be consistent, you must hold every other doctrine of the Christian system. Were it necessary, I should not find it a difficult task to produce arguments which would establish these propositions with all the certainty of demonstration; for these propositions are as susceptible of proof as are any propositions. If man is what the Bible says he is, none but God can save him. And if Jesus is the Saviour, the only Saviour of man, he must be God; and if this Salvation be not of works, it must be of grace; and if it is conditional, that condition must be faith; for as merit and works go together, so do grace and faith. Thus it is that all the parts of this wonderful and glorious system are connected; each one following the other as necessarily as effect follows cause, or as a *consequent* follows a given proposition. Take a single instance. If Jesus is David's God and David's son, then he must be both God and man: admit the former, and you must admit the latter. Let this suffice as an illustration and proof of what we claim.

Having discovered the *conditions* of moral power, specifying the *principles* with which this power is inseparably connected; and having shown that they are Pharisees, Sadducees, or Herodians, who do not possess the power and principles specified: and having established our position, as we believe, by Scripture, experience, and the facts of history, it only remains that we call attention to a certain evil, and point out that which is at once the preventive and the remedy.

The evil to which we refer is this: both individuals and churches who once possessed the power have lost it. This also is abundantly established by Scripture, history and experience. The primitive Christian Churches had the power, but it was not long before many of them, like that at Laodicea, lost it; and though they had the name to live, they were dead. For a time they retained "the form of Godliness," but it was not long till they even *denied* the power. And having returned to Pharisaism, Sadducism and Herodianism came in like a flood, and produced their legitimate fruits. Finally all the churches in the East became dead, corrupt, and corrupting masses; while Pharisaism, Sadducism, and Herodianism concentrated in the West, crushed out Christianity, and formed that horrible thing called Popery.

Turn to the Reformation of the sixteenth century. For a time the power was retained to a greater or less extent by the Protestant Churches on the continent of Europe; but they, too, soon lost the power, and, to an alarming extent, returned to Pharisaism. And, again, Sadducism and Herodianism made their appearance under new names, but essentially the same, as we have already shown. In England and Scotland, the same or a similar loss of life and power was experienced, and the same return to Pharisaism, followed by the same tendency to Sadducean unbelief, and Herodian carnal policy; accompanied, of course, by a corresponding amount of hypocrisy. Then God in mercy visited those churches with what is called the Wesleyan reformation, in the way which we have already described. As to how much of the primitive power of this last revival still remains, we do not take upon us to say; our present undertaking does not seem to require that we should take up this topic. It may be enough to say that while we all have abundance of cause to be ashamed, and to repent of our unfaithfulness to our God, and to the glorious dispensation of the Gospel committed to us, we have, at the same time, much cause to be thankful that so much of the primitive power still remains with us. But that we may not lose, either in whole or in part, the glorious power which our fathers had, and which they bequeathed to us, let us guard against those errors which have led to its loss in other churches, and this leads us to point out what is at once the *preventive* and the *remedy*.

Indeed we have done this already, if we are correct in what we have specified as the conditions of moral power. But that the whole may be seen at a glance, we will repeat in this connection, that the whole of genuine religion may be expressed in three terms, viz: DOCTRINE, EXPERIENCE, and PRACTICE. The first saves us from Latitudinarianism, Sadducism, and Scepticism of every kind: the second saves us from Pharisaism; and the third saves us from Herodianism, or Antinomianism; in a word, it regulates the life, and makes us do as well as say, sweeping away all hypocrisy. Without the doctrine there cannot be the experience, for it is by grace we are saved through faith; and without the experience there cannot be the practice, for an unholy nature cannot produce a holy life; and we cannot have a holy nature without regeneration and sanctification; and we cannot have the latter without justification; and we cannot have justification without faith; and we cannot have faith without doctrine; for "faith cometh by hearing the word of God," especially this word, "Believe on the Lord Jesus Christ and thou shalt be saved;" and this implies a knowledge of the condemnation, corruption, and helplessness which renders salvation necessary; and this again implies a knowledge of the *nature* and *extent* of the salvation needed; and all these unite to sweep away Pharisaism, root and branch, impressing upon the inmost soul the conviction, that *it is by grace we are saved through faith, and that not of ourselves; it is the gift of God.* Thus every process of just reasoning leads to precisely the same conclusion, showing most conclusively, that faith and the doctrines essential thereto, lie at the very foundation; and are essential to the very existence of Christian experience and Christian practice. It follows that, whether we would *obtain, restore,* or *retain,* the life and power of Christianity, we must embrace and hold the doctrines; especially the doctrine of the fall; that of the atonement, justification by faith, regeneration by the Spirit, the witness of the Spirit, and entire holiness through the all-cleansing blood of Jesus, by faith alone. And all these must be applied and enforced by the awful truth, that whoever is not thus saved must be damned. Let these doctrines go, and a return to Pharisaism and death is inevitable, and all the other errors will follow from time to time. But how is all this to be prevented? I answer, first—Keep a strict watch at the entrance of the pulpit, and allow none to enter that holy and exalted place but such as hold and can preach the Christian doctrines, and have the experience and the practice, which are at once the evidence and the fruits thereof. Second, Keep a strict watch at the door of the church, and let *doctrine, experience* and *practice* be the test of membership. This will do away with the low and pernicious ideas which are so generally entertained with regard to the Christian Ministry, and the fellowship of the saints. Then shall be fulfilled that Scripture—" For the Lord hath chosen Zion: he hath desired it for his habitation. This is my rest forever: here will I dwell: for I have desired it. 'I will abundantly bless her provisions: I will satisfy her poor with bread. I will also clothe her priests with salvation, and her saints shall shout aloud for joy." To be a minister or a member of such a church means something. The clothing here spoken of is very different from the ritualistic trumpery for which some priests contend so earnestly.

Seeing the Christian doctrines are so essential to the life, power, and prosperity of the Church, and even to the very existence of Christian experience and practice, we think it is matter for regret that the summary statement of our doctrines, as given in our Discipline, is not more complete than it is. True, all our doctrines may be found in our standard works, and in the works included in the Course of Study for the Ministry. But we humbly submit whether this is sufficient. If a minister in our church should reject the doctrines not specified in that summary, and preach accordingly, how would the church act in that case? If such a minister were brought to trial, as he certainly should be, would he be tried by all our standard works, or by the summary of doctrines found in the Discipline? If by the former, who shall decide as to what are our standard works? And if by the latter, how could you condemn him for not holding and preaching doctrines that are not contained in what is given as the summary of our doctrines?

I know it has been said that we depend, or have depended principally, upon the piety of the church for the preservation of her doctrines. If by piety is meant Christian experience and practice, then this theory represents the cause as depending upon the effect for its own existence, which is absurd and impossible. I admit that doctrine, experience, and practice, when they exist together, mutually support each other; but this is entirely consistent with our position, viz: that the doctrine is essentially necessary both to the *existence* and *continuance* of experience and practice. Take away the doctrine and there is nothing left; if the house was already built it falls when you take away the foundation; and if it was not, there is nothing upon which to build if you take away the foundation. Now the foundation of which we speak is said to be "the apostles and prophets, Jesus Christ himself being the chief corner stone;" and you take away this foundation when you take away the doctrines. The church must live so long as she properly holds the doctrines, especially those which we have specified. If the doctrine of salvation by faith properly embraced gives life, the same doctrine held fast must continue that life.

No church or individual ever fell, or ever can fall, while properly holding to this doctrine. "Take heed to thyself, and to the doctrine; continue in them: for in doing this thou shalt both save thyself, and them that hear thee." 1 Tim. iv. 16.

By turning to fallen churches we are admonished of another error, viz.: this, their depending upon the piety of the fathers, while they had none of their own. The fallen Jewish church kept crying, "We have Abraham to our father," when Christ said, "Ye are of your father, the devil." The fallen Christian church, too, was constantly talking and arguing about the fathers, even during the dark ages. As for the Church of Rome, she will have nothing but certain fathers; and, what makes the matter worse, she makes fathers of all sorts of sinners and errorists. Others talk about Martin Luther, John Calvin, John Knox, Lattimer, Ridley and others; while they are utterly destitute of their piety. And Methodists, too, are in danger of falling into the same error. Nay, many have talked loudly, and many still talk loudly about "old fashioned Methodism," who, we fear, were, or are, more nearly related to old fashioned Pharisaism; and the holy men to whom they claim kindred, would, we fear, be ashamed of them, and, perhaps, disown them, were they now living. If we would have the power, and retain it, let us guard against all these errors.

Once more. To retain this power, either as churches or as individuals, there must be CHRISTIAN PROGRESSION, and to this subject we will now turn our attention. All creation is moving, and it is absurd to suppose that either the church or the individual Christian can stand still. Mind moves everything, and thought moves mind. Hence, as the means of communicating thought become more and more abundant, we should abound more and more in Christian activities, and Christian progression. The reformers of the 1st, 16th, and 18th centuries had to travel principally on foot, or were carried occasionally by quadrupeds that could travel but little faster; hence the thinking agents and their thoughts moved slowly in those days. Now they move with marvellous rapidity, by the force of wind and steam. During the time that Paul travelled from Jerusalem to Rome, or Wesley from London to Dublin, a man may now pass from the Eastern to the Western Continent, and preach the gospel in both hemispheres. And as to thought, it is carried, not by two, or by four weary feet, but by the lightning, leaping from city to city, from island to island, and from continent to continent. Hence, even the lightning acts more efficiently now than it did in those days. Then it was satisfied to leap from cloud to cloud, and thence to the earth, and back again. But now, by means of the wire it leaps from continent to continent as readily as it then leaped from cloud to cloud. Then it carried no thought; now it comes freighted with thought every time It is unreasonable, therefore, to suppose that the Christian progression that sufficed to meet the claims of God in those days, will equally suffice in these days, when the means of progression are so much more abundant. Let us, therefore, carefully investigate this subject, the subject of CHRISTIAN PROGRESSION.

CHAPTER V.

THE NATURE, AND NECESSITY, OF CHRISTIAN PROGRESSION.

In support of this proposition the unchangeableness of God, and the essential activity of mind are referred to—*Progression* or *retrogression* inevitable—The word progress furnishes Bunyan with both the title and theme of his remarkable book—This idea runs through all the teachings of the bible—Many authors are quoted in support of this proposition, and many arguments advanced—Many illustrations are given, together with criticisms on the original.

To *develop* and *establish* this proposition, is the work to which we will now apply our best efforts, in the fear of God.

God is *unchangeable*, and he only. Of none but the *Infinite* can it be said that he is "the same yesterday, and to-day, and forever." Hence, all creatures are changeable, and this implies *progression*, or *retrogression*, for there are but the two directions in which the change can take place. This being true, the *necessity* of *progression* is indisputable; for that which does not *progress*, must *retrograde*, there being no medium.

Again, mind is active, *essentially so*. I cannot conceive of mind, or spirit, as being inactive; action is coeval with its existence, and co-extensive with its being. Matter is *inert*, but mind certainly is not. There can neither be action without mind, nor mind without action. Mere matter cannot move itself. Whether it has the solidity of the granite-rock, the elasticity of air, or the tenuity of the nebula, it is alike destitute of *self-action*. Not so mind; it is, I repeat, *essentially* active: action is one of its essential properties; when it ceases to act, it ceases to be mind, and when it ceases to be mind, it ceases to *be*. Mental action is moral action. You can no more divest mental action of moral quality, than you can divest mind of a moral nature. Moral action must be good or bad; to suppose it to be neither, implies a palpable contradiction; it may be good, better, or best; bad, worse, or worst; but neither good nor bad it cannot be, for the word *moral* implies *quality*, either good or bad; and this, again, implies progression, or retrogression, and is another argument in favor of the *necessity* of Christian Progression, seeing not to progress, is to retrograde, or, to use the common expression, *backslide*. So true it is, that "there is no standing still in religion." Nor is it any more possible to stand still in sin, nor in any thing. This law extends to all that is created, but is most strikingly seen in the vegetable, the animal and the mental departments; and still more so, perhaps, in the religious world, where *probation*, and *progression*, are so peculiarly connected.

The manner in which John Bunyan seizes and presents the principle of Christian progress is, we think, worthy of a passing notice. The word *progress*, furnishes the immortal dreamer with both the *name* and *subject* of his book. He does not call it the pilgrims' journey, the pilgrims' history, the pilgrims' adventures, or the pilgrims' conflicts; though all these ideas are included; no, he calls it "The Pilgrims' Progress," and from the title page, to the last page of his wonderful book, he never departs from, or loses sight of this grand principle He finds the subject of his wonderful narrative in "The City of Destruction;" and he represents that person as being moved to set out on the adventurous journey by a single idea, or conviction, viz., this, *if I remain here I will be destroyed!* And, let it be distinctly noticed, no one ever set out on that pilgrimage, or ever will, till moved by that same idea. "I perish," was the language of the prodigal son; and with this conviction in his mind, and these words on his lips, he started for his father's house, and to his father's house he came. Nor was it a mere illusion of the imagination that led the prodigal thus to think and act,; no, it was stern and terrible reality; for he certainly would have perished had he remained where he was, and he knew it; hence he rose and departed; nor does any one start on the Christian journey till moved by the same conviction. Therefore, let all who would move sinners to flee from destruction, labor to convince them of the certainty of their destruction, if they remain where they are. In this, as in other particulars, John Bunyan adhered closely to bible teaching.

But let us follow Bunyan's pilgrim a few moments that we may see how our dreamer develops his grand idea of Christian progress. Moved by this terrible conviction, the alarmed sinner starts; and when his neighbours would persuade him to remain, he stops his ears, and runs crying "life, life." He groans, however, under a heavy burden, but still he urges forward, as best he may, till he gets a sight of the *cross*, when the cords that bind the burden to his back are at once snapped in sunder, and the burden falling off, rolls into the open grave of a risen Saviour. Nor does he stop here, or at the Slough of Despond either, but still urges his way through and beyond. Neither is the progress terminated by the attractions of "Vanity Fair," nor by those of "By-path Meadow," nor even by "The Hill Difficulty;" still the progress is upward and onward. And even when the fields of "Beulah" are reached, "where the sun never sets," and where the pilgrim's locks are wafted by breezes from the promised land, still the progress is continued; onward and onward: now Jordan is reached, but even here, the pilgrim does not so much as pause, but dashes through the swelling flood, and is soon in "that good land beyond Jordan,"—

"Where everlasting spring abides
And never-withering flowers;"

and even now, the progress continues, and will, while endless ages roll; for immutability is as impossible in heaven as on earth; God alone is *immutable*.

It is not till we examine the Scriptures with regard to this great principle, that we discover the prominent place that it there occupies, and the frequency with which it is developed and inforced. Take a few instances—" Therefore leaving the principles of the doctrine of Christ, let us go on unto perfection." By reference to this passage, Heb. x., it will be seen that the Apostle inforces this exhortation lest we "fall away," showing that between *progression*, and *retrogression*, there is no medium, and this is as true of churches as it is of individuals! Again. "Not as though I had already attained, either were already perfect: but I followed after, if that I may apprehend that for which also I am apprehended by Christ Jesus. Brethren, I count not myself to have apprehended: but this one thing I do, forgetting those things which are behind, and reaching forth unto those things which are before, I press toward the mark for the prize of the high calling of God in Christ Jesus." So completely was Paul's mind occupied with the idea of progress, that he considered himself as having but "this one thing" to attend to, so far as he himself was concerned. Onward, and onward, with increased, and increasing speed, he urged his way, exclaiming, " This one thing I do, forgetting those things which are behind, and reaching forth unto those things which are before, I press toward the mark for the prize of the high calling of God in Christ Jesus." Deeply impressed with the glorious idea that his was a HIGH CALLING, Paul left behind, rose above, and even *forgot* what was little and low, comparatively, and rose higher and higher in his heavenward flight. As when the eagle soars aloft, the earth and earthly objects seem to become less and less, till they are wholly lost sight of, and even forgotten; while the sun toward which she flies seems constantly increasing in magnitude and splendor. In like manner, the things that Paul left behind seemed to become less and less, till they were wholly lost sight of, and even forgotten, while the object toward which he soared seemed to be constantly increasing in magnitude and splendor. This is the idea that Charles Wesley seized, and attempted to express in the following beautiful lines:—

> "Patient the appointed race to run,
>   This weary world we cast behind;
> From strength to strength we travel on,
>   The New Jerusalem to find:
> Our labor this, our only aim,
> To find the New Jerusalem.
>
> "Through thee, who all our sins hast borne
>   Freely and graciously forgiven,
> With songs to Zion we return,
>   Contending for our native heaven;
> That palace of our glorious King,—
> We find it nearer while we sing.
>
> "Raised by the breath of love divine,
>   We urge our way with strength renew'd;
> The church of the first-born to join,
>   We travel to the Mount of God:
> With joy upon our heads arise,
> And meet our Saviour in the skies."

Such pilgrims are journeying in what Bunyan calls "The land of Beulah," where the sun never sets;" such pilgrims "rejoice evermore, pray without ceasing, and in everything give thanks." And as to "The Slough of Despond," "Vanity Fair," and "Doubting Castle," they have long since been left far behind, out of sight, and are even forgotten. But still the progress continues, "from strength to strength," and "from glory to glory:" and as they go they exclaim, "Eye hath not seen, nor ear heard, neither have entered into the heart of man, the things which God hath prepared for them that love him." This progress must continue while endless ages roll, and at every period of duration it will remain strictly true, that eye hath not seen, nor heart conceived, save in part, what " God hath prepared for them that love him;" for, as Richard Watson beautifully observes, " God is *unsearchable.* All we see or hear of him is faint and shadowy manifestation. Beyond the highest glory, there is yet an unpierced and unapproached light, a track of intellectual and moral splendor untravelled by the thoughts of the contemplating and adoring spirits who are nearest to his throne. The manifestation of this nature of God, never fully to be revealed, because infinite, is represented as constituting the reward and felicity of heaven. This is ' to *see* God.' This is 'to be forever with the Lord.' This is to behold his glory as in a glass, with unveiled face, and to be changed into his image, from glory to glory, in boundless progression and infinite approximation. Yet, after all, it will be as true, after countless ages spent in heaven itself, as in the present state, that none by 'searching can find out

God,' that is, 'to perfection.' He will then be 'a God that hideth himself,' and widely as the illumination may extend, 'clouds and darkness will still be round about him.'"

But as we are speaking more especially of the *necessity of Christian progression*, progression in the present life, and of the frequency with which this idea is enforced in the Scriptures we will quote a few more texts. Psalm cii. 12, 13. "The righteous shall flourish like the palm-tree: he shall grow like a cedar in Lebanon. Those that be planted in the house of the LORD shall flourish in the courts of our God. They shall bring forth fruit in old age; they shall be fat and flourishing." It will be seen that the growth here spoken of is not stopped, nor even checked by old age, no, being "planted in the house of the LORD," they still *grow, flourish,* and *bring forth fruit.* The same truth is beautifully expressed by Hosea, chap. viii.: "I will be as the dew unto Israel; he shall grow as the lily, and cast forth his roots as Lebanon. His branches shall spread, and his beauty shall be as the olive-tree, and his smell as Lebanon." Our blessed Lord uses the same illustration for the same purpose, Mark iv. 26, 32. It is only necessary to remind the reader of the frequency with which the Apostles exhort Christians to *grow,* and give instruction as to how this growth is promoted. Take the following as instances. Eph. iv: "But speaking the truth in love, may grow up into him in all things, which is the head, even Christ." 1 Pet. ii. 2: "As new born babes, desire the sincere milk of the word, that ye may grow thereby. 2 Pet. iii. 18: "But grow in grace and in the knowledge of our Lord and Saviour Jesus Christ." Once more. Heb. x. 38, 39: "Now the just shall live by faith: but if he draw back, my soul shall have no pleasure in him. But we are not of them who draw back unto perdition; but of them that believe to the saving of the soul." Now, it is, we think, perfectly clear that in this passage the Apostle recognizes no medium between *going forward* and *drawing back*. And it is equally evident that while *life* and *salvation* are the result of going forward, *perdition* is the result of *going back!* Nor is it less evident that the Apostles connect with faith; *life, growth,* and *eternal salvation;* and consequently, *all power.* The soul by faith takes hold of the truth of God, all the truth; the *doctrines,* the *promises,* and the *precepts;* and with the truth of God, takes hold of God himself, of God in Christ; and thus makes God's power her own. Hence the Apostle says, "The life that I now live in the flesh, I live by the faith of the Son of God, who loved me, and gave himself for me." This faith so connects the soul with God in Christ, that the Apostle says, "I live; yet not I, but Christ liveth in me." O glorious union! I had almost said *oneness* with Christ, and, consequently, with God. I almost tremble to say it, and yet, what other words will express the sublime and glorious truth? "I am crucified with Christ: nevertheless I live; yet not I, but Christ liveth in me!" Paul lived in Christ, and Christ lived in

Paul! He is so lost in God, that when he says, "I live," he immediately corrects himself, and says, "yet not I, but Christ liveth in me." In an unexplainable, yet glorious sense, the light, the life, the wisdom, the power of Christ, are all his own. Or, as he himself expresses it, as far as human language can express it;—"But of him are ye in Christ Jesus, who of God is made unto us wisdom, and righteousness, and sanctification, and redemption: that, according as it is written, he that glorieth, let him glory in the Lord." And all this by faith! No wonder, then, that "all things are possible to them that believe." Truly "this is the victory that overcometh the world, even our faith." No wonder that Whitefield, Wesley, and other holy men, were a power, as well as the Apostles. They were united to God by faith; they lived in Christ by faith, and Christ lived in them. *He was their wisdom, their righteousness, their sanctification.* Dwelling in love, *they dwelt in God and God in them.* Hence God was their *strength*, as well as their *refuge*. Hence, too, *they had power with God and with man, and prevailed.* And all this by faith in Christ. And as their faith increased, which it did, they increased in wisdom and strength; they increased in all goodness; they grew "up into Christ their living head in all things." By faith they were justified, by faith they were sanctified, by faith they lived, by faith they conquered, by faith they "turned the world upside down." They understood this glorious doctrine; them with it was not matter of opinion, they knew it by happy experience. Hence Charles Wesley sang—

> "By faith we know thee strong to save:
>   (Save us, a present Saviour thou;)
> Whate'er we hope, by faith we have;
>   Future, and past, subsisting now.
>
> "To him that in thy name believes,
>   Eternal life with thee is given;
> Into himself he all receives,—
>   Pardon, and holiness, and heaven."

Again:—

> "Save us by grace, through faith alone,—
>   A faith thou must thyself impart:
> A faith that would by works be shown,
>   A faith that purifies the heart.
>
> "A faith that doth the mountains move,
>   A faith that shows our sins forgiven,
> A faith that sweetly works by love,
>   And ascertains our claim to heaven."

Again:—

> "Thy mighty name salvation is,
>   And keeps my happy soul above:
> Comfort it brings, and power, and peace,
>   And joy, and everlasting love:
> To me, with thy great name are given
> Pardon, and holiness, and heaven.
>
> "Jesus, my all in all thou art;
>   My rest in toil, my ease in pain;
> The medicine of my broken heart;
>   In war, my peace, in loss, my gain;
> My smile beneath the tyrant's frown;
>   In shame, my glory and my crown:

"In want, my plentiful supply;
　In weakness, my almighty power;
In bonds, my perfect liberty;
　My light in Satan's darkest hour;
In grief, my joy unspeakable;
　My life in death, my all in all."

Once more, listen to this sweet singer:—

"Up into thee, our living head,
　Let us in all things grow,
Till thou hast made us free indeed,
　And spotless here below.
Then, when the mighty work is wrought,
　Receive thy ready bride:
Give us in heaven a happy lot
　With all the sanctified."

Just so it was that John Wesley sang; take a single instance, the first that comes to hand:—

"Arm me with thy whole armor, Lord:
　Support my weakness with thy might,
Gird on my thigh thy conquering sword,
　And shield me in the threat'ning fight:
From faith to faith, from grace to grace,
　So in thy strength shall I go on;
Till heaven and earth flee from thy face,
　And glory end what grace begun."

Watts, too, is in raptures, while he attempts to express, in his heavenly numbers, the same glorious truths. Take a single verse from that beautiful and well-known hymn on p. 534 of our hymn book:—

"The men of grace have found
　Glory begun below:

> Celestial fruit on earthly ground
>   From faith and hope may grow:
> Then let our songs abound,
>   And every tear be dry:
>   We're marching through Immanuel's ground,
> To fairer worlds on high."

Newton, too, is in raptures when he attempts to express the same glorious sentiments in his exquisite numbers:—

> "How sweet the name of Jesus sounds
>   In a believer's ear;
> It soothes his sorrows, heals his wounds,
>   And drives away his fear.
>
>   . . . .
>
> "Dear Name, the rock on which I build,
>   My shield and hiding-place;
> My never-failing treasure fill'd
>   With boundless stores of grace."

Again:—

> "His name yields the richest perfume,
>   And sweeter than music his voice;
> His presence disperses my gloom,
>   And makes all within me rejoice;
> I should, were he always thus nigh,
>   Have nothing to wish or to fear;
> No mortal so happy as I,—
>   My summer would last all the year.
>
> "Content with beholding his face,
>   My all to his pleasure resign'd;
> No changes of season or place
>   Would make any change in my mind:
> While blest with a sense of his love,
>   A palace a toy would appear;

And prisons would palaces prove,
If Jesus would dwell with me there."

With similar sweetness and force the great and good Dr. Doddridge sings the same glorious truth, the same happy experience. Addressing his soul while urging onward in the Christian course, he says:—

" 'Tis God's all animating voice
  That calls thee from on high;
'Tis he whose hand presents the prize
  To thine aspiring eye.

" A cloud of witnesses around,
  Hold thee in full survey;
Forget the steps already trod,
  And onward urge thy way.

" Blest Saviour! introduced by thee,
  Our race have we begun;
And crown'd with vict'ry at thy feet,
  We'll lay our trophies down."

Again:—

" 'Tis to my Saviour I would live,—
  To him who for my ransom died;
Nor could all worldly honor give
  Such bliss as crowns me at his side.

" His work my hoary age shall bless,
  When youthful vigour is no more;
And my last hour of life confess
  His saving love, his glorious power."

Lest any one should attempt to dispose of the fine sentiments, the glorious truth, embodied in the above and similar verses, as mere flights of poetry, we beg to remind the reader of the experience of the Wesleys, Whitefield, Luther, and others already given. And as to John Newton, his remarkable conversion, and the holy, happy, and useful life which he afterward led, are well known. In short, what they have expressed in these heavenly songs, may be found in their sermons, and their other prose writings. And the whole comes to us supported and confirmed by their unmistakable consciousness, holy lives, and remarkable usefulness. Moreover, the same truths come to us with the seal of the Eternal Spirit, and may be found in God's own Book, confirmed to us by miracles and prophecies of which God alone can be the Author. It is only necessary to add, that the *vigorous growing faith* here exhibited, must result in *progression*, and the failure, or decline of faith, must as necessarily result in *retrogression*. If faith is the *condition* of life and power, it must be the *condition* of their *continuance* and *increase*. While a vigorous growing faith continues, there must be progression; for God has promised to such every possible good. Nor can the opposition of men and devils prevent the fulfilment of such promises, while the vigorous growing faith continues: on the contrary, "All things work together for good to them that love God; to them who are the called according to his purpose," which would not be true if any thing outside of them could prevent the progress of which we speak, and for which we contend. Moreover, the soul that is in possession of such faith, vigorous growing faith in Christ, must be active, and such action implies progress, as we have already shown. And where there is not progression, there is and must be retrogression, as we have also shown. Having spoken, more especially, of the *necessity* of Christian progression; we will now, more particularly, speak of

The Nature of Christian progression.—Perhaps the word *nature* but imperfectly expresses the distinction we desire to make; we use it as the best we can think of. The *nature*, and the *necessity*, of Christian progression are so closely connected, that neither can be discussed wholly independent of the other. Yet for the sake of clearness we have dwelt more especially upon the one, and will now dwell more especially upon the other, *viz.*, the *nature* of *Christian progress;* in other words, the *way* and *order*, in which the progress, or advance, is made.

The grand outlines of this subject may be found in the first chapter of the Second Epistle of Peter, from verse five to verse eleven. To our mind this is the finest exhibit of this subject that we have met with even in the word of God. The Apostle addresses himself "to them that have obtained like precious faith with us through the righteousness of our God and Saviour Jesus Christ." The entire introduction is sublimely beautiful, and inexpressibly rich. He desires that "grace and peace may be multiplied unto them through the knowledge of God, and of Jesus our Lord, according as his divine power hath given unto us all things that *pertain* unto life and godliness, through the knowledge of him that hath called us to glory and virtue, whereby are given unto us exceeding great and precious promises; that by these ye might be partakers of the divine nature, having escaped the corruption that is in the world through lust!"

To *escape*, to be *saved from* this corruption, and to be made *partakers of the divine nature*, are the grand objects to be accomplished; nothing short of this is Gospel Salvation, even in this life.

"And besides this," says the Apostle, "giving all diligence, add to your faith virtue." It will be observed that the Apostle commences the progress with *faith;* because the things which he exhorts Christians to add, never go before, but always accompany or follow this faith; I say *this faith;* for the faith of which he speaks is evidently that upon the exercise of which God justifies the ungodly; the same faith that the Apostles had: hence he says,—"To them that have obtained like precious faith with us." The same faith of which Paul speaks when he says, "Being justified by faith, we have peace with God through our Lord Jesus Christ: by whom also we have access by faith into this grace wherein we stand, and rejoice in hope of the glory of God." This is the faith to which the particulars here specified are to be added. You can no more add these particulars before you have this faith, than you can build the architectural structure before you lay the foundation. It is as true in the former, as it is in the latter case, that there is nothing *upon* which to build; nothing *to* which the additions can be made. Moreover, the Christian graces which the Apostle here specifies, cannot possibly have an existence before the sinner is justified. To deny this statement is to say, that the sinner can be a Christian before he is justified, and, consequently, before he is born again; and, also, without the agency and work of the Holy Spirit; which amounts to a denial of the whole Christian system. This is a point of great importance; for, to establish it, is to sweep away at a single stroke the whole system of pharisaism, the grand error of which consists in the assumption that the sinner may transform himself into a Christian before he is justified or regenerated; and, consequently, independent of the Holy Spirit, or the atonement! Let it be distinctly noticed, then, that the Apostle proceeds in the exact order in which the additions are made.

We are not to suppose, however, that any one may have this "precious faith," and yet be wholly destitute of the graces here specified. No, all who have this faith are justified, born again, adopted, sanctified, and, consequently, have all these graces, in a greater or less degree! But in the economy of grace each is to be increased in the way and order here specified; this is the work of the Christian life. In support of this view we refer to the criticisms of Doddridge, Wesley, Dr. Adam Clarke, and others, on the word *add*, here. In his paraphrase Doddridge says, "Be careful to accompany that belief with all the lovely train of attendant graces: *associate*, as it were, to your *faith*, *virtue*, true fortitude, and resolution of mind, which may enable you to break through that variety of dangers with which your faith may be attended." And in his accompanying note he adds, "The word ἐπιχορηγησατε properly signifies to *lead up*, as in a *dance*, one of these virtues after another in a beautiful and majestic order." In support of this view, he quotes several critics of high authority. It is assumed by the Apostle, that, having the "precious faith," he *has* these virtues in a greater or less degree, and, instead of shrinking from apparent danger, he is to lead up one of these virtues after another in a beautiful and majestic order, as a general would lead up one battalion after another into line of battle, as far, and as fast, as the opposing powers rendered this necessary. This is a beautiful and sublime idea. The Christian soldier is here represented as being supplied, *from headquarters*, with forces sufficient for any *emergency*, and as a moral agent he is to call them into action as the *exigency* may require; hence, if he does not conquer, the fault is his own, for the King in whose cause he fights keeps him well supplied *with forces sufficient for any occasion*, and he here gives him directions how to use these forces; and these directions being complied with, "One shall chase a thousand, and two shall put ten thousand to flight," shall "turn to flight the armies of the aliens;" in short, "No weapon formed against" such "shall prosper." In this way, while the moral agency of the Christian is preserved, and his heroism developed, the sufficiency is seen to be of God through the atonement. Hence it is, that certain men have been an all-conquering power, as we have seen in the case of Whitefield, Wesley, Luther, and others; while other pusillanimous creatures hid themselves, leaving the armies of the aliens to march forward and do their work of slaughter unresisted! The fact is, any man may be a *coward* or a *hero*, just as he pleases; and all men acknowledge this, in that they blame the coward for his cowardice, and praise the hero for his heroism: and God, the Almighty and infallible Judge, does the same! This same Peter acted the coward at one time, and the hero at another, and he is praised and blamed accordingly, and that by all worlds; hence, his exhortation is supported by his experience as well as by his inspiration. Thus much with regard to the entire passage, and with regard to the word *add, lead up*, or *associate*, in particular. We need not quote the other learned critics referred to, as their criticisms on this word are substantially the same as that of Doddridge, and are, doubtless, correct; only I do not like the reference to a *dance* for illustration; hence I have referred to the more noble action of a general in the field of battle: and in this particular I am supported by other Scriptures, which represent Christians as a noble army of soldiers, valiantly contending with opposing forces: but they never, I think, attempt to illustrate this noble action by the silly and ridiculous manœuvering in a dance.

CHAPTER VI.

Nature of Christian progression—Meaning of the word αρετην, courage. The command and promise of God are essential to Christian courage, and this courage is essential to Christian progression—Interesting examples are given, as Daniel and his three companions; and David slaying Goliath; Luther, also, and many other men of courage are noticed—This courage can only exist in connection with Christian faith—It does not precede, but results from faith—Faith and courage are specially necessary for the work of the minister of Jesus.

LET us now proceed to notice severally the noble forces specified by the Apostles, and the order in which we are exhorted to *associate* them with our faith, and lead them to the glorious contest.

"Add to your faith virtue." I have often been puzzled with the word virtue here, as I have no doubt others have been, and still are; for the word virtue may mean any one of a thousand good qualities. The fact is, in its *generic* form, the word αρετην, here translated *virtue*, has this general meaning; but in its *specific* form, as here, it means *courage*, or fortitude, as the critics above specified contend, and translate accordingly. Hence, *courage* is that which we are here exhorted to add to, or associate with, our faith. This is the noble force which the Christian believer is exhorted to lead at once into action, and thus set at defiance, resist, and conquer the opposing power, or powers. Thus it was that God exhorted Joshua when he appointed him to the place of Moses, as the great leader of the armies of Israel. This fine exhortation may be found in the first chapter of Joshua, from verse two to verse nine, and ends with the following remarkable words,—" Have not I commanded thee? Be strong and of a good courage; be not afraid, neither be thou dismayed: for the LORD thy God is with thee whithersoever thou goest." Three times in this short, but very comprehensive, and very forcible exhortation, Joshua is exhorted to be courageous;—verse 6. "Be strong and of a good courage:" verse 7. "Only be thou strong and very courageous:" and again in verse 9. "Have not I commanded thee? Be strong and of a good courage." Mark the *repetition*, the *variation*, and the connection, of the words *strength, courage, fear, dismay. Be strong: be of a good courage: be thou very courageous: be not afraid: be not dismayed.* Have courage in such measure as to exclude all fear but the fear of God. God exhorts to this end, and he positively commands;—" Have not I commanded thee? Be strong and of a good courage." Observe, too, the important fact, for it is a fact, and one that deserves the deepest attention; viz., that without this courage he could not obey the divine commands—" Only be thou strong and very courageous, that thou mayest observe to do according to all the law which Moses my servant commanded thee: turn not from it to the right hand or to the left that thou mayest prosper whithersoever thou goest. This book of the law shall not depart out of thy mouth; but thou shalt meditate therein day and night, that thou mayest observe to do according to all that is written therein: for then thou shalt make thy way prosperous, and then thou shalt have good success." Observe too, that all the motives to courageous action, are found in the commands and promises of God;—"Have not I commanded thee?"—"There shall not any man be able to stand before thee all the days of thy life: as I was with Moses, so will I be with thee: I will not fail thee, nor forsake thee." Again. "The LORD thy God is with thee whithersoever thou goest." Thus clearly are we taught that God's command and promise are the motives to courageous action, the sole rule of faith and conduct, the basis of faith and confidence, the spring of all right action, and the only ground upon which we can rationally hope for success. It is worthy of remark that the commission which JEHOVAH here gives to Joshua, is substantially the same as that which Jesus gave to his disciples,—"Teaching them to observe all things whatsoever I have commanded you: and lo, I am with you alway, *even* unto the end of the world." Those who have read the New Testament will remember how often Jesus exhorts his disciples not to be afraid, and, consequently, to be courageous; and he holds out precisely the same motives:—"Fear not, ye are of more value than many sparrows:"—"Lo I am with you alway:"—"Fear not them that kill the body:"—"The very hairs of your head are all numbered." The sum of all is contained in the good old promise, Deut. xxviii. 8. "And the LORD, he *it is* that doth go before thee; he will be with thee, he will not fail thee, neither forsake thee: fear not, neither be dismayed." In Heb. xiii. 5, 6, we have the same summing up, and the same application,—"Let your conversation be without covetousness; and be content with such things as ye have: for he hath said, I will never leave thee, nor forsake thee. So that we may boldly say: "The Lord is my helper, and I will not fear what man shall do unto me." It is quite evident, that the commands and promises of Jehovah in the Old Testament, and those of Jesus in the New, are essentially one, and prove conclusively that the Jesus of the New Testament, is the JEHOVAH of the Old. Though this is a point of the most vital inportance, we only notice it in passing, it being suggested by the Scriptures which our argument led us to quote; for it is evident that no *creature* can command and promise as above without blasphemously assuming what belongs to God only.

The command and promise of God are essential to Christian courage, and Christian courage is essential to Christian progression. Without this courage no man can do the work, fight the battles, or even profess the faith of the Christian; for the duties of the Christian life are such, that courage is in requisition much more frequently than some may be inclined to believe. This arises, in a great measure, from that opposition which the world and the devil present to every thing that is vital in religion. Hence it requires courage even for the young convert to obey that command, "Go home to thy friends, and tell them how great things the Lord hath done for thee, and hath had compassion on thee;" and even the old professor, under some circumstances, feels the need of courage to perform this important and very plain duty. But why is this? If one should become heir to a great property, a fine estate, with certain honorable titles attached to it, courage does not seem to be necessary to make these facts known: but when the sinner is converted, born again, he becomes heir to a glorious inheritance, to which the most honorable titles are attached, and yet he shrinks from the duty of making the facts known. Yea, and unless he adds to his faith courage, he will not do so, especially under some circumstances, and just here it is, in all probability, where the announcement is most needed, where it will do most good; yet he will surely fail to tell what God has done for him, unless he adds courage to his faith. Again, it will frequently require courage to obey that plain command, "Thou shalt in any wise rebuke thy neighbor, and not suffer sin upon him;" or as it is in the margin, "that thou bear not sin for him." The same duty is enjoined by our blessed Lord, "Go and tell him his fault between thyself and him alone," but plain as is this duty you will not perform it in one instance out of ten when it is your duty so to do, unless you add courage to your faith; you know it is God that commands you to do so, yet you will certainly disobey the command unless you add to your faith virtue.

The above are only a few of the instances which are of frequent occurrence; but there are other instances which, though they do not occur so often, require much more courage when they do occur; instances wherein fidelity to God will, apparently, at least, involve great risk. Take the case of the three Hebrew children: a snare is laid for them, and is laid with deep infernal cunning. An image is set up on the plain of Dura; it is made of gold, and is some ninety feet high. "The princes, the governors, and the captains, the treasurers, the counsellors, the sheriffs, and the rulers of the provinces, were gathered together unto the dedication of the image which Nebuchadnezzar had set up. And they stood before the image which Nebuchadnezzar the king had set up. Then a herald cried aloud, To you it is commanded, O people, nations, and languages, that at what time ye hear the sound of the cornet, flute, harp, sackbut, psaltery, dulcimer, and all kinds of music, ye fall down and worship the golden image that Nebuchadnezzar the king hath set up, and whoso falleth not down and worshippeth, shall the same hour be cast into the midst of the burning fiery furnace." The call has been given, and promptly has it been obeyed by the various nations and languages to whom it came. See! the vast plain of Dura, in the province of Babylon, is literally crowded from its centre to its circumference, and first and foremost in this crowd of idolators are seen multitudes of office-seekers, especially those who expect to fill the vacant offices of Shadrach, Meshach, and Abed-nego, when they shall have been consumed. The signal is given, and lo! the vast multitude lie prostrate before the image, *three only excepted*. Noble men! see how erect they stand amid the prostrate nations, even in sight of the furnace that burns with sevenfold intensity, flashing and flaming with infernal fury. But neither the fury of the king, nor that of the fiery furnace, can induce these men to bow in worship to any save the God of their fathers. Even now life and honors are offered to them if they will only worship like others; if they will fall down with the princes, and other office-seekers, with them, they are told, they shall share both offices and honors; but it is to no purpose that the king " in his rage and fury," threatens death, and offers his gifts: these heroes promptly reply, " O, Nebuchadnezzar, we are not careful to answer thee in this matter." Mark, their mind was fully made up; hence they did not ask time to think; this was entirely unnecessary; their judgment was already convinced, and their purpose firmly fixed as to the course they should pursue. Even to *hesitate* is a crime, where duty is clear; and those who do so, will surely yield to the temptation; and it were better to do so at once than to increase their guilt by equivocation and deception. But these honest courageous men at once gave the king to understand that it was simply impossible for him to fright them into submission, and that he would surely be disappointed if he should indulge any hope of succeeding by such measures. Hence they added, "If it be so, our God whom we serve is able to deliver us from the burning fiery furnace, and he will deliver us out of thy hand, O king, but if not, be it known unto thee, O king, that we will not serve thy gods, nor worship the golden image which thou hast set up." Whether we are, or are not, delivered, we will not worship thee or thine image! This was plain, honest, straightforward. It was just as it should be. Never before had the king of Babylon met with such men, never before had he heard such language: such language is used by none but the saints of the Most High. Such language is not, and never was, in the vocabulary of this world. As to office-seekers, it is foolishness unto them, neither can they understand it, for it is spiritually discerned, and spiritual discernment is a faculty that does not belong to courtiers and office-seekers; they have no use for it; the things they seek are discovered by a very different faculty. And as to the proud king of Babylon, this language was to him as inexplicable as it was offensive. The mysterious writing upon the palace, at an after period, was not more inexplicable to Belshazzar, than was this language to Nebuchadnezzar. The effect, however, was somewhat different, and is worthy of notice. "Then was Nebuchadnezzar full of fury, and the form of his visage was changed against Shadrach, Meshach, and Abed-nego; therefore he spake, and commanded that they should heat the furnace one seven times more than it was wont to be heated. And he commanded the most mighty men that were in his army to bind Shadrach, Meshach, and Abed-nego and to cast them into the burning fiery furnace." And they were cast in as he commanded. But their God was able to deliver them, and he did deliver them, he did save them, not *from* the flames, but *in* the flames. Thus he fulfilled his own promise, they passed through the fire, but it did not consume them. No, they still maintain, in the midst of the burning fiery furnace, the same erect position that they maintained in the midst of the idolatrous worshippers who lay prostrate before the image. Then the king drew near and said, "Lo, I see four men loose, walking in the midst of the fire, and they have no hurt: and the form of the fourth is like the Son of God." We may well say, "Who ever trusted in the LORD and was confounded:" "Blessed are all they that put their trust in him." Noble men! when I see them standing erect in the midst of the prostrate multitudes, defiant of all threats and all dangers, I almost feel like falling at their feet. But methinks I hear them say, "See thou do it not: for we are thy fellow servants, and of thy brethren the prophets, and of them which keep the sayings of this book: worship God."

These men by their courageous conduct did more for the cause of God, than was ever done by all the time serving pusillanimous creatures, since or before. By this heroic act they struck down the idols of Chaldea, so that they fell like Dagon before the ark of the Lord. As for the mean courtiers and office-seekers, they were covered with shame, while Nebuchadnezzar, and, it is hoped, many others, worshipped the true God; nor was there a single individual, for the present at least, who would dare to worship the image that the king had set up; for the threatening that had a little while previous to this act been hurled at the worshippers of the true God, are now hurled at all who would dare to worship any other. And three men achieved this mighty victory, and produced this glorious revolution, by simply *adding to their faith courage.*

Now, we ask, wherein did these men distinguish themselves from other men? was it in believing that the image of gold was not the true God? was not entitled to the worship of the nations? Certainly not. There were thousands there that day, who believed this as firmly as they did. Nor did they experience any difficulty in believing that the God of their fathers alone was entitled to worship. This was neither the point of *distinction,* nor the point of difficulty. What, then, was the difficult act by which they distinguished themselves, and by which they achieved the mighty victory? It was simply this *they added to their faith courage.* And: I aver, that this is the grand, the difficult act, by which the great and good have always been distinguished from other men, that by which they have surmounted the greatest difficulties, and produced the most glorious results. It was thus that Daniel triumphed in that same old city of Babylon. Daniel was a praying man, and the devil undertook to put a stop to his praying; and again he summoned to his help his old friends, the office-seekers; and they agreed upon the following plan: "Then these presidents and princes assembled together to the king, and said thus unto him: King Darius, live forever. All the presidents of the kingdom, the governors, and the princes, the counsellors, and the captains, have consulted together to establish a royal statute, and to make a firm decree, that whosoever shall ask any petition of any God or man for thirty days, save of thee, O king, he shall be cast into the den of lions. Now, O king, establish the decree, and sign the writing, that it be not changed, according to the law of the Medes and Persians, which altereth not. Wherefore King Darius signed the writing and the decree." This whole procedure was very cool, and it was as cunning as it was cool. They undertook to overcome the king by flattery, and Daniel by murderous persecution. With regard to the former they were successful, but with regard to the latter they failed, as signally as their brethren had failed in the case of the three Hebrew heroes, some forty-three years previous to this time. These men seem to have forgotten this humiliating defeat; or, these three champions having, in all probability, gone to their reward, it was probably supposed that courage had passed away with them; but God has always his man for the emergency, and having given Shadrach, Meshach, and Abed-nego, an opportunity to develop their courage, he now gives Daniel a similar opportunity. It is in this way that he makes the wrath of man to praise him while he restrains the remainder; in this way that he develops the manhood and moral power of his servants, and makes the abundant grace through the thanksgiving of many redound to the glory of God, and, at the same time, "all things work together for good to them that love God, to them that are the called according to his purpose." And such, unquestionably, have been the results in all the instances here noticed. If Daniel and his three friends had not been tested as they were, these glorious developments of moral courage had never been known, and these noble men had lived and died in comparative obscurity. And who can estimate the loss that the church and the world would have sustained in consequence. Who can fully estimate the effects, the glorious effects, which have been produced by the thrilling stories of the *furnace* and the *den* upon those who have heard those stories from that time to the present; and who can estimate the effects that will yet be produced by these wonderful stories.

But let us follow Daniel through his terrible conflict, and see how he triumphs over his enemies and turns to flight the armies of the aliens.

"Now when Daniel knew that the writing was signed, he went into his house; and his windows being open in his chamber toward Jerusalem, he kneeled upon his knees three times a day, and prayed, and gave thanks before his God, as he did aforetime."

Those vile courtiers and office-seekers well knew what Daniel's custom and practice were; they have watched him narrowly, and were convinced that the duties of his high and important office were discharged with ability and scrupulous fidelity, and that his life was irreproachable:—" Then said these men, we shall not find any occasion against this Daniel, except we find it against him concerning the law of his God." The snare was laid with deep, infernal cunning; they knew that he was as faithful to his God as he was to his king. Hence he will likely pray in spite of all consequences, and if he does, the lions shall have him, and if he does not, said the devil, I will have him: so that whatever course he takes, said his enemies, we are sure of him! but they were mistaken, and gloriously disappointed.

The hour for prayer is at hand; and the devil and his servants are anxiously watching to see what Daniel will do. He seems to be alone, for he is not said to have consulted his three faithful friends as formerly, they, as we have supposed, having gone, " where the wicked cease from troubling, and where the weary are at rest;" hence, Daniel is alone in Babylon, " and of the people," it would seem, " there were none with him," but his God is with him, and he is with God.

The hour for prayer has arrived: and Daniel is seen, " as aforetime," bending his steps toward the hallowed place of prayer. See! There he goes, wending his way from his office to his chamber, through the streets of Babylon, idolatrous Babylon!

Calm and thoughtful is his bearing as he approaches nearer and nearer to the mercy-seat. He seems to have forgotten all but his God, whom he "serves without fear," *for he has added to his faith courage.* His enemies are agitated, as they behold him from their hiding places. Devils are agitated, for they too behold him, as with firm step and thoughtful mien he wends his way to the place of prayer. All worlds view him with intense interest as he journeys on: and methinks I hear him sing—

> "While thou, Almighty Lord, art nigh,
>   My soul disdains to fear;
> Both sin and Satan I defy,
>   Still impotently near;
> Both earth and hell their wars may wage,—
>   I mark their vain design:
> And calmly smile to see them rage
>   Against a child of thine."

Noble man! truly thou hast *added to thy faith courage;* and noble were the acts that resulted from thy faith and courage. Here we may well take up the language of James and say,—"Seest thou how faith wrought with his works, and by works was his faith made perfect."

But he has reached the place of prayer, he is in his chamber, and has "kneeled upon his knees." "And his windows being open toward Jerusalem," he will not close them: defiant of his enemies, he "prayed, and gave thanks before his God, as he did aforetime," and this he did "three times a day." "Then these men assembled, and found Daniel praying and making supplication before his God.

Closely did they watch, and carefully did they record the facts: but he regarded them not. Methinks I hear him sing as he repeats his visits to that sacred chamber, that hallowed spot, "where prayer was wont to be made;"—

> "Sweet hour of prayer, sweet hour of prayer,
> That calls me from a world of care;
> And bids me at my Father's throne,
> Make all my wants and wishes known;
> In seasons of distress and grief,
> My soul has often found relief;
> And oft escap'd the tempter's snare,
> By thy return, sweet hour of prayer."

And, let it be distinctly noticed, this was really *the only* way of *escape* that was left for him at this time. If he prayed not, he is conquered, he is undone; but praying he is victorious, he triumphs over all his enemies. But mark! to pray at this time required courage; courage was absolutely necessary: there was nothing, absolutely nothing, that would substitute for it. When Daniel prayed, no man *would* or *could* pray without courage, even such courage as *only* springs from faith in God. And such was Daniel's courage, for he *added it to his faith*. This courage never goes before faith: when it exists at all, it accompanies or follows faith, even the faith by which a sinner is justified before God.

When these men found Daniel praying, and had proved the fact against him, they thought they had him sure enough; and insisted that he must be cast into the den of lions, and cast in he was. But "man's extremity is God's opportunity." This proved specially true in the present instance; for lions and political office-seekers are alike under God's control. In proof of this we have only to glance again at the history before us. "My God," says Daniel, "hath sent his angel, and hath shut the lions' mouths, that they have not hurt me: for as much as before him innocency was found in me; and also before thee, O King, have I done no hurt." He was upright before God and man. But that very thing made him the more hateful to those mean hypocritical office-seekers and court flatterers. When the king found that Daniel was unhurt, "Then was the king exceeding glad for him, and commanded that they should take Daniel up out of the den. So Daniel was taken up out of the den, and no manner of hurt was found upon him, because he believed in his God. And the king commanded, and they brought those men who had accused Daniel, and they cast *them* into the den of lions, them, their children, and their wives; and the lions had the mastery of them, and broke all their bones in pieces or ever they came at the bottom of the den." This is only one out of many warnings to which sinners, especially office-seeking sinners, would do well to take heed. There is no help for them in the lions' den; no angel there to shut the mouths of the lions when such men are in the den. But the holy, the believing, and courageous Daniel, was as safe there as he was when praying in his chamber. In fact, the lions' den became a praying chamber as soon as Daniel was cast into it; and these savage creatures, the lions, were more affected by Daniel's prayers than were the still more savage creatures, the office-seekers. God says: "I will that men pray everywhere;" and the possibility of doing so cannot be doubted, when we remember that Jonah prayed in the whale's belly, and Daniel in the lion's den.—

"From every stormy wind that blows,
From every swelling tide of woes,
There is a calm, a sure retreat;
'Tis found beneath the mercy-seat."
. . . .
"Ah! whither could we flee for aid,
When tempted, desolate, dismayed?
Or how the hosts of hell defeat,
Had suffering saints no mercy-seat?

"Jesus, thou sov'reign Lord of all,—
 The same through one eternal day,—
Attend thy feeblest foll'wer's call,
 And O, instruct us how to pray!
Pour out the supplicating grace,
And stir us up to seek thy face."
. . . .
"Come in thy pleading Spirit down
 To us who for thy coming stay;
Of all thy gifts we ask but one,—
 We ask the constant power to pray:
Indulge us, Lord, in this request,
Thou canst not then deny the rest."

And help us to add to our faith courage. Make us, like thy servants of old, "very courageous."

A few additional remarks, and we will take our leave of these heroes. *First:* the noble acts by which they achieved such glorious victories were voluntary acts, as are all such acts. Before being cast into the furnace and the den, they were not subjected to violence of any kind, either by God or man. God promised and commanded, and gave the necessary grace, on the one hand; while man commanded, promised, and threatened, on the other. That was all. But these men disregarded the threatenings, and disobeyed the commands of men, while they believed the promises and obeyed the commands of God. That was all. *Second:* Shadrach and his noble companions could have bowed with the multitude before the image, just as easy as turn their hand; and with equal ease Daniel could have suspended his daily devotions; but if they had, they would have lost their power for good; like Sampson, they would have been shorn of their strength instantly; they would have been as powerless as other sinners. But, *third;* they added to their faith courage, adequate to the emergency, and thus retaining their strength, they vanquished their enemies, God was glorified, their strength was renewed, and they went on from conquest to conquest, rejoicing in the Lord and joying in the God of their salvation.

Now, I maintain that this is the way, the only way, in which moral power is retained and increased. It is common to talk about great men as though they rose by chance, by a happy turn of the wheel of fortune. No such thing. I admit that some men rise like floodwood, but they fall with the receding tide as fast as they rose. Or by cunning and wickedness they rise like Haman, and like Haman they fall. They build upon the sand, and for awhile they may glitter in the sunbeams, but by and by, the rain descends, the floods come, and the winds blow, and their building falls, and great is the fall thereof; while they, themselves, are like the chaff which the wind driveth away. Not so, men who are truly great: they rise in spite of winds and tides. They rise from their fallen state by faith in Jesus, and by adding courage to this faith they continue to rise despite the opposing powers of earth and hell. See there, that blustering Philistine, Goliath of Gath. He has a helmet of brass upon his head; his coat of mail weighs five thousand shekels of brass; he has greaves of brass upon his legs, and a target of brass between his shoulders; the staff of his spear is like a weaver's beam, and his spear's head weighs six hundred shekels of iron. Hark how he blusters and shouts! "I defy the armies of Israel this day, give me a man that we may fight together." O! bless me! His appearance and his words are alike awful. Hence "when Saul and all Israel heard those words of the Philistine, they were dismayed, and greatly afraid." And who would not be afraid? I will tell you. He who has faith in God, and who adds to that faith *courage* adequate to the occasion. He, and he only, will not be afraid. And just such a man God has prepared for the emergency. See! there he comes, a mere stripling, a ruddy youth. "What shall be done," inquired the youth, "to the man that killeth this Philistine, and taketh away the reproach from Israel? for who is this uncircumcised Philistine, that he should defy the armies of the living God." Well said, David. That is a new idea; it is against God that this uncircumcised Philistine hurls his threats. This idea had not occurred to the people: hence, "all the men of Israel, when they saw the man, fled from him, and were sore afraid." And, poor frighted creatures, they do not get the grand idea even now. Hence, "Eliab's anger was kindled against David, and he said, Why comest thou down hither? and with whom hast thou left those few sheep in the wilderness? I know thy pride, and the naughtiness of thine heart; for thou art come down that thou mightest see the battle." The battle! My dear sir, there is no battle! with what face can you talk about a battle when you are all fleeing, being terror-stricken by the very sight of the giant of Gath? Fleeing, not fighting, is your present policy. Truly it is with a poor grace that such men talk about a battle. But it is just such men who do talk and bluster, and say all manner of evil against men of real worth. Saul, too, tried to dissuade the youth from such a bold undertaking. But David said to Saul, "Let no man's heart fail because of him; thy servant will go and fight with the Philistine." When Saul further talked about David's youth, and about the marvellous prowess of the Philistine, David replied, "Thy servant kept his father's sheep, and there came a lion, and a bear, and took a lamb out of the flock: and I went out after him and smote him, and delivered it out of his mouth: and when he arose against me, I caught him by his beard, and smote him, and slew him. Thy servant slew both the lion and the bear: and this uncircumcised Philistine shall be as one of them, seeing he hath defied the armies of the living God. David said, moreover, The LORD that delivered me out of the paw of the lion, and out the paw of the bear, he will deliver me out of the hand of this Philistine. And Saul said unto David, Go, and the Lord be with thee." Now here is genuine courage; no fanaticism, no foolish temerity, but true intelligent courage. And Saul caught the grand idea, and so did others, doubtless, and it put new life in them. God having thus prepared his man for the emergency, he went forth with his staff, his scrip, his sling and his stone, saying as he met the boasting Philistine, " This day will the LORD deliver thee unto mine hands; and I will smite thee, and take thine head from thee; and will give the carcasses of the host of the Philistines this day unto the fowls of the air, and to the wild beasts of the earth: that all the earth may know that there is a God in Israel. And all this assembly shall know that the LORD saveth not with sword and spear: for the battle is the LORD's, and he will give you unto our hands." The next moment the giant lay dead at David's feet. " So David prevailed over the Philistine with a sling and with a stone, and smote the Philistine and slew him; but there was no sword in the hand of David." But the sword of the giant was now David's sword, and with that he cut off the giant's head. Thus it is that God transfers the power of the wicked into the hands of men who have *faith* and *courage*, not into the hands of unbelieving cowards. No, "to him that hath shall be given; and from him that hath not shall be taken away even that which he hath."

Here again, the faith and courage of a single man, saves a nation from ruin, and with it the church of God; while their enemies, their boasting and almost triumphant enemies, are confounded, routed and slain. And herein the promise of God is fulfilled, "One of you shall chase a thousand, and two shall put ten thousand to flight." Rest assured of it, God's promises mean something. In fact they "are all yea and amen in Christ Jesus."

It is only necessary to remind the reader that David achieved his victories in precisely the same way that the other heroes, whom we have mentioned, achieved their victories. He could have allowed the lion and the bear to have carried off the lambs and the sheep unheeded. And he could have whined and scolded like his brother Eliab, leaving the church and nation to fall, while, like others, he fled before the conquering armies of the Philistines. But he did not. On the contrary, he met and conquered the enemy, and saved both the nation and the church. And he did so, because *he had faith in God, and added to that faith courage.* In short, we might bring forward, in support of this position, every real hero of whom we know any thing, and

CHRISTIAN PROGRESSION. 217

show that the same *faith* and *courage*, were the mighty, the all-sufficient forces by which they were moved to deeds of daring and conquest. They were not mere machines, no, they were moral heroes; and they were so, because they had faith in God, and added to that faith courage. In the face of his enemies, who included almost the entire world, Luther published his ninety-five theses, and nailed them to the very door of the church of Rome, with which he thus joined issue defiant of all consequences. At another time, when that same Rome, to all human appearance, had shut him in on every side, and threatened him with speedy destruction, he exclaimed, "Living I will be her enemy, and dying I will be her death." Nor were they vain words. Living he was her enemy, her conquering enemy, nor did she kill him either, for he died in peace. And at this very day that same Rome is reeling to her fall under the mighty blows of his faith and courage. Zwingle too, actuated by the same faith and courage, published his sixty-seven theses in Switzerland shortly after Luther published his ninety-five in Germany. And having challenged the champions of Rome to meet him in Zurich, he stood up in their midst and said, "I have preached that salvation is found alone in Jesus Christ, and on account of this assertion I have been designated, throughout all Switzerland, a heretic, a seducer, and a rebel." . . . . "Now, therefore, in the name of God, I make my appearance here." . . . . . "If there is any one present who has any thing to say, let him come forward." . . . . . . "I implore all those who have accused me, and I know that in this hall there are many such, to come forward and answer me, for the love of the truth." In the presence of this valiant soldier of the cross the enemies of the gospel were frighted into profound silence, no one daring to accept the challenge. In view of this, says D'Aubigne, "the counsel declared that Master Ulrich Zwingle, not having been answered by any one person, would continue to preach the holy gospel, and that all the other priests of the canton should only be allowed to teach those things which they are able to establish by reference to the Holy Scriptures." On hearing this Zwingle exclaimed, "Praise be to God, who desires his holy word to rule and reign both in heaven and upon earth." Writhing under these killing blows of the courageous reformer, an advocate of popery, one Faber, was at length moved to say, "The theses of Master Ulrich are contrary to the honor of the church and the doctrine of Christ, and I will prove it." "Do so," replied Zwingle. But Faber, conscious of his inability to do so, refused to offer his proof, save in Paris, Cologne, or Friburg. To this Zwingle replied, "I desire no other judge but the gospel." "The gospel," said Faber, "always the gospel. It would be possible to live in a holy manner, in peace and charity, even although there were no gospel." In these brief utterances of Zwingle on the one side, and those of Faber on the other, you have the sum of all religious truth, and the sum of all religious error. "Salvation is found alone in Jesus Christ." "The gospel, the gospel, nothing but the gospel." "I desire no other judge but the gospel." This is Zwingle's position. "It would be possible to live in a holy manner, in peace and charity, even if there were no gospel." This is Faber's position. We could be *holy, peaceful,* and *loving,* without the gospel, and, consequently, without Jesus Christ. This is Rŏmanism, this is Deism, this is infidelity: aye, and this same thing, this sum of all religious error, is still very prevalent, and very popular: only it is now called *natural theology, natural religion, natural and moral philosophy; innate ideas, intuitive knowledge, necessary intuitions,* by which we have, or may have, *a knowledge of God, of morals, of duty and accountability, and of a future retribution.* And to convince us of the truth of all this, we are told wonderful things about conscience; and amongst other things, that it is *an infallible guide,* more *reliable than the dictum of any prophet or seer.* Nor is there any remedy for these errors but that which was employed by those great reformers, those men of faith and courage whom we have noticed. True to these great principles this same Ulrich Zwingle aimed at nothing less than sweeping out of the church every human invention, all but Jesus and his gospel. Hence, assisted by faithful colleagues, such as Oswald Myconius, and Leo Judas, he, in 1525, restored to the church the Lord's Supper, and caused it to be administered with primitive simplicity. The supper was thus administered in Zurich, for the first time, on Holy Thursday, Passion Friday, and Easter Sunday. "The people knelt down on their knees," says D'Aubigne, "the bread was served round in large covers or dishes of wood, and every one broke off a morsel of it; afterwards the wine followed in wooden goblets." What a glorious scene was witnessed in Zurich on these three days. The people crowded to their places at the feast, and blessed the founder's name. As in Samaria of old, when Philip preached the gospel there, so in Zurich, "there was great joy in that city." Nor did the good effects end with the holy exercises of these days. "Peace now dwells in our city," said Zwingle, soon after, "among us there are no longer witnessed scenes of dissimulation, dissension, envy, or quarrelling. Whence can have proceeded an agreement so general, if it be not from the Lord, and in consequence of the fact that the doctrine which we proclaim assures to us a state of innocence and peace."

But this glorious reformation was not brought about without faith and courage on the part of these noble reformers. Indeed, the Swiss reformers, under the noble leadership of Zwingle, went even farther than did Luther. They not only swept away *transubstantiation*, but also *consubstantiation*, together with numerous traditions and ceremonies of human invention, by which the word of God was made of none effect. And in this they were followed by John Calvin, and also by the Scotch reformers, Knox and Walsh. Hence it is, that the Presbyterian Church is freer from human inventions than the Church of England is, or ever has been. And for this they are indebted, under God, to the courage and fidelity of the Swiss reformers, and specially to their noble leader Zwingle. Had it not been for his intelligent courage and fidelity, the Presbyterian Church might have been as zealous in the advocacy of *ritualism* and other human inventions to-day, as is the Church of England. O how much good may be done by the faith, courage, and fidelity of a single man!

In conclusion, then, let it be remembered that this *Christian* courage can only exist in connection with Christian faith, the faith that justifies the penitent sinner, for it is to this faith that this courage is *added*. Without this faith there cannot be this courage, and without this courage there can be no *progression*, and where there is no progression, there must be *retrogression*, there being no medium. In support of this position, I again appeal to the facts of history and experience, and to the plain word of God. You cannot point to a single instance of *reformation* and *progression* that was not in connection *with* the faith, aye, and in proportion *to*, the faith and courage of the reformers. O for more such reformers! Let no one suppose that they are no longer needed—such a supposition is a grand mistake—they are always needed. And to-day the Luthers, the Zwingles, the Latimers, the Ridleys, the Knoxes, the Walshes, the Whitefields, and the Wesleys, are needed, probably as much as they were in the sixteenth and eighteenth centuries. But alas! the pusillanimous souls of the present day are in the habit of apologizing for their time-serving cowardice by assuming that they are more re-

19*

fined than the rough reformers of those days. As illustrative of this I give the following. Conversing with a certain gentleman in the city of ———, on this very subject, only a few days ago, he told me the following incident. Conversing with a well-known friend, that friend said to him, "I wish you had heard our minister last Sunday evening; the sermon was so fine, there was not a coarse word in it, he was too refined for that, he never used the word hell or devil once."—Talk about such men reforming the church and the world! No such thing; they are destitute of the reforming power; they have neither faith nor courage; and God cannot exert his power through them; there is a moral obstruction in the way of his doing so; their thoughts are not God's thoughts, neither are their ways God's ways. They even claim to be more refined than the Holy Spirit, so much so, that they would not use the language that He uses; no, they would not offend the refined taste of their *elite* audience; hence, they "never use the word hell or devil once." About the time that God raised up Whitefield and the Wesleys, a certain minister, of great refinement of course, venturing, on one occasion, to warn outbreaking sinners, said, "If you do not reform, you will go to a place that I will not name before this respectable audience." And this was going much farther than many popular ministers would dare to go.—Gentlemen, allow a plain man to ask you a few plain questions. Do you believe that sinners, open, daring sinners, are in danger of going to hell? Do you believe that they are in the direct road to hell? that except they repent they shall perish? that he that believeth not shall be damned? that except they are born again they cannot see the kingdom of God? If so, why not lift up your warning voice and announce to them the startling fact: will they in the day of judgment thank you for allowing them to run the whole way to hell unwarned, rather than offend them by announcing God's truth, and faithfully warning them to flee "from the wrath to come?" What will it profit you, though you should gain the whole world, if you save neither yourself nor those who hear you, if both you and they drop into hell together? O be honest, and, to this end, if you do not believe the Bible, say so, but if you do, then declare the whole counsel of God, alike regardless of the deceptive smiles, and the threatening frowns, of man whose breath is in his nostrils. And if you have neither faith nor courage, cry mightily to God, and never rest till you have both. Nor must you stop here, but proceed at once to make the next addition, in its appropriate place, for unless you do so you can progress no further.

CHAPTER VII.

Add *knowledge*—This is essential to the development of the preceding graces—How these graces mutually increase each other—Luther, Zwingle, and others, are produced as examples—Consequences of not adding knowledge are specified, specially in the case of Ministers.

BUT if you would continue to progress, add to both the preceding, *knowledge*. Unless you increase in knowledge, how can either your faith or your courage increase? And even if they could increase without an increase of knowledge, how could you intelligently direct their operations? Under such circumstances your faith, no doubt, would degenerate into fanaticism, and your courage into rashness and foolhardiness, especially if your teachers were as ignorant as yourself. And it is precisely in this way, if I mistake not, that thousands have become raving fanatics, noisy dreamers; whereas, had they increased in knowledge, they would have increased in *faith, courage*, and *usefulness*. Wisdom, being the right use of knowledge, my wisdom cannot exceed my knowledge; neither can my faith, for I cannot believe what I do not know. An uncertain knowledge, if there be such a thing, can only result in conjecture, at the best; it cannot result in faith, properly so called. In like manner, courage, being the legitimate offspring of faith, and also faith's armor-bearer, it must, of course, be subject to the same limitation. Or, as I said before, if it could increase without an increase of knowledge, how could it operate without a corresponding increase of knowledge to direct its operations? If it operate at all, it must, as I said before, result in blunder and disaster. The fact is, courage, like love, must have an object. As I cannot love what does not exist, neither can my courage lead me to the conquest of an enemy that does not exist, or of whose existence I am entirely ignorant: it cannot carry me over a mountain or river that does not exist, or of which I am as yet entirely ignorant. If I pass over such a mountain or river, while ignorant thereof, it must be by chance, or by some other power, not by courage. I may have power to love that which does not exist, or of which I am ignorant, but as yet I do not actually love it. In like manner, I may have power courageously to attack and conquer an enemy that does not yet exist, or of which I am ignorant; but the courage cannot actually exist till the enemy exists and is known *as such*. I say *as such*, for I cannot courageously attack as an enemy, though he is such, one whom, in my ignorance, I still recognize to be a friend. From these considerations, and from many others that might be adduced, it is, we think, quite evident, that my faith, love, and courage, cannot exist or increase beyond the limit of my knowledge, though they may come far short of it, which is always criminal.

Courage and knowledge mutually support and

increase each other. For instance: if I put forth noble deeds of courage, I am thus made to know, as I otherwise could not have known, what courage can do—what I can do—thus my knowledge is increased. And this knowledge leads to other noble deeds, that I have supposed to be impossible. Hence, as long as I make a good use of the increase of either one, the increase of that one will lead to the increase of the other; and thus the mutual increase continues. It is thus that some men can do what others conceive to be impossible. And when a mishap occurs, it is because knowledge and courage are not reciprocal in *proportion* and *operation*. It is equally clear, that knowledge without courage is useless, and even pernicious. For instance: when Luther obtained a knowledge of the doctrine of justification by faith, what would that knowledge have accomplished if he had not had courage to embrace it for himself, and proclaim it to others, defiant of the Roman Pontiff, Charles the Fifth, and all their combined forces? To this question there is but one answer. It would simply have increased his guilt. But Luther added courage to his faith, and thus conquered the Pope, the Emperor, the world, and the devil, and saved himself and multitudes of others; yea, though dead, he yet speaketh. The very same did Zwingle; and every advance step that these noble men took in their illustrious career, demanded the mutual action of their *faith, courage,* and *knowledge*. For instance: when the contest was raging with regard to the Sacrament of the Supper—Rome contending for the dogma of Transubstantiation, attempting to support it by the words, "This is my body"—Zwingle examined the divine teaching on this subject in the Hebrew and Greek. The result was, a very important increase of knowledge; and to this knowledge he added courage. Hence, in the midst of the grand council in Zurich, he announced the startling discovery, viz., that there is no word in the Greek language but εστι (is) to represent the idea *signify*, and that, consequently, it is used in the Greek language to convey this idea. In support of this position, he referred to Exod. xii. 11, where the *seventy* use it for this purpose in translating the words, "Ye shall eat it in haste; it is the LORD's passover." Thus guided by the Hebrew and Greek texts, by the obvious sense in which the *seventy* used the word *esti;* by the common consent of all as to the meaning of the text in Exodus; not that the lamb was the LORD's passover, but that it *signified* his passing over the Israelites when he smote the Egyptians. And finally, guided by our Lord's comment upon his own words, he triumphantly proved to the grand council that the words, "This is my body," "This is my blood," mean, this *signifies* my body, this *signifies* my blood, as the lamb *signified* his passage over the Israelites when he slew the Egyptians. Zwingle, having thus added knowledge, he added corresponding courage, and demanded that the *mass* and *transubstantiation* should be swept out of the church, together with *consubstantiation*, and that the sacrament of the supper should take the place of these human inventions, and be administered according to the original institution. "And it was so." For, as D'Aubigne states, "The altars were taken away, and simple tables, covered with the bread and wine of the eucharist, were substituted in their place, while an attentive crowd eagerly sought to find a place at these tables. A very solemn aspect was presented by the action of this multitude." In this way was the Lord's Supper restored to his church in Switzerland. And this holy feast, the first after many long ages of darkness and sacrilegious fraud, lasted three days in Zurich, "and there was great joy in that city." The feast was truly a *eucharistic* feast.

But what we more especially desire to be noticed, is the important fact that this victory on behalf of God's church and cause, was not achieved without *courage*. When the change was proposed, strong men trembled, and apprehended the most awful consequences. Thus to sweep away, at a stroke, the holy mass, the transubstantiated body, blood, soul, and divinity of Jesus Christ, together with the long-established faith and customs of the church, which, to the eyes of hoary-headed sages, appeared gray and venerable with age, was an act that was thought to be as daring as it would be disastrous. But Zwingle and his noble colleagues were undaunted, and fearlessly did that very thing which so much frighted their neighbors, and woke the thunders of the Vatican, causing them to roll down from the seven hills with sevenfold fury; and these thunders were to exhaust all their fury upon Zwingle and the men who united with him in this work of reformation. But, defiant of all that men could say or do, Zwingle said it shall be so; "and it was so." Now, how did those men perform those noble acts, which resulted in this glorious reformation? I answer, *by adding to their faith courage, and to their courage knowledge.* Their *faith*, their *courage*, and their *knowledge*, wrought together, mutually supporting and increasing each other. Zwingle was at Zurich, and Erasmus was at Bazil. Zwingle did much, Erasmus did little—perhaps I might say, *nothing*—in the work of the great reformation. In this work, Zwingle was a power, Erasmus perfect weakness. Why? Did Zwingle understand the Hebrew and the Greek languages better than Erasmus? No. Did not Erasmus know, as well as Zwingle, the meaning of the word εστι, in the passages referred to? Doubtless. Did he not know, as well as Zwingle, that transubstantiation was a human invention, involving contradiction and absolute impossibility? He did. Why, then, did he not say and do as did Zwingle? Why did he not unite with the Swiss and German reformers in their noble efforts to beat back the powers of darkness, and deliver the people from tyranny here, and destruction hereafter? Why did he not on this occasion come up "to the help of the LORD against the mighty?" I answer, simply because he did not add courage. He courted the smiles, and feared the frowns of Rome, while Zwingle and the other reformers did neither. Moreover, while Erasmus added the knowledge of letters, he did not add the knowledge of God and the things of God. His faith, his knowledge, and his courage, did not act in harmony—they did not mutually support and increase each other. Hence, there was no *Christian progression*, either *in him*, or *produced by him*. This progression is only found where men add to their faith courage, and to courage knowledge. In short, it is simply impossible to progress save in that way that God has marked out by his servant Peter. And, remember, to enter upon this way you must be justified by faith; before this, no child of Adam can enter upon it. And when you are in this way, you must progress or leave it; and to progress, you must "add to your faith courage, and to courage knowledge"—"grow in grace, and in the knowledge of our Lord and Saviour Jesus Christ"—"desiring the sincere milk of the word, that ye may grow thereby." "For the soul to be without knowledge is not good;" but "this is life eternal, to know thee, the only true God, and Jesus Christ whom thou hast sent." For want of observing these important teachings of the Holy Spirit, there are ministers who could have preached better, more intelligently, more efficiently, twenty years ago, than they can to-day; though they still retain sufficient bodily strength. O, what have such added to their faith during those long and precious years of opportunity! Surely, these things ought not so to be. But this is but a small part of the evil of not progressing.

CHAPTER VIII.

Add *temperance*. Erroneous views exposed, and the meaning of the word εγκρατεια given—Christian temperance is dwelt upon at great length, and its nature and extent specified—Mr. Wesley's definition and views of temperance—Scripture teachings on this subject—Erroneous views farther exposed—Defects of modern temperance lectures, and temperance movements—It was by not adding temperance that Solomon and multitudes of others were ruined—It was by not adding temperance that the primitive churches were ruined, and the dark ages brought on—The activity essential to the Christian character will lead to ruin if temperance does not keep pace with it.

AND having progressed thus far, if you would continue to progress, you must make the next addition just here, by adding to your knowledge *temperance*. But what is temperance? In these days of temperance movements, temperance lectures, temperance papers, temperance societies, temperance festivals, temperance lodges, temperance flags, temperance passwords, temperance grips, temperance signs, temperance songs, temperance leagues, and temperance laws; some may think that the question is a very tame one, and that the subject is already well understood. But, alas! we fear this is far from being the case. Indeed, in popular phrase it has come to mean no more than total abstinence from intoxicating drinks. We do not believe, however, that it ever has this meaning, and we know it has not this meaning in the text before us; though we are perfectly willing, nay, more, very desirous that men should thus abstain from such drinks. But God never commands us to be temperate in what is positively wrong; with regard to such things total abstinence is always the law. But *temperance* is enjoined with regard to such things as may be used, but are liable to be abused. At best, the temperance contended for by temperance lectures, and temperance societies, makes but a small part of Christian temperance, which is the temperance enjoined by the Apostles in the passage under consideration. A man who never saw strong drink may be as intemperate as Cain, or as Judas was; and if he should die in his sins, may become as intemperate as the devil himself, who is the embodiment of all intemperance, though it will not be claimed, we presume, that he ever drank any spirituous liquors. It follows, that one may resemble the devil in badness, and yet, never be guilty of the intemperance against which temperance lectures declaim. It follows too, that temperance societies, so called, are a poor substitute for the church of God, and temperance lectures a poor substitute for the gospel ministry: yet it is not an uncommon thing for men who have been solemnly consecrated to this ministry, to leave it and turn temperance lecturers. But this, alas! is only one of the many improvements of this age of improvements; only one of the new discoveries for which this our day is so remarkable. Let it be remembered then, that one may be a thorough temperance man, according to modern phrase, and yet be as bad as Cain, or Judas; and even resemble the devil himself in badness. This being the case we cannot believe that the subject of temperance is sufficiently understood, even yet.

But the question still recurs, what is temperance? We mean what is that temperance which the Apostle exhorts the Christian to add to the faith, courage, and knowledge which he already has? Certainly it cannot be the mere abstinence from intoxicating drinks; to suppose that this is the temperance here enjoined, is to suppose that a man may have the high Christian character here developed by the Apostle, before he is thus temperate; which is to suppose what is contradictory and impossible. To suppose that the Apostle exhorts such a Christian to add this kind of temperance to his faith, courage, and advanced Christian knowledge, is absurd; for a man cannot have any of these Christian graces, or be a Christian at all, before he is thus temperate. It were too late, then, for the Apostle to come to such holy persons with such an exhortation. Hence, the question still recurs, What is the temperance which the Apostle exhorts the Christian to add to the bright constellation of graces already possessed? To answer this question, it will be necessary to ascertain the meaning of the word ἐγκρατεία, for this is the word here used by the Apostle. This word, says Parkhurst, is "from ἐγκρατης," and means self-government or moderation with regard to sensual-pleasures, temperance, continence." In proof of this he quotes several texts, and amongst the rest that now under consideration. It means, says Greenfield, "moderation, continence, self-control, temperance;" not moderation with regard to what is absolutely forbidden, but with regard to what is allowable to a moderate extent. *Self-government.* This is a word of more extensive signification; it means such a control of all inward and outward action as preserves from extremes on every hand; such a control as subjects the whole man to the will of God, causing all his powers to act in harmony with God's will as revealed in his word, and is opposed to undue fasting as well as to undue eating. Those who kill themselves by fasting, and those who kill themselves by eating or drinking, are alike guilty of self-murder and are alike intemperate. There are many killed by intemperate drinking, but I am inclined to think that a still greater number are killed by intemperate eating, while others are killed by *smoking;* some are killed by doing nothing, while others are killed by over exertion: but all are intemperate; and the remedy for all these evils, and a thousand others, is that here prescribed by the Apostle; *add temperance* to the other good qualities which you may possess. Working, resting, sleeping, waking, eating, drinking, loving, hating, hoping, fearing, saving, spending, giving, receiving, resisting, yielding; all, all are good, when in harmony with the divine will; and this is the case when temperance has her perfect work, and then only. "Now the

Spirit speaketh expressly, that in the latter times some shall depart from the faith, giving heed to seducing spirits, and doctrines of devils; speaking lies in hypocrisy, having their conscience seared with a hot iron; forbidding to marry, *and commanding* to abstain from meats, which God hath created to be received with thanksgiving of them which believe and know the truth. For every creature of God is good, and nothing to be refused, if it be received with thanksgiving: for it is sanctified by the word of God, and prayer. If thou put the brethren in remembrance of these things, thou shalt be a good minister of Jesus Christ, nourished up in the words of faith and of good doctrine, whereunto thou hast attained. But refuse profane and old wives' fables, and exercise thyself unto godliness." I have quoted the above passage, because I believe it develops in a very striking manner the meaning of the word under consideration. Whoever will critically examine the word, or carefully notice its meaning as given by lexicographers, will see, I have no doubt, that this one word sanctions and forbids, all that is sanctioned and forbidden in the above passage, and much more. The Pope claims to be very temperate, forsooth, because he forbids what God has commanded, and commands what God has forbidden; but by so doing he practices and promotes *intemperance*, not *temperance*. But instead of giving such teachers credit for temperance, the Spirit charges all such with "departing from the faith, giving heed to seducing spirits, and doctrines of devils," and "profane and old wives' fables." Mr. Wesley's definition of temperance is in his characteristic style, *laconic*, and yet comprehensive and forcible.—" The voluntarily abstaining from all pleasure that does not lead to God." Among all our temperance lecturers can you find one who ever *thought* of such a definition of temperance as that here given? Nor will you find in all the rules of our temperance societies any thing superior to the following from the same great teacher—"Buying or selling spirituous liquors, or drinking them, unless in cases of extreme necessity." His preaching, too, was in keeping with this:—Take the following from his sermon entitled "The use of money," and discussed under the following three heads, *viz.:* "Gain all you can." "Save all you can." "Give all you can." Under the first head he shows that we may not gain at the expense or injury of others. After dealing some heavy blows upon doctors, merchants, gold-dealers and others, he puts his whole strength to it and strikes after this fashion;—"Neither may we gain by hurting our neighbor in his body. Therefore we may not sell any thing which tends to impair health. Such is, eminently, all that liquid fire, commonly called drams, or spirituous liquors. It is true these may have a place in medicine, they may be of use in some bodily disorders; although there would rarely be occasion for them, were it not for the unskilfulness of the practitioner. Therefore such as prepare and sell them only for this end, may keep their conscience clear. But who are they? Who prepare them only for this end? Do you know ten such distillers in England? Then excuse these. But all who sell them in the common way, to any that will buy, are poisoners general. They murder his majesty's subjects by wholesale, neither does their eye pity or spare. They drive them to hell like sheep: and what is their gain? Is it not the blood of these men? Who then would envy their large estates and sumptuous palaces? A curse is in the midst of them: the curse of God cleaves to the stones, the timber, the furniture of them! The curse of God is in their gardens, their walks, their groves; a fire that burns to the nethermost hell. Blood, blood is there: the foundation, the floor, the walls, the roof, are stained with blood. And canst thou hope, oh thou man of blood, though thou art clothed in scarlet and fine linen, and farest sumptuously every day; canst thou hope to deliver down thy *fields of blood* to the third generation? Not so; for there is a God in heaven: therefore, thy name shall soon be rooted out. Like as those whom thou hast destroyed, body and soul, 'thy memorial shall perish with thee!'" In a word, "Gain all you can," but injure no man in body or soul, hold sacred all his interests, for time, and for eternity.

The next proposition in this good old temperance sermon is, "save all you can." Don't waste any thing to gratify the *flesh*, the *eye*, or the *pride of life;* for this would be to spend this "precious talent," your money, to increase your unholy passions. "And why should you throw away money upon your children, any more than upon yourself." Neither "leave it to them to throw away." ...... "How amazing then is the infatuation of those parents who think they can never leave their children enough! What! cannot you leave them enough of arrows, firebrands, and death? Not enough of foolish and hurtful desires? Not enough of pride, lust, ambition, vanity? Not enough of everlasting burnings! Poor wretch! Thou fearest where no fear is. Surely both thou and they, when ye are lifting up your eyes in hell, will have enough of 'the worm that never dieth,' and of 'the fire that never shall be quenched!'" "Save all you can," but not in any of these ways, this is not to save but to destroy; this is the veriest *intemperance*, not *temperance*. Neither "can a man be properly said to save any thing, if he only lays it up. You may as well throw your money into the sea, or bury it in the earth. And you may as well bury it in the earth, as in your chest, or in the bank of England. Not to use, is effectually to throw it away." As yet here is no *temperance*, but *intemperance*. If you stop here you are no better than a thief or a robber; you rob both God and man of their due. What then? Why, there is but one remedy; here it is, "Give all you can;" not to build monuments to gratify thy vanity, but to feed and clothe the poor, and promote the cause of God in the earth. Do this, or thy *gaining* and *saving* are the veriest intemperance: give, give, "or as the Lord liveth and as thy soul liveth," thou art undone: to gain and save, and yet not give, is to turn these blessings into the most terrible curses. "Waste nothing," says the holy man. "Waste nothing, living or dying, on sin or folly, whether for yourself or your children; and then, give all you can, or, in other words, give all you have to God. Do not stint yourself, like a Jew rather than a Christian, to this or that proportion; render unto God, not a tenth, not a third, not half, but all that is God's, be it more or less." "No more sloth!" he exclaims again; "whatsoever your hand findeth to do, do it with your might! No more waste! Cut off every expense which fashion, caprice, or flesh and blood demand. No more covetousness, but employ whatever God has entrusted you with in doing good, all possible good, in every possible kind and degree, to the household of faith, to all men!"

Thus it was that John Wesley preached temperance, in all its compass; not that narrow thing now called temperance—the mere abstinence from intoxicating drinks. Nor did he preach in vain. No. Multitudes, sunk and sinking in all kinds of intemperance, became thoroughly temperate, in every sense of the word. His societies, or churches, were the grand temperance societies of those days. He did not give his people into the hands of infidels, that *they* might form them into societies and teach them temperance. Not so; he proclaimed salvation —all salvation—*by grace through faith : salvation to the uttermost.* And all who accepted salvation on these terms, the only terms upon which salvation can be had, he gathered together into the sacred fold, according to divine appointment; and being satisfied with a place in this sacred enclosure, among God's people, they sweetly sang,—

> " Let us then sweet counsel take
> How to make our calling sure ;
> Our election how to make,
> Past the reach of hell, secure,
> Build we each the other up ;
> Pray we for our faith's increase ;
> Solid comfort, settled hope,
> Constant joy, and lasting peace."

And again,—

> " O, do not suffer him to part
> The souls that here agree ;
> But make us of one mind and heart,
> And keep us one in thee.
>
> " Together let us sweetly live,—
> Together let us die ;
> And each a starry crown receive,
> And reign above the sky."

And yet again :—

> " Let worldly minds the world pursue,
> It has no charms for me :
> Once I admired its trifles too,
> But grace hath set me free.
>
> " Its pleasures can no longer please,
> Nor happiness afford :
> Far from my heart be joys like these,
> Now I have found the Lord."

This is gospel salvation. The heart is weaned from all forbidden things, and made to delight in God and the things of God. Then, and not till then, will a man "Gain all he can;" "Save all he can;" and "GIVE ALL HE CAN!" This is temperance in earnest. And, observe, a greater authority than John Wesley speaks words still more pointed and terrible, aiming them directly at all those who *gain* and *save*, but do not *give*. "Go to now, ye rich men, weep and howl for your miseries that shall come upon you. Your riches are corrupted, and your garments are moth-eaten, your gold and silver are cankered; and the rust of them shall be a witness against you, and shall eat your flesh as it were fire. Ye have heaped treasure together for the last days."

It is easy to see that these men meant something when they preached. John Wesley struck heavy blows, but James struck heavier still. John said strong things about laying up treasure upon earth, but James, I think, has said still stronger things to the same characters. And, it may be well to say in passing, that John Wesley practiced what he preached It is said that he gave away in the course of his life not less than *one hundred and fifty thousand pounds sterling!* And when he died he had just about enough left to pay his funeral expenses. This is what he had long before promised the world he would do, and gave them leave to call him a thief and a robber if he would do otherwise. Truly here is temperance in preaching and practice. O what a difference, both in practice and theory, between this great temperance preacher, and the bulk of temperance lecturers who in the present day try to make a fortune by lecturing on temperance, and then do little more than make the people laugh. John Wesley did more to promote genuine temperance in all its branches, than such men ever did, or ever will do, even though they were as numerous as the armies of Artaxerxes, or even as the frogs of Egypt. Yet such lecturers would have us believe that the pulpit had proved a signal failure, and that the world, especially Christendom, was just at the point of ruin when they appeared on the stage; and all would certainly have been lost long since, had they not come to the rescue. I myself heard a lecturer say this much, and more than this, for he specified the Bible as well as the pulpit. I make these remarks because I would have it understood that it is by *declaring the whole counsel of God* that the world is to be saved, not by telling humorous stories, one half of which, perhaps, are not true. And, be it understood, Gospel Salvation includes temperance in all its latitude and longitude! Go, then, and preach as did Paul, Peter, James, Luther, Zwingle, Whitefield, Wesley, and other holy men who preached the preaching that God commanded them to preach: and pay no attention to those who would have you turn your churches into places of amusement, and your ministers into humorous lecturers and story-tellers.

I have dwelt upon Wesley's temperance preaching not only to show, if possible, the extensive meaning of this important word, but because he anticipated the very same evil that is anticipated in the Scripture under investigation, and, consequently, gave temperance the very same place among the

Christian graces, that is given to it by the Apostle Peter. With his characteristic discrimination, he saw that a genuine Gospel ministry would cause the people to become *intelligent, active, prudent,* and *economical:* and that the natural result of this, together with God's blessing upon such a life, would be, that they would become rich. He saw with equal clearness that unless their temperance would keep pace with their prosperity, this very prosperity would prove their ruin. Hence he frequently touched upon this subject in his sermons, and finally took it up in good earnest, frequently preaching from the text, "Lay not up for yourselves treasures upon earth," etc., etc. Introducing in connection with this text these words of our Lord, "If any man be willing to do my will, he shall know of the doctrine whether it be of God," he gives the following incident to show why men do not know, or pretend not to know, so plain a text: "Two as sensible men as most in England, sat down together, some time since, to read over and consider that plain discourse on 'Lay not up for yourselves treasures upon earth.' After much deep consideration, one of them broke out, 'Positively, I cannot understand it. Pray do *you* understand it, Mr. L.?' Mr. L. honestly replied, 'Indeed, not I. I cannot conceive what Mr. W. means. I can make nothing at all of it?'" Such was the decision of "Two as sensible men as most in England," "after much deep consideration," on Mr. Wesley's "plain discourse" upon "Lay not up for yourselves treasures upon earth." The reason Mr. Wesley assigns for the obtuseness of these two very sensible men, with regard to his plain temperance sermon, is found, he says, in that text, "If any man be willing to do my will, he shall know of the doctrine whether it be of God." In this sermon which these gentlemen found so hard to be understood, Mr. Wesley talks after this manner:—"How does experience confirm this? Even after God hath opened the eyes of the understanding, if we seek or desire any thing else than God, how soon is our foolish heart darkened? Then clouds again rest upon our souls. Doubts and fears again overwhelm us. We are tossed to and fro, and know not what to do, or which is the path wherein we should go. But when we desire and seek nothing but God, clouds and doubts vanish away." .... "God showeth us the path wherein we should go, and maketh plain the way before our face." This not laying up treasure upon earth, this desiring and seeking God alone, this *single eye*, is temperance in earnest, Scripture temperance, the temperance which John Wesley preached, and which these sensible gentlemen could not understand, no not "after much deep consideration." After dwelling at some length upon this subject, Mr. W. adds, "And it is also matter of daily experience, that by grace we are [thus] saved through faith." Thus he not only shows what true temperance is, but also, how it is obtained. Nor will it ever be either understood, or experienced till it is sought in the way here stated, "By grace through faith." Mr. W. also shows, that between a *single*, and an *evil* eye, there is no medium. And in this particular also, he teaches just what Christ teaches,—"But if thine eye be evil thy whole body shall be full of darkness." Hence Mr. Wesley's, as well as our Lord's sermon, is all mystery to certain gentlemen, they can "make nothing at all of it!" Particularly when he says, "With regard to most of the commandments of God, whether relating to the heart or life, the heathen of Africa or America stand much on a level with those who are called Christians. The Christians observe them (a few only being excepted) very near as much as the heathens. For instance: the generality of the natives of England, commonly called Christians, are as sober and as temperate as the generality of the heathen near the Cape of Good Hope. And so the Dutch or French Christians are as humble and as chaste as the Choctaw or Cherokee Indians. It is not easy to say, when we compare the bulk of the nations in Europe with those in America, whether the superiority lies on the one side or the other." After saying a great deal more of this kind, and all addressed to those who seek and lay up treasures upon earth, he exclaims, "Hear ye this, all ye that dwell in the world, and love the world wherein ye dwell! Ye may be highly esteemed of men; but ye are an abomination in the sight of God! How long shall your souls cleave to the dust? How long will you load yourselves with thick clay? When will ye awake and see, that the open, speculative heathen are nearer the kingdom of heaven than you? When will you be persuaded to choose the better part, that which cannot be taken away from you? When will ye seek only to lay up treasures in heaven; renouncing, dreading, abhorring all others? If you aim at 'laying up treasures on earth,' you are not barely losing your time, and spending your strength for that which is not bread; for what is the fruit if you succeed?— You have murdered your own soul! You have extinguished the last spark of spiritual life therein. Now, indeed, in the midst of life, you are in death! You are a living man, but a dead Christian."..... "Your love, your joy, your desire, are all placed on the things which perish in the using. You have thrown away the treasures in heaven. God and Christ are lost! You have gained riches,—and hell fire!"

Alas! how many are there now, who understand this kind of preaching just as little as did the two gentlemen who said, "Positively, I cannot understand it." "I cannot conceive what Mr. Wesley means, I can make nothing at all of it!" Well, whether you understand Wesley, or not, do you understand Jesus, when he commands you not to "Lay up treasure upon earth;" when he exhorts that your *eye be single, not evil*, and assures you the former is a state of *light*, the latter a state of *great darkness*? If we do not understand this, it is with a poor grace that we talk either about *Christian temperance*, or *Christian progression*.

In his sermon entitled *the wisdom of God's counsels*, he takes occasion to lift up his warning voice thus, upon this same subject:—"Once more, therefore, I say, having gained and saved all you can, do you give all you can? else your money will eat your flesh as fire, and will sink you to the nethermost hell! O beware of 'laying up treasures upon earth!' Is it not treasuring up wrath against the day of wrath? Lord, I have warned them! but if they will not be warned, what can I do more? I can only 'give them up unto their own heart's lusts, and let them follow their own imaginations.' By not taking this warning, it is certain many of the Methodists are already fallen; many are falling at this very time; and there is great reason to apprehend, that many more will fall, most of whom will rise no more!"

In his sermon "on riches," and while dwelling on the topic, "denying ourselves," after saying much, and bending all his strength to it, he thus touchingly exclaims, "O that God would give me acceptable words! and cause them to sink deep into your hearts! Many of you have known me long, well nigh from your infancy: you have frequently helped me, when I stood in need. May I not say, you loved me? But now the time of our parting is at hand: my feet are just stumbling upon the dark mountains. I would leave one word with you, before I go hence; and you may remember it when I am no more seen. O let your heart be whole with God! Seek your happiness in him, and in him alone. Beware that you cleave not to the dust! This earth is not your place! See that you use the world as not abusing it: *use* the world, and *enjoy* God. Sit as loose to all things here below, as if you were a poor beggar. Be a good steward of the manifold gifts of God; that when you are called to give an account of your stewardship, he may say, 'Well done, good and faithful servant, enter thou into the joy of thy Lord!'"

Thus did Mr. Wesley clearly see, and faithfully show, that previous attainments, though in themselves great blessings, would be turned into the veriest curses, if temperance were not added. And this is precisely the evil that is anticipated, and guarded against in the Scripture under consideration, and which so clearly points out the path, the only path, of Christian progress. Having advanced so far, in faith, courage, and knowledge, now add *temperance*. We are not to suppose, of course, that this grace did not exist previous to this time, but having made these advances in temporal, as well as in intellectual and moral attainments, there are stronger temptations to *intemperance*, and, consequently, additional reasons for fortifying yourself in that direction. For instance, you are more liable to become proud of your *attainments*, than you were to become proud of your *destitution;* and pride is the worst kind of intemperance. You are more liable to think more highly of yourself than you ought to think, in view of your attainments in knowledge, than you were in view of your ignorance, especially if other attainments are not equal, for, in this case at least, "knowledge puffeth up." Moreover, when you were poor, in temporalities, almost as poor, though as holy, as Lazarus, it was not possible for you, in your pride and self-sufficiency, to exclaim with the Laodiceans, "I am rich, and increased with goods, and have need of nothing:" nor was it possible for you, then, to be enamored with a well-furnished mansion, and a splendid equipage; for you neither had, nor could have, any thing of the kind; and, perhaps, you neither desired nor thought of such things, but would have been well satisfied with an humble, though comfortable home. And it was equally impossible for you to be "clothed in purple and fine linen, and fare sumptuously every day." In these ways, and many others, it was not then possible for you to become intemperate; but having become rich and honorable, by the Christian attainments above specified, it is quite possible for you to become *intemperate* in all these ways, and many others; indeed you are surrounded with many and strong temptations to become intemperate; and the flatterers by whom rich and honorable men are always surrounded, are amongst their most dangerous tempters.

Hence the necessity of now adding temperance, and guarding against intemperance, to an extent that was not previously necessary. If Nebuchadnezzar had been a poor man, he never had said, "Is not this great Babylon, that I have built for the house of the kingdom, by the might of my power, and for the honor of my majesty;" and, consequently, would never have been thus intemperate—would never have had his "dwelling with the beasts of the field," where he was caused to "eat grass as oxen." For the same reason, if the primitive Christian churches had never become rich and honorable, the great apostacy had never taken place; nor would it have taken place, if they had taken the advice of that Apostle, whom, without reason, they claimed to be their patron. No; the apostacy never could have taken place, if they had added to their knowledge, temperance. But they became intemperate, and thereby turned all their blessings into curses; and ruin, universal ruin, was the result—the inevitable result. This was specially the case under Constantine. Then, position in the Christian church became very desirable. Hence it was sought by men of worldly aspirations; and soon these honor and pleasure seeking dignitaries took the places of the holy and humble primitive pastors of Christ's flock, and, like their Jewish ancestors, another apostate generation, they "beat one, and killed another, and stoned another." And having thus killed off the faithful pastors, and, as far as possible, Jesus also, they said, "Let us seize upon his inheritance." And they did so; and to this day they are living, upon that inheritance, a life of *intemperance* and *infamy;* and that which was a fruitful field, a paradise, when they seized it, has long since become a waste howling wilderness, full of ravenous beasts and venomous serpents. And so it will remain, doubtless, till the Lord of the vineyard destroys those murderers, and gives his vineyard to others who shall render him the fruits in their seasons.

Once more. Solomon, too, had a good beginning. He evidently had faith, and the concomitant graces to a very encouraging extent. And, we presume, he added courage; and it is quite certain he added knowledge, and that to an unprecedented extent. So that for a time he had an illustrious career; but, alas! he did not add *temperance adequate to his circumstances.* And just here progress terminated, and retrogression commenced, and, like his intemperance, continued till this once illustrious monarch became a degraded idolator, and sunk down into the veriest whirlpool of intemperance under a cloud of unmitigated darkness which rests on his grave to this day! Here is a man that had placed before him one of the brightest prospects, perhaps the brightest, that ever stretched out before a human being, and every thing was in his favor: he had riches, honors, knowledge, fame, to an incredible extent. Yet this same Solomon, so famous for wisdom at one time, finally died a fool! Why? Simply because he had not wisdom enough to add to his knowledge temperance. This one mistake proved his ruin! Had Solomon done what the fisherman of Galilee here advises, his progress without doubt had continued, and his career would have been one of the most illustrious ever known among men. O that I could move all Christians, especially rich Christians, to study, prayerfully study, these few verses, this single passage of holy writ, and put its sublime and heavenly teachings into practice. To this end I beg that you will yet sit with me at the feet of this great teacher, and hear with the profoundest attention the marvellous instructions which he is here imparting.

CHAPTER IX.

Add *patience*. This is shown to be absolutely necessary to Christian progress; for, the more Christian activities abound, the more is patience rendered necessary—The peculiar work of patience at different periods in the Christian life—No other grace can take its place and do its work—Sometimes one grace must take the lead, sometimes another—Judgment must lead up first one, and then another, according to circumstances; as an experienced General will lead up to the front, first one division, and then another, according to the necessities of the occasion—Meaning of the word υπομενω is given—It always springs from, and is supported by faith, as are all the Christian graces—It is distinguished from stoicism, and from the natural power of endurance as seen in the camel or the ox.

HEAR him—"And besides this, giving all diligence, add *patience*, otherwise your progress must terminate just here. For, one who is in possession of the faith, courage, knowledge, and temperance, here specified, must travel at an uncommon speed, and, consequently, must come in contact with the *unbelieving, cowardly, ignorant, intemperate* creatures, who will, doubtless, view him as being very singular, if not very offensive. And singular he is, not because he is right, but because the bulk of mankind are wrong. Indeed, it would be strange, passing strange, if he would not come in violent collision with some of the multitude, who are either moving in an opposite direction, or moving very slow, while he is moving very fast. Nor would it be strange if he should find it necessary to shove some of them out of the way, or even to tramp right over them! And then, of course, their anger and opposition would know no bounds. And here, certainly, if not before, he must add patience, without delay, or he will surely be overcome, by partaking of their spirit, and imitating their example, even by "rendering railing for railing." Just here it is that he must imitate his master, who, "when he was reviled, reviled not again;" yea, "as a sheep before her shearer is dumb, so he opened not his mouth." But to this end he must *add patience*, nothing else will do. Or, if he does not choose to be "dumb," he must do as this same Peter directs—act still more contrary to his scolding and cursing neighbors, by not only "not rendering railing for railing, but, contrariwise, blessing." And to this end, he must add love as well as patience, otherwise he will not bless lovingly, if he does patiently. But if he adds patience sufficient for such an emergency, his triumph is easy, and his progress sure; he will pass on, leaving the angry cursing creatures far behind, too far even to be heard. And this very conduct, while it preserves the soul of the unoffending party in peace, will greatly increase the rage of the other. Now it is that the rage of *Shimei* knows no bounds, hence he commences to throw stones, as well as curse, while patient David travels on, simply saying, let "*Shimei* curse David." But these very words wound Shimei more than the stones wound David. And if the Christian, when thus treated, has the spirit of song, as well as that of patience, it may be wise to sing the following, or similar lines,—

> "Lord I adore thy righteous will,
> Through every instrument of ill
> My Father's goodness see;
> Accept the complicated wrong
> Of *Shimei's hand* and *Shimei's tongue*
> As kind rebukes from thee."

Such a song as this, if sung very *patiently*, sweetly, and lovingly, may silence *Shimei* altogether. Be this as it may, "In your patience possess ye your soul," and you will continue to progress despite a host of angry, noisy, *Shimeis.* And in view of such noble conduct another Wesley may sing something like the following to your praise:

> "Let Shimei curse: the rod he bears
> For sins which mercy had forgiven;
> And in the wrongs of man reveres
> The awful righteousness of heaven."

And while patience thus triumphs, all the other graces will participate in her victory, and increase in strength. No marvel, then, that such patient conquering heroes exclaim with Paul,—"We glory in tribulation also; knowing that tribulation worketh patience; and patience, experience; and experience, hope; and hope maketh not ashamed: because the love of God is shed abroad in our hearts by the

Holy Ghost which is given unto us." The Christian graces, like the members of Christ's mystical body, have a mutual sympathy: when one suffers, all suffer; and when one triumphs, all participate in that triumph. But, although all engage in every battle, one or other of the graces takes the lead, according to the nature of the contest or character of the opposing power. When the contest is like that in which David and the three Hebrew children engaged in, courage must take the lead; but when the contest is like that in which Job engaged, then patience is called upon to act the most prominent part. As an experienced general would lead up that battalion, or division, that is most adapted to the occasion; so judgment, in this case, must act a similar part, leading up to the front that grace which is most adapted to the occasion. For instance, it would be folly to expose meekness or patience in the front of the battle that was fought with the angry king and his vile courtiers on the plain of Dura. There courage was the proper force to take the lead, hurling defiance at the enemy, and exclaiming as in tones of thunder, in the very face of the king, "Be it known unto thee, O King, that we will not bow down to thine image, nor worship it!" Never was a battle better ordered, or better fought, than that in which courage took the lead during that terrible contest on the plains of Babylon, in the vicinity of a furnace which flamed and roared with infernal fury. This was not the place for weeping damsels, like meekness and patience to lead the van. No, no, this was the place for courage to shout to the battle, in tones that rose higher and louder than the threatenings of the king, and the roaring of the furnace, when commingling with "all kinds of music." But under such calamities as fell upon Job, it was equally proper that meekness and patience, clothed in sackcloth and bathed in tears, should lie in the dust, crying with tremulous voice in weeping and subdued tones, "The Lord gave, and the Lord hath taken away, and blessed be the name of the Lord." Here in the land of Uz, meekness and patience acted as noble a part, as did faith and courage on the plain of Dura. But, whatever grace takes the lead, faith is the base, so to speak, from which all the supplies are drawn, and drawn as needed. At other times faith itself may be said to take the lead, as in the taking of Jericho; then, of course, all the walls fell down *flat*, and every gun was taken, with the city itself, and the victory was complete; so much so, that Jericho never rose again!

At other times the progress is continued principally under the leadership of *patience;* then it is not uncommon to hear the pilgrims sing this song, especially when "passing through the valley of Baca,"—

> "Patient the appointed race to run,
>   This weary world we cast behind;
> From strength to strength we travel on,
>   The New Jerusalem to find:
> Our labor this, our only aim,
> To find the New Jerusalem."

Or this—

"Come, let us anew our journey pursue,
  Roll round with the year,
  And never stand still till the Master appear.
His adorable will let us gladly fulfil,
  And our talents improve,
  By the patience of hope, and the labor of love."

Under such circumstances patience makes a good leader, but let her be well supported by all the other graces—" My brethren, count it all joy when ye fall into divers temptations; knowing *this*, that the trying of your faith worketh patience. But let patience have her perfect work, that ye may be perfect and entire, wanting nothing." "Let patience have her perfect work," let faith, hope, love, temperance, courage, even all the graces, render her proper assistance, but let none of them attempt to take her place. Courage is a good leader, none so good, when angry kings, murderous office-seekers, lion's dens, and fiery furnaces, are to be met; when it comes to a hand to hand fight with all the armies of the aliens on the plains of Babylon, or in the valley of Armageddon. But in the valley of Baca, the Island of Patmos, the cells of the Inquisition, the sick bed, or a place with Lazarus at the rich man's gate, or with Job on the dung-hill; patience makes an excellent leader, yea, and an excellent nurse too. In such circumstances she exhibits inimitable charms, is the veriest *Dorcas*, and even *makes all the bed of the afflicted.* If she does not *stop the mouths of lions,* and *quench the violence of* fire, and *turn to flight the armies of the aliens,* she utterly annihilates enemies not less dangerous; such as, *murmuring, complaining, fretfulness, ingratitude,* and even *rebellion,* and the worst of all enemies, *despair itself!* Therefore, "Let patience have her perfect work, that ye may be perfect and entire, lacking nothing!" Truly very excellent things are spoken of this same patience. Indeed it is difficult to speak too highly of her. It would even seem that every other grace receives its complete finish, its highest polish, under her hand, for it is only when she has "her perfect work," that we are "perfect and entire, lacking nothing." We are to "bring forth fruit with patience;" "patience worketh experience;" under her soft hand we "quietly wait" for all that is the object of hope. Indeed, it is "through patience and comfort of the Scriptures that we have hope." Even Apostles "approved themselves as ministers of God in much patience." "Truly the signs of an Apostle were wrought among you in all patience." It seems, then, that an Apostle could not be known as such without the finish of her wonderful hand; without it both he and his signs would be rejected as spurious. Strength too, it would seem, must be perfected by patience, for we are "strengthened with all might, according to his glorious power, unto all patience and long-suffering with joyfulness." Strength is not only no substitute for patience, but in some cases it is useless without patience. Sampson had strength enough to subdue all the Philistines, but he had not *patience* enough to bear the teasing of Delilah: strength was very important in a contest with the Philistines, but it was useless in a contest with Delilah. Supported by *patience* and *faith* the Thessalonians conquered all their persecutors; hence Paul says, "we ourselves glory in you in the churches of God, for your patience and faith in all your persecutions and tribulations that ye endure." Their *patience* and *faith* stood side by side, and bore them safe through a sea of persecution and tribulation. In 1 Tim. vi. 11, we find *righteousness, godliness, faith, love, patience,* and *meekness* united, and Timothy is exhorted to "follow after" them. Here is a glorious troop, a kind of body-guard, that would keep Timothy safe in the midst of the greatest perils. Indeed it is "through faith and patience" that we are to "inherit the promises." The same authority says: "Ye have need of patience, that, after ye have done the will of God, ye might receive the promise." So then, we can neither do the will of God, nor inherit the promises of God, without *patience!* Truly, Paul, you may well say, "ye have need of patience." "Let us run with patience the race set before us." Truly, *patience* is "a friend that sticketh closer than a brother," when we run, as well as when we suffer. From Rev. i. 9, we learn that patience was the *companion* of John and others in their *tribulations.* And, finally, we are told that the good being himself, is "the God of patience."

We may now safely conclude, we think, that patience is essential to Christian progress; without her it is not possible to "run the race that is set before us," especially when we are called to pass through the valley of *Bochim*, where the journey is *long* and *lonely*, and the burden presses heavy. Here it is that we must *add patience;* and here it is that she must "have her perfect work." It was while passing through this dreary valley that she was the most intimate companion of the holy Apostle John: and very lovely does she appear in this valley, close by the side of *love*, with *meekness* and *long-suffering* upon her left hand. With such companions, it is always safe to travel this valley, nay, it is profitable, so much so, that by the time the pilgrim passes through the entire valley, accompanied by these four excellent companions, *faith* leading the way, and searching out the land, he is sure to be "perfect and entire, wanting nothing."

But, to do away with figure, what is this patience of which such excellent things are spoken? The Greek word is ὑπομηνω, from ὑπω, under, and μενω, to remain. *Patience* then, or the patient Christian, remains under the cross, in other words, under all the burdens incident to the Christian life, without complaining, never saying, "I neither can nor will bear it any longer," for such Christians both can and do bear the burdens of life, whether the time be long or short, till God releases them from the last burden, saying, "'tis enough;" then, and not till then, are they heard to say with the good and patient old Simeon, "Now let thy servant depart in peace, according to thy word, for mine eyes have seen thy salvation." Unsupported by patience, the burdens of life kill, "the sorrow of this world worketh death;" but supported by Christian patience, which always springs from faith, as we have already shown, these burdens are borne with meekness and cheerfulness; nor do they injure at all, but "work together for good;" so that the patient traveller journeys on, waxing stronger and stronger, singing as he goes:—

> "Vain, delusive world adieu,
>   With all of creature good:
> Only Jesus I pursue,
>   Who bought me with his blood:
> All thy pleasures I forego;
>   I trample on thy wealth and pride;
> Only Jesus will I know,
>   And Jesus crucified."

Again, methinks, I hear these patient pilgrims sing, right in the depths of the Valley of *Bochim*:—

> "Here fierce temptations beset me around,
>   Yet I am blest, I am blest.
> Here I must weep while my foes me surround,
>   Yet I am blest, I am blest.
> Let them revile me, and scoff at my name;
> Laugh at my weeping, endeavor to shame,
> I will go forward, for this is my theme,
>   There, there is rest, there is rest."

Let no one attempt to confound *this Christian patience* with stupid unfeeling stoicism, it is as different therefrom as is light from darkness. It is not the stubborn resolution, or the indifference of the stoic, neither is it the dull endurance of the ox or the camel, *mere natural fortitude:* no, it is one of the Christian graces, and is only found in connection with faith in Jesus, the faith that *justifies*, that *saves*. Nor is it possible for *Christian progression* to continue without it. Without it, *sour discontent* will spring up and corrode the very vitals of the soul; or senseless levity will be substituted for Christian cheerfulness, and will kill the last vital principle of the Christian life. Then God and heaven will be forgotten, and this present world will be loved and sought, and this alone! Hear, then, O ye Christians, the exhortation of the holy Apostle, and obey it, by *adding* to the previous graces PATIENCE; and, to this end, "Give all diligence." Then you, too, will continue the glorious Christian progression, and unite with the holy company in singing the pilgrim's song, even in the valley of *Bochim*.

CHAPTER X.

Add *Godliness*. Both action, and inaction, may result either from knowledge or ignorance. Hence there may be something very like courage, or patience, when there is no Godliness—Godliness results from a knowledge of God, and faith in God—Godliness consists in doing and suffering in the spirit of devotion to God. In other words, doing because God has commanded, or not doing, because he has forbidden—Calmet's definition of Godliness—Godliness in practice, is to imitate God in every thing—Godliness in character is to be like God—ευσεβεια, always has reference to God—Parkhurst is quoted—No act can be acceptable to God that is not Godly; various arguments are employed to prove this, also, to show the necessity of adding Godliness just here.

AND, if you would continue thus to progress, you must be careful to ADD GODLINESS. That is, *do, and suffer, every thing in the spirit of devotion to God.* It is thus that the Christian is distinguished from the mere philosopher, so called, as well as from the stoic and the infidel. The latter do and suffer uncomplainingly, it may be, not in the spirit of humble devotion to God, but because it would be *unphilosophical, unmanly*, not to do so. This may be called *fortitude*, but is not Christian fortitude; it is not *godliness*. Wirz had fortitude, or something like it, but he certainly had not *godliness.* Either action, or inaction, may be the result of ignorance, or the result of knowledge: I may fear where no fear is, or I may not fear when I should fear: I may not place confidence where I should, or I may place confidence where I should not: but my *trepidation* in the one case, and my *intrepidation* in the other, are equally the result of ignorance; and those who are as ignorant as myself, may give me credit for both prudence and fortitude: yet all was the result of ignorance, and must, consequently, be very different from Christian prudence, and Christian courage, which result from *Christion knowledge,* and *Christian faith*, not from *ignorance* and *unbelief.* It is equally certain that what results from ignorance, whether action or non-action, confidence or fear, cannot be godliness; but is, I apprehend, ungodliness; for godliness results from a knowledge of God, and faith in God; while the other particulars result from the very reverse of these, viz., ignorance and unbelief. Godly acts, are intelligent acts; and consist in doing what God has commanded, and that *because* he has commanded it; and in not doing what he has forbidden, and that because he has forbidden it; and all this *believingly, cheerfully, lovingly.* This is GODLINESS: and this is what we are to add to all the previous graces. That is, let your courage, your knowledge, your temperance, and your patience, all be *Godly.* "Whether you eat or drink, or whatever you do, do all to the glory of God." Do not "sacrifice to your own net, and burn incense to your own drag:" do not say, "my power, and the might of my hand hath gotten me this wealth. But thou shalt remember the LORD thy God: for it is he that giveth thee power to get wealth" Therefore say continually, "Not unto us, O Lord, not unto us, but unto thy name give glory, for thy mercy, and for thy truth's sake." This is *godliness*, and every thing short of this, is *ungodliness*, nay, it is *idolatry*, for it is giving to the creature what belongs to God. And, let it be distinctly noticed, all your offerings must be through Jesus, for it is only through him that our offerings, and ourselves, can be acceptable to God. Therefore, "whatsoever ye do in word or deed, do all in the name of the Lord Jesus, giving thanks to God and the Father by him." Nothing short of this is *Christian godliness*. And the act that is not *thus godly*, cannot be pleasing to God, nor can he accept it.

Calmet's definition of this word is worthy of notice here: "GODLY, that which proceeds from God, and is pleasing to him; it also signifies conformity to his will, and an assimilation to his character." (See his Dictionary.) This is an excellent definition; and what is here said of *godliness*, is true of every thing in genuine religion. Indeed, every thing that proceeds from God, is *like him*, so far as its nature will admit of such likeness; and its design and tendencies are to lead to God. You may be well assured, that whatever has not these characteristics, is not of God. All that comes from God to man, is characterized by *Godlike* wisdom, goodness, truthfulness, and holiness; and is both designed and calculated to lead man to God. And the religious system or principle that has not these characteristics, is not of God. It is true that there have been, and still are, many attempts to imitate God, to counterfeit what comes from God; and while some of these are very clumsy attempts, there are others which, to the superficial observer, may appear as genuine; but, upon closer observation, they will be found entirely destitute of the two grand characteristics, namely, *likeness* and *tendency* to God. History shows that all erroneous religious systems and principles have led from God, not to him; and, whatever might be their *appearance* to the superficial observer, they really were not like God; they had not the stamp of his wisdom, goodness, truthfulness, holiness. Both they and their votaries were destitute of godliness, or *godlikeness*. Those who have carefully examined God's account of himself, as given in the Scriptures, will easily discover that the various anti-scriptural systems and principles of this, or any other age, or country, are entirely destitute of a *likeness* to the account which he has given of himself and of his government. Nor is it difficult to see that the same principles and systems are *designed* to lead from the *Creator* to the *creature*. For instance, it is easy to see that every thing in Popery *points* and *leads* to the *creature*. The mind of the worshipper is constantly directed to the departed saint, the living priest, the lifeless image, and the senseless ceremony. All this is *ungodly*, essentially so; and must be hateful to God, and ruinous to man; for its sole tendency is, to lead from the *Creator* to the *creature*. Hence, as it did not proceed from God, it has not the stamp of his wisdom, goodness, truthfulness, and holiness. On the contrary, the grand characteristics of the whole are *folly, badness, falsehood,* and *sinfulness.* Other systems and principles, though not so *obviously ungodly,* are, nevertheless, equally so. Such are all systems which do not point man *to God in Christ for all good*—for *pardon, holiness,* and *heaven.* They are all *ungodly,* and lead from God. But the godly teacher, and the godly teaching, constantly say, "Behold the Lamb of God, who taketh away the sins of the world!" *This is Christianity; this is Christian progression.* Christian progression is always to God in Christ; retrogression is always from God—there is no medium. The utmost, or farthest departure from God, is the deepest hell. The nearest approach to God, is the highest heaven. This is to "see the King in his beauty, in the land that is far away." Far away, indeed, from all that is *low, sinful, evil. This is to see God's face; to see him as he is; to be* LIKE HIM. To the same effect is that sublime prayer of our blessed Saviour, "God manifested in the flesh": "Father, I will that they also, whom thou hast given me, be with me where I am; that they may behold my glory which thou gavest me." The holy Apostles were permitted to have a glimpse of this glory while on earth, particularly Peter, James, and John, in the Holy Mount. Hence, John says, "The word was made flesh, and dwelt among us, (and we beheld his glory, the glory as of the only begotten of the Father,) full of grace and truth." And even in heaven, the approach to the Infinite Majesty is *through Christ;* and the glory of that Majesty, is seen *in Christ,* as far as it is secable. "Father, I will that they also, whom thou hast given me, be with me where I am; that they may behold my glory." It follows, that the utmost progress is the nearest approach to God, in heaven as well as on earth, and this approach, even in heaven, is through our blessed Saviour, who is "the way, the truth, and the life," *even there!*

Godliness in *practice,* is to imitate God in every thing;—"But I say unto you, love your enemies, bless them that curse you, do good to them that hate you, and pray for them which despitefully use you, and persecute you; that ye may be the children of your Father which is in heaven: for he maketh his sun to rise on the evil and on the good, and sendeth rain on the just and on the unjust." Those who thus imitate God, are *godly; they are like their Father in heaven.* Godliness is also a moral likeness to God,—"Be ye therefore holy, for I the *Lord* your God am holy." This is to be "partakers of his holiness," "partakers of the divine nature," and therefore, to be *like God,* or *godlike.* Then God sees and loves his own image in the human soul: then shall Christ "see of the travail of his soul, and shall be satisfied;" and then too, shall his people "be satisfied, when they awake with his likeness," the likeness to God in which they were originally created, and in which they are now "created anew in Christ Jesus." God and his people are now satisfied, the former, because he has restored what was lost, the latter, because they have received *back* what was lost. Nothing short of this moral assimilation to God, can produce this mutual satisfaction of the created and the Infinite Mind. And this is *godliness, perfect godliness.*

Finally, we beg to remind the reader, that the word ευσεβεια, translated godliness, always has reference to God: and when it is used as the designation of certain acts, it always means such acts as have God for their object; acts of piety, acts of devotion to God. And as it includes that holiness of *nature* from which such acts spring, the moral nature of God, and that of the holy worshipper, it follows, that it is a very comprehensive word. It means, says Parkhurst, "godliness, or the whole of true religion; so named, because piety towards God is the foundation and principal part of it. See Heb. xi. 6; Matt. xxii. 37, 38; 1 Tim. iv. 7, 8; vi. 6. Comp. 1 Tim. iii. 16." In short, it means all that is morally good in your *courage,* your *temperance,* your *patience:* all that is morally good *in your heart and in your life.* In other words, *all your acts and tempers are good and acceptable, only so far as they are godly.* The word being now understood, any one can see the *importance,* and feel the *force* of the exhortation, "add godliness," especially here, where there is so much danger of your abounding activities lacking this essential quality, GODLINESS!

CHAPTER XI.

Add *brotherly kindness.* Your duty to God will not substitute for your duty to your brother—God will not allow the creature to take his place, nor will he take the place of the creature—Love is varied both by its subject and object—God will not accept your gifts, if you have no gift for your brother—He who loveth God, loveth his brother also—He hates who does not love—Both the *subject* and *object* of this love must be a brother—The difference between kindness and brotherly kndness—A striking illustration—God alone can make a brotherhood, men may assume, or give the name but they cannot impart what that name imports—Each preceding grace is essential to that which follows—This order must not be broken; to progress, you must make each addition in its place.

BUT having made all these additions, do not suppose that *Christian progression* ends here. Not so. Just here you must *add brotherly kindness.* Do not suppose that your duty to God is a substitute for your duty to your fellow. It was this mistake that led men to flee to the desert, and become monks and hermits; and in this way they soon became as destitute of godliness as they were of brotherly kindness. The Christian graces go together, support each other, and will not be divorced: no one of them can live alone: united they live; separated they die. God will not allow the creature to take his place in your heart, nor will he take the place of the creature. Godliness does not exclude brotherly kindness, nor does brotherly kindness exclude godliness. On the contrary, these graces mutually support and increase each other. These graces exist in the heart, or are absent from it, in reciprocal proportion. "If a man say, I love God, and hateth his brother, he is a liar. For he that loveth not his brother, whom he hath seen, how can he love God, whom he hath not seen? And this commandment have we from him, That he who loveth God, loveth his brother also." Brotherly love is simply a modification of that love which has God for its object, for love may be varied by its object as well as by its subject: and the gift of this love may be called brotherly kindness, when a brother is the recipient of that gift. But when God is the object of this love, it is not thus modified; his infinite perfections, and his munificent and unmerited gifts, call forth this love as no other object can;—"We love him because he first loved us." But although God is loved in *unlimited measure* and *fervor*, the brother is not excluded from his place; on the contrary, brotherly love, or kindness, increases, by a kind of *reflection*, just in proportion as love for God increases. My loving God with all my heart, does not hinder me from loving my neighbor as myself, nor from loving my brother with a brotherly love; indeed, the latter is the necessary result of the former; for the love that embraces God, embraces the family of God. If a man should profess to love me while he hated my family, I should not believe his profession, especially if I knew that my family were deserving of his love. And just so it is, precisely, that God treats such a profession, as is clearly seen in the quotations given above. To the same effect is the following:—" Therefore, if thou bring thy gift to the altar, and there rememberest that thy brother hath aught against thee, leave there thy gift before the altar, and go thy way; first be reconciled to thy brother, and then come and offer thy gift." You may offer your gifts to God, but if you have no gifts for your brother, no brotherly kindness, God will not accept of your gifts: hence you are as destitute of godliness as you are of brotherly kindness. If "thy brother hath aught against thee," (and he certainly has, if you have no brotherly kindness,) God also has a charge against thee; he unites his charge with that of the injured brother, and till you are reconciled to your brother you cannot be reconciled to God:—" Verily, I say unto you, inasmuch as ye have done it unto one of the least of these my brethren, ye have done it unto me." Again, " Verily I say unto you, inasmuch as ye did it not to one of the least of these, ye did it not to me. And these shall go away into everlasting punishment: but the righteous into life eternal." It is clear, then, that godliness and brotherly kindness are inseparable, and that where the latter is not, neither is the former. Away, then, with your monkish nonsense, which would separate godliness from, or substitute it for, brotherly kindness. When you separate yourself from your brother you separate yourself from God:—" These be they who separate themselves, sensual, having not the Spirit." God has not a place for you, either in heaven or on earth, where you may, as his children, live separate from his children. God's house is not thus divided against itself: no, that which separates you from God's children, separates you from God himself; and that which unites you to God, unites you to his people! "He that hath an ear let him hear" these teachings of the Holy Spirit! Have zeal for God, but let it be "according to knowledge;" see that brotherly kindness is added to your godliness, and never dream that you can have the one without the other, for you cannot; any more than you can have matter without figure, or fire without heat, or a sun without light, or design without a designer, or thought without a thinking agent; or any other thing without its essential property; for brotherly kindness is an essential property of the godliness here specified. "This commandment have we from him, that he who loveth God, loveth his brother also." "If a man say, I love God, and hateth his brother, he is a liar. For he that loveth not his brother, whom he hath seen, how can he love God, whom he hath not seen?" Who is he, then, who undertakes to do this *impossible* thing, and at the same time, to make the command of God of none effect? I answer, that man who professes, or tries, to be godly, while destitute of brotherly kindness; who professes to love God, while he hates his brother, that is, does not love him, for there is no medium between hatred and love: he hates who does not love. Hatred, like love, may have its degrees;

but the proper object of love must be hated in some measure, if it is not loved at all.

It should be remembered, however, that brotherly love, or kindness, must have a brother for its object, as well as for its subject. It is as true in the spiritual, as it is in the natural order, that I cannot love as a brother, if I am not a brother. I say I cannot: I may, and should, have a feeling of kindness, but it is not brotherly kindness, if I am not a brother. I cannot have feelings of brotherly kindness before I am a brother, any more than I can have *humane* feelings, before I have the human nature. For the same reason I cannot love *as a brother*, one who is not a brother; I cannot have feelings of brotherly kindness for one who is not a brother. It were absurd in the extreme, to require me to have the very same feelings of affection, the same brotherly kindness, for the son of an unknown woman, that I have for my brother, the son of my mother. I may, and should have feelings of kindness for such a man, and these feelings will be increased by a further knowledge of his amiable qualities; but the sight or death of my own brother will stir feelings away down in the depths of my nature, as they are not, and cannot be stirred by the sight or death of that stranger. For the same reason, the laws, both of God and man, require me to act toward a brother as they do not require me to act toward any other being. As illustrative of this truth, let us suppose a case. See that fine mansion; and see that old man, weary and wayworn, as with trembling steps he approaches the door. It is cold, and his garments are scanty and torn. The bell is rung, and at its call a well-dressed and fine-looking lady opens the door, and is thus briefly addressed by the wayworn stranger, "Madam, I am hungry and cold, and am not able to go farther; will you allow me shelter in your house for the night?" The good lady takes him by the hand, leads him to one of her comfortable rooms, causes him to be stripped, washed, and clothed. He is then fed with food convenient for him; he is invited to bow with the family in the devotions of the evening; and, finally, he is led to a comfortable bedroom, where he rests in peace, and is refreshed, body and soul. In the morning, the good woman shows him similar kindness, and after worship and breakfast, she opens the door for his departure, slips a sum of money into his hand, and bids him good morning, never again expecting to see him in this world. Now, her conscience approves of her conduct toward this old man; and the word of God adds its stamp of approval; and her neighbors admire and praise her truly Christian hospitality; and who does not? But suppose that, upon opening the door, she discovered that this wayworn old man was none other than her own brother; yes, her brother Edwin, with whom, long, long ago, she was wont to play in her father's lawn, and repose on her mother's lap. Yes, this same Edwin, after so many years, and after strange reverses of fortune, now unexpectedly stands before her, a wayworn old man, trembling with cold, weary with his journey, faint with hunger, and weary of life! Now, suppose she should receive this same Edwin, knowing him to be her brother, and treat him with all the kindness we have supposed in the former case, and then in the morning, coolly send him away, never again expecting to see her brother Edwin in this world; would her neighbors, and the word of God, to say nothing about her conscience, approve of, and praise her conduct in this instance? No, they would all condemn her, and so would her conscience, if she had any. Why so? Simply because the stranger was entitled to kindness, and he had it; but the brother was entitled to brotherly kindness, and he had it not. The fact is, however, a woman who would treat a stranger as we have supposed, could not possibly treat a brother in the same way. No, the first sight of her own brother Edwin would rouse a sister's feelings, which a sister could not control, and for which she was neither to be praised nor blamed: but the extent to which she might cultivate, or destroy, such feelings, would be just cause for praise or blame. It is certain, however, we think, that most sisters, or brothers, would never allow poor unfortunate Edwin to leave that rich mansion till he should be carried to his resting-place in the city of the dead: and we are sure none would, who would add to their godliness brotherly kindness.

Let it be well observed then, that a brother is entitled to brotherly kindness, and he only. And let it also be well observed, that none but a brother can impart brotherly kindness, for he only has it to impart, and none can give what they do not possess. I may, and should show kindness to a horse, much kindness; and, if I mistake not, I have had horses, and dogs too, which have manifested much kindness toward me; but in all this there was no *brotherly* kindness, and could not be. Why? Because we were not brothers, and could not be. Now, I rejoice to know, and believe, that there is a sense in which all men are brothers: but I also believe, that there is a sense, a very important sense, in which all men are not brothers; and, consequently, a sense in which all men have not brotherly kindness for each other; and never will till in a corresponding sense they are brothers. And in that sense God alone can make them brothers, either natural brothers, or spiritual brothers. Neither legal documents, so-called, nor mathematical instruments, nor monastic vows, nor priestly ceremonies, nor jesuitical combinations, nor inquisitorial tribunals, nor pharisaic righteousness, can make men brothers; neither can all of them put together, nor any thing else that man can do. There are but two ways in which human beings are constituted brothers, viz: by a natural, and by a spiritual birth. The former are born of the flesh, the latter of the Spirit; the former are a brotherhood having a man for their parent, the latter are a brotherhood having God for their parent; and by this birth they have mutual brotherly affections which nothing else can possibly give them. After this birth, brotherly kindness may be vastly increased by proper cultivation and the grace of God; or it may be partially impaired, or wholly destroyed, by sin: but to expect this brotherly kindness without the *birth*, is like expecting a crop without the seed; to expect a spiritual brotherhood, without a spiritual birth, is like expecting a human family without the human nature.—"Verily, verily, I say unto thee, except a man be born again, he cannot see the kingdom of God." . . . . . . "Verily, verily, I say unto thee, except a man be born of water, and of the Spirit, he cannot enter into the kingdom of God. That which is born of the flesh, is flesh; and that which is born of the Spirit, is spirit. Marvel not that I said unto thee, ye must be born again." Men may assume or give the name, but they cannot impart what that name imports; and it imports something without which no son or daughter of Adam can *see* or *enter* the kingdom of God. If God has any other way of constituting the children of men brothers, with brotherly kindness, he certainly has not revealed it. And to give or receive the name without the thing which that name imports, is like the practice of those maniacs who give or receive the titles of kings and princes, while they are absolutely destitute of all that such titles imply. Hence, as we observed at the very outstart, the Apostle addresses this exhortation "to them that have obtained like precious faith with us through the righteousness of God our Saviour Jesus Christ." He does not exhort unbelievers to add these things, for they have not the faith to which all these things are to be added, just as all the stones in a building are to be added to the foundation. He who undertakes to add these things before he is justified by faith, undertakes to build without a foundation. This is the error of the Pharisee; and the things he substitutes for *these* things are like *wood, hay, stubble,* which will be consumed in the day of the Lord. "Every man's work shall be made manifest: for the day shall declare it, because it shall be revealed by fire; and the fire shall try every man's work, of what sort it is;" and nothing will stand the test of that fire but the things here specified. With these things the three Hebrew children were *fire-proof* even in Nebuchadnezzar's furnace, but wood, hay, and stubble, would have offered little resistance to that *sevenfold heat;* and the inventions of men shall offer still less resistance to the fire that shall try their work in the great and terrible day of the Lord, when "the fire shall try every man's work of what sort it is."

Once more. Let it be well observed, that in this divine summary of the Christian graces, each following grace is *added* to that which went before, and which, consequently, previously existed; whether by this is meant the addition of the entire specification, or that of a larger measure of it, the fact is the same.—Thus, courage is added to faith, which is the basis upon which the whole column rests; while faith itself rests upon the atonement. And knowledge is added to courage, and temperance to knowledge; patience to temperance, godliness to patience, and brotherly kindness to godliness. Hence, the existence of each preceding grace, is essential to the existence of that which follows. Neither one can precede the foregoing in the sense in which we are here exhorted to make the addition. This divine order demands strict attention, for it is the order in which Christian progression is conducted, and it is essential to its continuance. For instance; under certain circumstances I may be very willing to add knowledge, temperance, or patience; but may not be so willing to add godliness; or I may be willing to add godliness, in my way of thinking, but may not be at all willing to add brotherly kindness; but I cannot choose and reject in this way; God's order will not be reversed and thrown into confusion in this way; and if I do not add brotherly kindness, progression will terminate just here. Neither can I retain my previous position; for, in the absence of brotherly kindness, all the preceding graces must languish and die, it may be, by almost insensible degrees. And just in this way, it is, I apprehend, that thousands backslide. Let us, then, carefully observe the divine order, and make every addition in its proper place, and that with promptness and earnestness; for, to hesitate, in a single instance, when the peculiar addition is called for, particularly that of brotherly kindness, to hesitate, I say, may result in a conclusion not to make the addition; and then retrogression immediately takes place, for there is no such thing as standing still: onward or backward, is the fixed unalterable law. And if you have progressed thus far, and an addition of brotherly kindness is called for just here, and it is called for, even by the progress you have made, then make the addition, with promptness and full-heartedness, and you have passed the point of danger; and have only to spread your sails to catch the increasing heavenly gale, which will carry you with increased and increasing speed directly towards the port of glory

CHAPTER XII.

Add *Love*, which takes a much wider range than brotherly kindness. How Peter was led to make this addition, and how his other graces were increased thereby—Had he not made this addition here, he would have progressed no further, but would have backslidden, as many do just at this point—A striking resemblance between Peter and John Wesley at this point—How they and others continued to be a power, while others ceased to be a power—There is nothing that will substitute for this love—A striking incident in illustration—The addition of love is shown to be absolutely necessary.

AFTER this you may have fair sailing for a time, wind and tide being both in your favor; but do not suppose that no further addition is to be made, or that between you and the distant port there is no other point of danger. Not so: the fisherman of Galilee had a very different experience, and accordingly, gives very different advice. Here it is:— *And to brotherly kindness add love.* Peter had a goodly measure of this excellent grace, brotherly kindness, before he had the vision in the house of "one Simon a tanner, by the sea-side;" but he was not so well supplied with that thing called *love*. This takes a much wider range than brotherly kindness. The latter extended very readily to his brethren in Judea, who were Christians of the stock of Abraham; but it did not extend to the "unclean" creatures who were *far off among the Gentiles*—these were not the proper objects of "brotherly kindness;" and Peter, the Jew, though now a Christian, will leave these unclean creatures where they are, and as they are, unless *love* is added to his brotherly kindness. And unless this is done, he will backslide, as sure as he lives. Yes, he will surely backslide, unless he carries the Gospel to the perishing Gentiles; and this he will not do, unless love is added. We have known a great many who actually did backslide, just at this point; and all will, who do not add love just here, and that in sufficient quantity to carry them far hence to the Gentiles. To make this addition was no easy matter in the case of Peter. His Jewish ignorance and prejudices had to be removed, and his judgment corrected. To do this, God employed the singular vision recorded in the tenth chapter of the Acts of the Apostles, and to which it is only necessary to refer, it being well known. But, what deserves special notice, is the fact, that his Christian progression was continued in precisely the same way that is marked out in the Scripture under consideration. He had faith, and, in short, all the other particulars; but they must all be increased, and increased now; and that by making additions as here directed. His knowledge was increased, especially, by adding this important truth, viz: that "God is no respecter of persons; but, in every nation, he that feareth God, and worketh righteousness, is accepted of him." Nor had he this increase of knowledge, till he added sufficient courage to enable him to go with the three strangers, and enter into the midst of those Gentiles who, in the vision, had been represented to him by a variety of unclean and dangerous creatures. Nor can we doubt that this required considerable courage, especially when we take into the account his previous views, and the opposition, the conscientious opposition, that he knew he would have to meet with from his own countrymen, and even from his own Christian brethren. His temperance, too, underwent quite a change. Hitherto, his feelings and views, and, consequently, his conduct toward the Gentiles, were very intemperate, and even superstitious. But now he is wonderfully changed in all these particulars. His godliness, too, is vastly increased. He now feels, and thinks, and acts, more like God, than he ever did before. His brotherly kindness, also, is wonderfully increased. It now extends to all who fear God and work righteousness, even among the Gentiles; and still more to those who are made partakers of like precious faith with himself. I presume he has now as much brotherly kindness for the Gentile as for the Jewish Christians. And he evidently has a degree of *love* that he never had before. And this increase of love so swells his old Jewish heart, that it embraces the entire Gentile world. Hence, he preaches just as well in Cesarea as he did in Jerusalem, and with similar effect. And, what wonderfully surprised, and equally delighted, the honest fisherman, was the fact, that he thus records, in answer to those who "contended with him, saying, Thou wentest in to men uncircumcised, and didst eat with them."

After relating how God led him to do so, and also stating what he preached, he adds, "And as I began to speak, the Holy Ghost fell on them as upon us at the beginning. Then remembered I the word of the Lord, how that he said, John indeed baptized with water; but ye shall be baptized with the Holy Ghost. Forasmuch then as God gave them the like gift as he did unto us, who believed on the Lord Jesus Christ, what was I, that I could withstand God. When they heard these things they held their peace and glorified God, saying, then hath God also to the Gentiles granted repentance unto life." See what good resulted from the Christian progression of one man! To himself and others, both Jews and Gentiles, in Joppa, in Cesarea, in Jerusalem, and elsewhere; and the good results continue to this day. Had not Peter added courage, by which he obeyed the divine command, followed the leadings of providence, went and preached to the Gentiles, and thus made glorious additions to all his Christian graces, he would have progressed no further, but would have remained in Joppa, and, it may be, have died there a backslider. O how many remain at Joppa, when they should go on to Cesarea and preach the gospel to the perishing Gentiles! Nor is there any remedy for this sore evil, but that here recommended by this same Peter; make all these additions as here directed, and especially add *love*, without which you will never go and preach the gospel to those perishing creatures who were represented to Peter by what he saw in the sheet: a sight that will frighten any one that has not a large and increasing amount of *faith, courage, knowledge, temperance, patience, godliness, brotherly kindness,* and LOVE! It will be seen, too, that by continuing to progress, Peter continued to be a power. His day of power did not end with the day of Pentecost; no, he was the same man of power in Cesarea that he had been in Jerusalem. And that power produced among the Gentiles the very same effects that it produced among the Jews. Now, I ask, would this have been the case if he had disobeyed the divine call and remained at Joppa when he was ordered to Cesarea? To this question there is but one answer, and that is *no*. And he certainly would have remained there, would not have went to Cesarea, had he not made the necessary additions as above stated, without the necessary faith, courage, knowledge, godliness, and love; he would not, he could not, have went on that mission; and he could have offered as good reasons for not going, as those which are offered by thousands as an excuse for similar disobedience. But their excuses do not alter the fact, viz: that they remain at Joppa while men like Peter go on to Cesarea. The result is, of course, that the latter progress and continue to be a power, while the former backslide and become powerless, like other men. It must be so; it positively cannot be otherwise; the contrary supposition is downright *antinomianism!* O ye who are at Joppa when ye should be at Cesarea, lounging and sleeping away your time at the house of some friend by the sea-side, when you should be preaching the gospel to the perishing Gentiles; hear the call of God before it be too late; hark, it comes even to you. "Rise, Peter! Behold three men seek thee. Arise, therefore, and get thee down, and go with them, nothing doubting: for I have sent them." Yes, God calls; "the Master calleth for thee;" the perishing Gentiles call for thee, and men are even now at thy door imploring help; and God says: "Go with them, nothing doubting: for I have sent them." It is folly, worse than folly, for you to dream and talk about power, till you obey that call. If you are in Joppa when you should be in Cesarea, you may remain there, talking about power, and about entire sanctification, till the last trumpet sounds; but you will talk, yea, and pray in vain, till you obey that call. God says: "What doest thou here Elijah?" or the Spirit says, as he did to Peter, "Arise, go!" and unless you do as he commands, you may talk ever so prettily about "power, holiness, entire sanctification, and men of power," but the first power that will reach you will be the power that punishes the disobedient. God save us from that power, and, to that end, save us from *disobedience*.

The fact, that there is a striking resemblance between the case of Peter and that of John Wesley, deserves a passing notice just here. Peter, even after his conversion, was so controlled by prejudices resulting from the erroneous teachings of Scribes and Pharisees, that he would not go in unto the

Gentiles and preach the Gospel unto them, till God corrected his judgment, and increased his love, as stated above. Just so it was with John Wesley, till God corrected and qualified him as he did Peter. In reference to this fact, Mr. Wesley makes the following record.—" Saturday, March 31, 1839. In the evening I reached Bristol, and met Mr. Whitefield there. I could scarce reconcile myself at first to this strange way of preaching in the fields, of which he set me an example on Sunday; having been all my life (till very lately) so tenacious of every point relating to decency and order, that I should have thought the saving of souls almost a sin, if it had not been done in a church." Just so it was with Peter; he, too, was still adhering to the rules of "decency and order" as laid down by Scribes and Pharisees, who had long *made the word of God of none-effect by their traditions.* The Scribes and Pharisees of olden times talked largely and loudly about the *temple*, the *temple;* but would leave the Gentiles to perish, unwarned and unpitied. Just so the Scribes and Pharisees of later times; they, too, talked largely and loudly about the *church*, the *church;* but, like their ancestors, they, too, would leave the poor Gentiles to perish unwarned and unpitied; and all this they called "decency and order." What strange ideas Pharisees have of "decency and order!" But the God who delivered Peter from this dreadful delusion, also delivered the Wesleys, Whitefield, and others. And the result was, they became a power for good. The power that was felt in the dwelling of Cornelius in Cesarea, was now equally felt in the humble dwellings of the poor in England; and not less so in the streets, the highways, and the fields; while the Scribes and Pharisees, as of old, adhered to their own inventions, boasted of their vast stone buildings, and were satisfied with the form without the power. But the gospel, which had been excluded from those old gray temples, triumphed in the dwellings of the poor, in the streets, the lanes, the highways, and the fields; and was felt to be "the power of God unto salvation," in London and Bristol, just as much so, as it had been in Jerusalem and Cesarea, when Peter preached it in those places. And why? Because it was again preached by men who followed the Lord fully; men who did not remain at Joppa, but went on to Cesarea at the command of the Lord; men who "added to their faith, courage; and to their courage, knowledge; and to knowledge, temperance; and to temperance, patience; and to patience, godliness; and to godliness, brotherly kindness; and to brotherly kindness, *love*." And, observe, others would have been a similar power, had they been equally obedient to the heavenly calling. But, instead of this, they remained Pharisees, Sadducees, or Herodians; or having started, they continued the progress for a time, and becoming weary of well-doing, they refused to *add love;* refused, consequently, to go on to Cesarea; sat down and fell asleep at Joppa; and died there! while Wesley and others, went on singing,

> "O that without a lingering groan,
> I may the welcome word receive;
> My body with my charge lay down,
> And cease at once to work and live."

Thus, obedient to the heavenly calling, they pursued their illustrious career, exclaiming, "the love of Christ constraineth us," "so that from Jerusalem, and round about unto Illyricum," they "fully preached the gospel of Christ." But those who did not *add love*, were constrained by a very different influence; constrained, not to urge their way "through every city and village," like their Master, "preaching the gospel," but to settle at Joppa, or some other watering place, and there in ease and indolence end their days in obscurity. There is nothing in the gift of God that will substitute for this love; nothing that will constrain men to live and labor as did the Apostles, the Wesleys, Whitefield, and others, but this love: no, *nothing*. And, as Christian progress implies a life of benevolent toil for the good of others, and for the glory of God; it is folly to talk about Christian progress, unless you add love to all your other attainments; that is, unless you *grow* in love, as well as knowledge; not "brotherly kindness," but *love* that extends to, and embraces every child of man. Without this your Christian progress must terminate just here; without it further progress is simply impossible. You might as well expect a man to walk without feet, or a bird to fly without wings; as expect a man to do the work of a Christian without love. The following incident may serve as an illustration of this truth. A young man who had been brought up in easy circumstances, and received a liberal education, was offered as a candidate for the Ministry in the British Conference. The Rev. Richard Reece, with whom the writer had the pleasure of being acquainted, and from whom he received wholesome counsel when a youth, had some doubts about the young man, and thus put him to the test; —" Now," said the venerable itinerant, addressing himself to the young candidate, "as a minister among us, you will have to travel long journeys, in all weathers, by night and by day; often over bad roads, sometimes hungry; and will have to sleep, it may be, in cold houses and damp beds; and, in short, submit to many other inconveniences." The young man heard all this with profound attention, and wisely concluded that he would not be an *itinerant:* for the special measure of love that always accompanies the special call, being wanting, he could not do that special work. But, observe, I do not say that this love is rendered necessary merely by those physical difficulties which accompany the work of the Christian: these, doubtless, have their influence in keeping men at Joppa when they should go on to Cesarea: but this love is *morally* and *absolutely* necessary, as the brotherhood is properly, and necessarily, the object of "brotherly kindness;" while the love here specified has God for its object, and also *the whole human family*, not brethren merely, whether natural or spiritual. In short, there is much of the Christian work that cannot, or will not, be performed, when this love is wanting;

and if it were performed, as to the outward act, it would not be acceptable to God, not having the necessary moral quality. Therefore, to all the preceding graces, add love, or your Christian progress must terminate just here; and where progression terminates, there retrogression commences.

CHAPTER XIII.

All "these things" are to be "in you," and are the fruit of the Spirit—The grand distinction between a Christian and a Pharisee—They are all of grace, yet not without the willing co-operation of the subject—All these things being in you, they are to abound—Between this and retrogression there is no medium—Meaning of the words $αργους$, and $ακαρπους$—These things being in you and abounding, you cannot possibly be inactive, and the action is of such a nature that fruitfulness must be the result—This action is irresistible, bidding defiance to every opposing power—Hence all such Christians progress, and are a power—Idleness, inaction, or slothfulness, must result from a want of *faith*, *courage*, or *love*—Faith, courage, and love are the great moving powers; those who have them are ready for every good work, making tents like Paul; or, like Jesus, preparing a breakfast for the hungry disciples by the sea-shore, when necessary—A country inhabited by such a people must be prosperous—All this is confirmed by the facts of history—A point of great importance—The Apostle connects all with the knowledge of our Lord Jesus Christ—A man may be idle and unfruitful in the knowledge of Plato, Socrates, and other men of fame, but not in the knowledge of our Lord Jesus Christ—To have life and power, we must be connected with Jesus in the way specified by the Apostle, for no other being has either life or power to give to man.

BUT having made all these additions, what then? Has Christian progression now reached its utmost limit? So far from this, the Apostle conveys the idea that you will now progress with a rapidity which was hitherto rendered impossible by the imperfect development of your intellectual and moral character. Hear him. "If these things be in you, and abound, they make you that ye shall neither be barren nor unfruitful in the knowledge of our Lord Jesus Christ." Observe, all these things are IN YOU. Here is the first grand characteristic of a genuine Christian, and that by which he is *essentially* distinguished from a Pharisee. The things by which the latter would recommend himself to God, such as "mint, anise, and cummin," are in his garden, or elsewhere, not *in him*. His acts of devotion too, are merely outward, they do not spring from the inward living principles here specified; these are only in the genuine Christian and are directly from God, "who worketh all in all." This grand idea is beautifully expressed by Charles Wesley in the following lines:

>"Thou all our works in us hast wrought:
> Our good is all divine:
> The praise of every virtuous thought
> And righteous word, is thine.
>
>"From thee, through Jesus, we receive
> The power on thee to call.
> In whom we are, and move and live:
> Our God is all in all."

Yes, the eight principles here specified by the Apostle, are "the fruit of the Spirit," and have their seat in the soul; while the things which constitute the religion of the Pharisee are merely *outward*, and *natural;* not *supernatural,* not the *work,* not the *fruit,* of the Spirit. And as he has nothing but what results from the exercise of his natural powers, independent of this peculiar work of the Spirit, and equally independent of the atonement, he is said to "exalt himself," or to attempt so to do. Nor does the righteousness of the Pharisee include any one of the eight particulars here specified; he is absolutely destitute of *Christian faith, courage, knowledge, temperance, patience, godliness, brotherly kindness,* and *love. Being ignorant of God's righteousness, and going about to establish his own righteousness, he has not submitted to the righteousness of God. " For Christ is the end of the law for righteousness to every one that believeth."* Pharisaism excludes alike, *the Christian doctrine, the Christian experience,* and *the Christian practice.* Hence a Pharisee, *as such, has no hope, and is without God in the world.* If the Pharisee, *as such,* can make good his claim, the Bible is not true; it is not possible to unite Pharisaism and the Bible; he who embraces the one, must absolutely reject the other: the more I investigate, the more I become convinced of the absolute antagonism of these two systems. Hence, as I attempt to develop the great principles of the Christian system, I find Pharisaism meeting and opposing me at every step. This is my apology for so often adverting to it; it is not possible to defend the one, and not oppose the other.

But, although all the above particulars are *in* the Christian, and are produced by the direct agency of the Holy Spirit, this is not done without the willing co-operation of him who is the subject of this work of the Spirit. Indeed, the very *nature* of each particular implies this. But this *willing co-operation* is itself *the result of free grace*, by which fallen man is enabled, though not forced, to co-operate with the Spirit in his renewing operations. And the reason why any man is not renewed, or does not progress, is to be found in the fact that he does not co-operate with, but resists, the Holy Spirit. Hence the charge, "Ye do always resist the Holy Ghost; as your fathers did, so do ye." Hence, too, the exhortation, "Work out your own salvation with fear and trembling; for it is God which worketh in you to will and to do of his good pleasure." *Work, for God works.* If God did not work, no child of man would ever work, in the sense here specified. Nor can we work *any longer* than God works. The Christian work is one of co-operation with God, which co-operation is itself the result of free grace. We may well sing,—

"O! to grace how great a debtor."

The works which do not result from the operations of the Holy Spirit, St. Paul calls "the works of the flesh." Nothing can exceed the clearness and force with which this Apostle presents this whole subject, in the fifth chapter of his Epistle to the Galatians. And the principles involved, being of such vital importance, I have concluded to give the entire passage in this connection.

"This I say then: Walk in the Spirit, and ye shall not fulfil the lust of the flesh. For the flesh lusteth against the Spirit, and the Spirit against the flesh; and these are contrary the one to the other; so that ye cannot do the things that ye would. But if ye be led by the Spirit, ye are not under the law. Now the works of the flesh are manifest, which are *these*—Adultery, fornication, uncleanness, lasciviousness, idolatry, witchcraft, hatred, variance, emulations, wrath, strife, seditions, heresies, envyings, murders, drunkenness, revellings, and such like—[for this is only a sample]—of which I tell you before, as I have also told you in time past, that they which do such things shall not inherit the kingdom of God."

Observe, not only are these the legitimate "works of the flesh," of "the natural man," but they are done despite the teachings and influences of the Spirit, despite that "measure of grace that is given to every man to profit withal;" despite that "true light that lighteth every man that cometh into the world." And when the Spirit and grace of God, coming to him through the atonement, succeed in checking this vile wretch in his mad career, so that he is saved from outbreaking sins, then, forsooth, he gives himself credit for the whole, turns Pharisee, and claims heaven on the principle of *merit*; pronounces himself meet for, and entitled to "an inheritance among all them that are sanctified;" among those "who have washed their robes and made them white in the blood of the Lamb!" To me, this seems to be the highest pitch to which madness and wickedness can be carried. AND THIS IS PHARISAISM! "But the fruit of the Spirit is love, joy, peace, long-suffering, gentleness, goodness, faith, meekness, temperance; against such there is no law. And they that are Christ's have crucified the flesh, with the affections and lusts. If we live in the Spirit, let us also walk in the Spirit. Let us not be desirous of vain-glory, provoking one another, envying one another." It is by the life-giving energy of the Holy Spirit that the dead soul is first quickened into life; and having thus lived by the Spirit, Paul says, "let us walk by the Spirit." Thus, Christian *life* and Christian *progression* are, alike, the result of the Spirit's *life-giving* and *life-increasing* influences. This is Christianity, and all beside "is enmity against God."

But the Apostle not only says that all "these things" are to be "in you," but that they are to "abound;"—faith, courage, knowledge, temperance, patience, godliness, brotherly kindness, and love; all in the soul, and each in its place; all acting, and acting in harmony. Here is a system, infinitely more glorious than the Solar System; here is harmonious action, more glorious than the dance of the spheres. And from the harmonious action of this complete system, results Christian progression, glorious progression; for by their mutual action they necessarily support and increase each other. Every power of the soul, in its action, is under the influence of its appropriate grace; while all are under the influence of the Holy Spirit. Yet the will is still free, and, consequently, may still resist any or all of these influences, or comply with any or all of them. If it does the latter, action and progression continue. But if it does the former, the *brake* is on, and both the action and the progression are retarded or wholly stopped—while a very different action is introduced, resulting in *retrogression*, as far as it extends, for the *brake* may only be applied, say, to brotherly kindness; but, by a kind of sympathy, all the active powers feel the shock, and are more or less enfeebled in their action. But so far as the will has positively forbidden right action, there is action in the contrary direction; for here there is no standing still—onward, or backward, is the unalterable law with regard to this machine.

"For," says the Apostle, "if these things be in you, and abound, they make you that ye shall neither be barren nor unfruitful." It is obvious that the words "barren," and "unfruitful," are of synonymous import; not so the original Greek words which they are designed to represent, ουκ αργους ουδε ακαρπους. The latter word, *akarpous*, means barren, or unfruitful; but the former, *argous*, means *unemployed, inactive, idle, slothful*. It is so rendered by Parkhurst, Greenfield, Whitby, Wesley, Dr. Adam Clarke, and, in short, all whom I have consulted. With this criticism the Apostle's words are at once seen to be *accurate, expressive*, and *important*, in the last degree. "If these things be in you, and abound, they make you that ye shall neither be inactive nor unfruitful." The person in whom all these principles are in lively operation, and *abounding*, cannot possibly be *unemployed, idle, slothful, inactive*. To say he can, implies a positive contradiction. You might as well talk about a perfect *locomotive* being inactive with a full head of steam on, as to talk about such a man being *inactive*, or idle. What the Apostle says, is strictly and absolutely true. *These things being in you, and abounding, they make you that ye shall not be idle, slothful, inactive.* The man in whom all these principles are in harmonious action, *must* move, and move *in the right direction too.* The harmonious action of *faith*, courage, knowledge, temperance, patience, godliness, brotherly kindness, and love, *must* move in the right direction. Love guided by knowledge directs to its proper object as truly as the needle points to the pole. The same is true of *brotherly kindness, courage*, and *godliness;* while the impetuous onward rush of the more ardent affections are tempered, softened, and controlled by *temperance* and *patience.* Meantime, the whole soul rests upon the atonement by *faith,* moving, so to speak, as upon a pivot, while in holy affection she turns to every object that legitimately claims her attention. See that holy Apostle Paul, for example, as he flies from Jerusalem round by Illyricum, exclaiming "The love of Christ constraineth us, because we thus judge, that if one died for all, then were all dead." Yet, while he is thus flying to the rescue of Jew and Gentile, barbarian, Scythian, bond and free, he exclaims, "The life that I now live in the flesh, I live by the faith of the Son of God, who loved me, and gave himself for me." Again, "I determined to know nothing among you, save Jesus Christ, and him crucified." Again, " The law of the

Spirit of life in Christ Jesus, hath made me free from the law of sin and death." And yet again "Nay, in all these things we are more than conquerors, through him that loved us. For I am persuaded, that neither death, nor life, nor angels, nor principalities, nor powers, nor things present, nor things to come, nor height, nor depth, nor any other creature, shall be able to separate us from the love of God which is in Christ Jesus our Lord." Thus does his soul cleave to and rest in Jesus by faith, while in holy and ardent affection he flies to the help of every child of man. Truly here is action, powerful, irresistible action; and that in the right direction. I say, irresistible action; for, heroically and triumphantly, he bids defiance to all the opposing powers that were, or that could be brought against him; exclaiming, "None of these things move me, neither count I my life dear unto me, so that I might finish my course with joy." And waxing still more bold he exclaims, "Who shall separate us from the love of Christ?" Then specifying every conceivable evil principle and agency, such as, *tribulation, distress, persecution, famine, nakedness, peril, sword,* and numerous others; he sets them all at defiance, and gives to all worlds the most convincing proof that his boasting is not in vain, by going right forward in the face of every enemy, and in the midst of perils by sea and by land; shouting as he goes, "Thanks be unto God which always causeth us to triumph;" adding, "If God be for us, who can be against us?" To this challenge all his enemies were silent, hence he went on from conquest to conquest, till he finished his course with joy! Nor has the challenge been taken up to this day, though the church has been repeating it from then till now. And it is firmly believed that it never will be taken up. And, what is still more strange, many a poor saint, not worth a dollar in the world, has repeated this challenge, and many such are still repeating it, and hurling it right in the face of all their enemies; but as yet no one has ever dared to join issue: and we confidently believe that it may be repeated with perfect safety by the poorest and the feeblest of all who trust in Jesus. And it is quite certain, that having these things in them and abounding, they will not be *inactive, idle* or *slothful.* No, they *will* act, they *will* go forward, they *will* go about doing good, regardless of every threatening, every enemy, every danger. If their duty leads them to Jerusalem, Corinth, Rome, or Worms, they *will* be there, though there were as many devils there as there are tiles upon the house-tops. Yes, they *will* go, despite every threat, if they have in them faith, courage, knowledge, temperance, patience, godliness, brotherly kindness, and love, ABOUNDING according to the demands of the occasion. Nor is it possible even to conceive of a reason why they *should* not proceed when God thus calls and qualifies; and pledges his infinite perfections in their defence.

Idleness, inactivity, or slothfulness, must result from want of *faith, courage,* or *love;* or because all three are defective. For instance, you hear a man take the name of God in vain; or in some other way sin against God: and you know, consequently, that he is in danger of perishing: yet you do not reprove or warn him, though God has commanded you to do so. Now, why do you not? Evidently because you lack *courage,* or *love,* or *both:* if you loved him, you would try to save him, regardless of any supposed inconvenience resulting from your efforts to that end. Would a mother, on beholding her child in danger of perishing, begin to count up the little inconveniences that would probably result from her attempts to save her child? No, her love would move her to instant and energetic action, not allowing her even to think of her own safety, much less probable inconveniences. Your faith, too, is defective in such instances of *inaction:* you do not believe God's threatening, either as it regards your own disobedience, or your neighbor's daring sins; or, it may be, you do not believe that your reproof or warning would have any good effect upon the offender. In either, or all of these ways, your unbelief may prevent your acting in the case. But if you firmly believed both the command and the threatening, you would certainly reprove and warn your neighbor, especially if you loved him as you should. Take another instance. You are commanded to wait upon God in his appointed means of grace, say, the weekly prayer-meeting: and to this command also he adds exceeding great and precious promises; yet you absent yourself from the prayer-meeting, and that, perhaps, habitually. Why? Evidently because you lack faith, or love, or both. You do not love to be there. And you do not love to be there because you do not love God, or his cause, or his people, as you should. And your faith, too, is defective! You do not believe God would meet with you there and bless you. You say, "What should we be profited if we should pray unto him?" Neither do you believe that "his blessing maketh rich." If you did, you would certainly be there, and seek his blessing earnestly, knowing that "every one that seeketh findeth." But you say, it may be, "The evening is cold," or, "it is wet," and this, you think, fully accounts for your not being there. But I do not think so. Allow me to ask a single question. Suppose you fully believed that you would receive ten dollars by going that distance at the same hour, and that you would lose that sum if you did not go, would you go? Yea, verily, and that for a much less sum, even if it were both colder and darker than it is on prayer-meeting night. In this way any one may easily judge of the strength of his faith, and also of the value he places upon God's blessing! If he would go farther to obtain a few dollars, than he would go to obtain God's blessing, his promised blessing in his own appointed means, it is evident that his faith, and his love, and his estimate of the divine blessing, are very small. To such it is, that God says, "Go to the ant, ye sluggard." Here, too, all may see, who are willing to see, why there are so many idlers in matters of religion; they lack these holy active graces of the Spirit, for if these things were in them, and abounding, they would not, they could not, be idle. O! ye idlers, hear ye the word of the Lord, and add these things to your faith, if you have any faith, and if you have not, repent and believe the gospel, otherwise you will be damned, for the mouth of the Lord hath spoken it. "He that believeth not shall be damned."

The Apostle not only says, "these things being in you, and abounding, make you that ye shall not be idle," but he adds, "nor unfruitful." This, too, is *strictly* and *necessarily* true. Such action must produce fruit, good fruit, and much of it. To all such actors, God himself says, "Your labor shall not be in vain in the Lord." Such vigorous plants of grace must, and do, produce fruit; "some thirty, some sixty, and some an hundred fold." Nor is this true in regard to spiritual things only. Such persons are "not slothful in business," while they are "fervent in spirit, serving the Lord." While these principles moved Paul to fly "from Jerusalem round by Illyricum," for the glory of God and the salvation of souls; they also moved him to make tents, when that was necessary; while other disciples were moved to "go a fishing," when that was necessary. And Jesus was with them when they were fishing, as well as when they were preaching; yea, and assisted in preparing a breakfast for those fishermen, as well as in helping them to catch the fish. To see Jesus standing by that "fire of coals," by the sea of Galilee, "and fish laid thereon, and bread," and to hear him say, "Bring of the fish which ye have now caught;" and, finally, "Children, come and dine," is to my mind one of the most sublime, instructive, and affecting scenes ever witnessed; while it is a withering rebuke to proud *idlers*. "He went about doing good," saying, "knowest thou not that I must be about my Father's business;" I must work the work of him that sent me;" "My meat is to do the will of him that sent me." He fed the hungry disciples by the sea-shore, and the hungry multitudes in the wilderness. "He went about all the cities and villages, teaching in their synagogues, and preaching the Gospel of the Kingdom, and healing every sickness, and every disease among the people. But, when he saw the multitudes, he was moved with compassion on them, because they fainted, and were scattered abroad, as sheep having no shepherd. Then saith he unto his disciples, The harvest truly is plenteous, but the laborers are few. Pray ye, therefore, the Lord of the harvest, that he will send forth laborers into his harvest." Truly, Jesus was neither *idle* nor *unfruitful;* neither are his disciples, for they are influenced by the very same principles that influenced their Master; *they have the mind that was in Jesus,* every one of them, without a single exception; for "if any man have not the spirit of Christ, he is none of his." Hence, they labor as he did, going about doing good; to the bodies as well as to the souls of their fellows, in every possible way; feeding the hungry and clothing the naked; visiting those who are sick, and those who are in prison; willing to cook a meal of victuals, make a tent, or go a fishing, when necessary; singing as they go,—

"Jesus, confirm my heart's desire,
  To work, and speak, and think for thee;
 Still let me guard the holy fire,
  And still stir up thy gift in me.

"Ready for all thy perfect will,
My act of faith and love repeat,
Till death thy endless mercies seal,
And make the sacrifice complete."

It is evident that a country inhabited by such a people, a people having "these things in them, and abounding," must prosper every way. "The wilderness and the solitary place shall be glad for them; and the desert shall rejoice, and blossom as the rose. It shall blossom abundantly, and rejoice, even with joy and singing: the glory of Lebanon shall be given unto it, and the excellency of Carmel and Sharon." Where such people dwell for a given period, hamlets, towns, and cities, will rise all over the land. Here "the pastures of the wilderness, and the little hills rejoice on every side. The pastures are clothed with flocks; the valleys also are covered with corn; they shout for joy, they also sing." Such people are "like a tree planted by the rivers of water, that bringeth forth his fruit in his season, their leaf also shall not wither, and whatsoever they do shall prosper." Being influenced by the principles, and guided by the knowledge here specified, they cannot be either inactive or unfruitful. This is the godliness that "is profitable unto all things, having the promise of the life that now is, and of that which is to come." They "have their fruit unto holiness, and the end everlasting life." Such a people are emphatically a power for good; they have "power with God and with men," and they prevail. "They turn the world upside down," and under their culture the wilderness becomes a fruitful field, in every sense of the word, *and that just in proportion as these things are in them.* All this is confirmed by the most incontestable facts of history. *Weakness, indolence,* and *unfruitfulness,* ever have been, and now are, the characteristics of the people who have been, or now are, destitute of these principles. If, being forced, such people have built pyramids, or other monuments, to gratify the pride of tyrants, this affords no exception to the rule: so far as any people are destitute of these principles, they are indolent, weak, and unfruitful; and such has ever been the fact, and ever will be. What has paganism done for this country? What has it done for any country? What has been done for any country by those religious systems which were, or are, destitute of the principles here specified? The facts of history afford but one answer to this question. On the other hand, it is equally clear that wherever these divine principles have been in any people under the whole heaven, they have been *active, powerful,* and *fruitful,* and that just in the proportion that these things were in them and were abounding. O how marvellously has the fisherman of Galilee seized upon all the great principles of *action, power,* and *fruitfulness!* But the secret is simply this, *he wrote and spoke as he was moved by the Holy Ghost.* Had it not been so, he never could have declared, in a few words, what was never known, or conceived, much less taught, by the wise men, so called, of Greece and Rome: never could have said, in a few words, more than was ever known by any uninspired man, however learned, either since or before. How abundantly has that modern saying been admired and praised, "Knowledge is power." But this saying sinks into insignificance when compared with these few words of the Apostle Peter; yet how few have been particularly struck with them! The fact is, mere knowledge is not power; to be a power it must be properly applied. The devil has a vast amount of knowledge, doubtless, *yet he has no power for good: absolutely none.* Whereas the man who has the knowledge and the other particulars specified by the Apostle, is such a power that he triumphs over every opposing power: he "has power with God and with men, and prevails;" and triumphs over the powers of darkness also!

But observe, for it is a point of great importance, the Apostle connects all with "the knowledge of our Lord Jesus Christ." Without this knowledge we are powerless, whatever else we may have; but every man who has it, is a power, especially if he is careful to add to it, the other particulars here specified; then he will "neither be idle nor unfruitful in the knowledge of our Lord Jesus Christ." A man may be idle and unfruitful in the knowledge of Plato, Socrates, and other men of fame; but not "in the knowledge of our Lord Jesus Christ." "This is life eternal, that they might know thee the only true God, and Jesus Christ whom thou hast sent." To have life and power, we must be connected with Jesus Christ in the way here specified by the Apostle; for "Jesus is the way, the truth, and the life;" and "all power is given unto him in heaven and in earth." Hence no other being can give either life or power to fallen man; for no other being has either one or the other to give. In view of this fact, how forcible are the words of the beloved disciple:—"This is the true God, and eternal life. Little children, keep yourselves from idols. Amen."

CHAPTER XIV.

To make the additions here specified, we must give all diligence. "These things" do not come by chance—Having seen the consequences of making these additions; and abounding, we are now shown the awful consequences of not doing so—All this is addressed to them that have obtained Apostolic faith—The distinctive characteristics of those who do, and of those who do not, make these additions—Some thoughts with regard to those who have backslidden as here stated—The infallibility of those who "do these things."

To make the additions here specified we must *give all diligence.* These things do not come to us by chance, nor are they forced upon us by any power, either human or divine. I may be courageous or pusillanimous; I may seek and find knowledge, or I may live and die in ignorance; I may be temperate or intemperate; I may be patient or peevish; I may be godly or ungodly; I may be kind or unkind; I may love or hate; I may increase or diminish the good that is already in me; I may be idle or active; fruitful or unfruitful. All this is matter of fact and experience. These are among the things that are only found by seeking for them. And to obtain them we must seek with diligence. Nor will ordinary diligence suffice for this purpose.

Therefore the Apostle exhorts us to *give all diligence*. That is, I suppose, make a wise use of all the knowledge and grace you have, and use all the means in your power to obtain more. Ask, seek, strive. "Be instant in season and out of season." Leave no stone unturned. "Buy the truth, and sell it not." "What thy hand findeth to do do it with thy might." O what a change would soon be witnessed in the church if all her members would faithfully practice these teachings of the Apostle! and what a change would soon be witnessed in the world, as well as in the church! Doubtless we would soon witness such revolutions as were witnessed in apostolic times. But alas! while few are giving all diligence to obtain these things, they are multitudinous who are seeking ritualistic trumpery and other carnal gratifications; while others are so indolent and useless, that it is extremely difficult to say why God permits such useless lumber to remain on the earth, seeing they are only a burden to themselves and others; mere stumbling-blocks over which others stumble and fall.

Having exhorted us to add these things and to give all diligence to that end; and having shown the happy consequences of so doing, the Apostle now shows the consequences of not doing so "But he that lacketh these things is blind, and cannot see afar off, and hath forgotten that he was purged from his old sins." Such are the consequences of not adding. If you do not add, you will lose what you have; if you do not progress you will retrograde. This is evidently the teaching of the Apostle in the passage before us. And in view of this, he again urges the necessity of diligence. "Wherefore the rather, brethren, give diligence to make your calling and election sure: for if ye do these things ye shall never fall." If you add these things, giving all diligence to that end: if you have all these things in you, and all abounding, you thus "make your calling and election sure," and "shall never fall." "But he that lacketh these things," that is, does not add them, "is blind, and cannot see afar off, and hath forgotten that he was purged from his old sins."

Now, let it be remembered, that the Apostle addresses all this to them that have obtained like precious faith with us through the righteousness of God our Saviour Jesus Christ;" and then still more pointedly, to each one as having been "purged from his old sins." Remember, too, that none but those who have this faith can make these additions, for it is to this faith that all these things are added, as we formerly showed. It follows, that this very individual, who had this "precious faith," and had been "purged from his old sins;" "is blind and cannot see afar off, and hath FORGOTTEN that he was purged from his old sins;" and all this is in consequence of lacking these things; and he lacks, or is destitute of these things, because he did not add them; and he did not add them, because he did not "give diligence" to that end. In a word, *he did not progress, and therefore backslid.* Forward or backward is the fixed and unalterable law in Christian morals!

Now let us more carefully notice the state of this backslider, as here described by the Apostle. "He is blind, and cannot see afar off, and hath forgotten that he was purged from his old sins." I doubt whether I can do better than give Dr. Adam Clarke's comment upon these words; I will therefore lay it before the reader, as he may not have the doctor's Commentary.

"Verse 9. *But he that lacketh these things.*] He, whether Jew or Gentile, who professes to have FAITH in God, and has not added to that FAITH *fortitude, knowledge, temperance, patience, godliness, brotherly kindness,* and universal *love,* is *blind*—his understanding is darkened, *and cannot see afar off,* μυωπαζων, *shutting his eyes against the light, winking,* not able to look truth in the face, nor to behold that God whom he once knew was reconciled to him: and thus it appears he is *wilfully blind,* and *hath forgotten that he was purged from his old sins,* has at last, through his non-improvement of the grace which he received from God, his faith ceasing to work by love, lost the evidence of things not seen; for, having grieved the Holy Spirit, by not showing forth the virtues of him who called him into his marvellous light, he has lost the testimony of his sonship; and then, darkness and hardness having taken place of *light* and *filial confidence,* he first calls his former experience into doubt, and questions whether he has not put enthusiasm in place of religion. By this means his darkness and hardness increase, his memory becomes indistinct and confused, till at length he forgets the work of God on his soul, next denies it, and at last asserts that the knowledge of salvation, by the remission of sins, is impossible, that no man can be saved from sin in this life. Indeed, some go so far as to deny the Lord that bought them; renounce Jesus Christ as having made an atonement for them; and finish their career of apostacy by utterly denying his Godhead. Many cases of this kind have I known; and they are all the consequences of believers not continuing to be workers together with God, after they had experienced his pardoning love."

Unquestionably the doctor has seized the leading ideas of the Apostle, but whether he has, or has not, stated the exact way in which the retrogression takes place, the fact that it has taken place, or that it may take place, and that to the extent specified by the Apostle, remains indisputable. Nor can the *way* in which the apostacy takes place, be better stated than it is stated by the same inspired authority that states the fact of its possibility:—*If you add these things, if they are in you and abound, you must be active, and fruitful; and can neither backslide or apostatize; but he that lacketh these things is blind, and cannot see afar off, and hath forgotten that he was purged from his old sins.*" This is the sum and substance of the Apostle's teaching. And the state here described, call it that of an apostate, or any thing else you please, is certainly an awful state: and it is, or may be, the state of one who once had like precious faith with the Apostles, and had been once purged from his old sins. *These are the facts!*

One characteristic of unbelievers, as given in Scripture, is, that they look at the things that are temporal, the things that belong to this world; while the grand characteristic of believers is, that they look at the things that are spiritual and eternal. The objects and rewards of faith, are represented by our Apostle as being "far off," so far that the man who "lacks these things" cannot see them: and, like one who is short-sighted, and who tries to see a distant object, that his neighbor speaks of, and sees clearly, he contracts and dilates his eyes, and after thus squinting and trying his best, and yet failing to see the object, he finally concludes there is no such object to be seen, that it is his neighbor that is mistaken not himself! Just so the blind man spoken of by Peter; blind as to the objects and rewards of faith, he hears others talk about these things, but after a kind of squinting effort, and utterly failing to see them, because they are far off, he finally concludes there are no such things, and settles down as a believer in all unbelief; is henceforth content to confine his attention to those things which he can see with such faculties as he has; and all this is quite natural; though he has no right to conclude that others cannot see distant objects, simply because he cannot. The blindness here spoken of by the Apostle, is spoken of with equal distinctness by our blessed Lord, in John xiv. 16, 17. "And I will pray the Father, and he shall give you another Comforter, that he may abide with you forever; even the Spirit of truth; whom the world cannot receive, because it seeth him not, neither knoweth him: but ye know him; for he dwelleth with you, and shall be in you." The same fact is thus stated by Paul; "But the natural man receiveth not the things of the Spirit of God; for they are foolishness unto him; neither can he know them, because they are spiritually discerned." Now, the man of whom Peter speaks, though once enlightened, and purged from his old sins, is again in this state, and is so for the reasons specified by the Apostle. If the world cannot see because it receiveth not the Spirit, neither can this man, because he has grieved away the Spirit. The reason is precisely the same in each case. When the light is taken away or extinguished, he who had it is no better off than he who never had it, unless so far as he may remember what he once saw: but the memory had also suffered, in the man of whom Peter speaks, so that he had "forgotten" what he once knew; he had both lost sight of, and forgotten, what he once knew and saw. We may not be able to understand these mental and moral *phenomena*, but the fact is indisputable, being matter of observation and experience.

But, bad as is the case here described by the Apostle, I am not prepared to say that it is hopeless. Formerly, when he was both blind and dead, Jesus gave him eyes to see, and quickened him into life, and he may be able to do so again. But, to this end, he must cry, like blind Bartimeus, "Jesus, thou son of David, have mercy on me." The Holy Spirit may still be given to him if he will ask him; and in his light, and under his life-giving influences, he may yet "remember from whence he has fallen, and repent and do his first works." And unless he do so, it is quite certain that he will perish. True, his last state may be worse than the first; but it is equally true that the dead may still hear the voice of the Son of God; equally true that Jesus still gives eyesight to the blind, hearing to the deaf, utterance to the dumb, and feet to the lame. Yea, he still cleanses the lepers, and raises the dead. And even now, he cries, long and loud, to dead Laodiceans; and knocks at the closed door, intreating an entrance, and promising that he will come in and sup with them, if they will only grant him an entrance. O, let us not limit the Most High: for he is still "the LORD, the LORD God, gracious and merciful, long-suffering, and abundant in goodness and in truth, forgiving iniquity, and transgression, and sin." But if such backsliders will still persist in their own ways, still persist in closing their eyes, their ears, and their hearts; the time will certainly come, when even this merciful God will cease to be gracious, when his mercy shall be clean gone, when he shall even swear in his wrath that they shall not enter his rest. O ye blind and dead, *twice dead*, Laodicean backsliders, cry, cry mightily to God, and give him no rest till he restore unto you the joys of his salvation. And if you are again saved by grace through faith, see to it that you "add to your faith courage, and to courage knowledge, and to knowledge temperance, and to temperance patience, and to patience godliness, and to godliness brotherly kindness, and to brotherly kindness love." And see that all "these things" are not only "in you," but that they ABOUND. Then ye shall no longer be either idle or unfruitful.

"Wherefore," says the Apostle, in view of the stupendous interests that are pending, in view of the fact that "some, concerning faith have made shipwreck," in view of the awful danger of your coming short of heaven and perishing forever; "wherefore," in view of all these considerations, and many others, not to be expressed, or even conceived; "Wherefore the rather, brethren, give diligence to make your calling and election sure: for if ye do these things ye shall never fall." "Give diligence," "add these things;" have them "in you," and have them *abounding*, and "ye shall never fall." The same truth is declared in the fifteenth Psalm, "He that doeth these things shall never be moved." No, never. "He shall be as Mount Zion, which cannot be moved." Suns, moons, and stars may, yea, and will fall: but "He that doeth these things shall never be moved," much less fall! Such believing, courageous, progressing Christians, can, yea, and do sing: "God is our refuge and strength, a very present help in trouble. Therefore will not we fear, though the earth be removed, [mark their faith and courage,] and though the mountains be carried into the midst of sea; though the waters thereof roar and be troubled, though the mountains shake with the swelling thereof. Selah." No, for being thus faithful, they have the blessed assurance, "that neither death, nor life, nor angels, nor principalities, nor powers, nor things present, nor things to come, nor height, nor depth, nor any other creature, shall be able to separate them from the love of God which is in Christ Jesus, our Lord." "Here is the patience of the saints," and here is the *infallibility* of the saints; and in this infallibility I believe with my whole soul. IF YE DO THESE THINGS YE SHALL NEVER FALL. SELAH. "The mouth of the LORD hath spoken it." And though men may *gainsay* it, neither man nor devil can *unsay* it.

CHAPTER XV.

The final result of the progression—An "abundant entrance into the everlasting kingdom of our Lord and Saviour Jesus Christ"—These wonderful words and thoughts could only come to us by inspiration—An attempt to explain the word πλυδιως—The question, shall all who finally reach heaven, have this *abundant* entrance ministered unto them, is examined, and answered in the negative—It is again shown why some are a power, while others are not—Even for the same reason that the glorified shine as stars of different magnitudes—The word of God holds out no encouragement, no reward, to *idleness*.

For so an entrance shall be ministered unto you abundantly into the everlasting kingdom of our Lord and Saviour Jesus Christ." Such is the issue to which the Apostle conducts this glorious Christian progression. He conducts his conquering hero to a KINGDOM, an "EVERLASTING kingdom;" and leaves him in quiet, *undisputed, indisputable,* and *eternal* possession of it. The words with which the Apostle concludes this glorious progression, and the ideas which they are employed to express, are alike marvellous. All attempts to improve the language, or swell the ideas, must prove a failure. This may be seen in the attempts which commentators have made to this end. Mr. Wesley on the place, says, "Ye shall go in full triumph to glory." Doctor

Doddridge says, "Ye shall be received into it with circumstances of solemn pomp and distinguished honor." Dr. Clark says, "An abundant, free, honorable, and triumphant entrance shall be ministered to you into the everlasting kingdom. "This is very well, and probably the best that can be said, if the words of the Apostle be at all departed from. But it is easy to see that all such attempts fall immeasurably below the original.

While we would not attempt to improve, or in any way change, a single word in this truly wonderful conclusion, we may be permitted to call *special* attention to the marvellously expressive words which the Apostle employs, and which are well translated in the common version.

Observe then, the progression of which the Apostle has been speaking is represented as terminating in a KINGDOM; and the triumphant hero is represented as now entering into this kingdom 'for the *first time*. The kingdom is that of "our Lord and Saviour Jesus Christ." Hence, the entrance into it is said to be *ministered unto you*, not by ministering angels, but by the king himself, the Lord Jesus, who is "the king eternal, immortal, invisible," "the King of kings, and Lord of lords." He does not enter into his kingdom by ancestral right, nor by right of conquest, nor by any other right, save that which is derived from the atonement of Jesus Christ, whose is the kingdom. Hence the entrance is *ministered as the gift of grace*, to the finally faithful. The same truth is thus expressed by the Apostle Paul.—"I have fought a good fight, I have finished my course, I have kept the faith: henceforth there is laid up for me a crown of righteousness, which the Lord, the righteous judge, shall *give* me at that day: and not to me only, but unto all them also that love his appearing." Thus it is that Jesus is "the author and finisher of our faith;" he lifts the believer out of the horrible pit, sets his feet upon the rock, establishes his goings, supports, defends and leads him throughout the entire *progression:* and, finally, raises him to participate in his own throne and kingdom, placing the crown upon his head with his own hand. And the crown and kingdom thus *graciously bestowed*, can never be alienated either by fraud or force : the parties to whom the entrance is thus *ministered*, "shall reign forever and ever." Thus it is that Jesus " saves to the uttermost." And all, from first to last, is *the gift of grace*, "through the righteousness of our God and Saviour Jesus Christ." O how wonderful the words, and how glorious the thoughts, that God here proclaims to us from the lips of the humble fisherman of Galilee! Short of *inspiration* no human mind could originate these sublime conceptions, nor is it possible for human lips to express them as they are here expressed, till first touched with a live coal from the heavenly altar. Here the progressive life of the Christian is delinated with infallible accuracy from its commencement to its consummation; and that consummation is the gracious bestowment of an everlasting kingdom, even the kingdom of our Lord and Saviour Jesus Christ, who with his own hand places the crown upon the victor's head, and shares with him his own throne and kingdom. To express all this Peter says, "An entrance shall be ministered unto you ABUNDANTLY." The word πλουσιως, here translated *abundantly*, is very significant: it is used to express the greatest abundance of riches, both temporal and spiritual. Hence, in Eph. ii. 4, it is used to express the abounding mercy of God. And in 2. Cor. viii. 9, it is used to express the eternal and ineffable dignity, glory, and felicity of Christ before his incarnation. See also Col. iii. 16, Titus iii. 6, and Rev. ii. 9, where the same word occurs.

But while we make this feeble attempt to assist the reader to understand these inspired and truly glorious words, we are more delighted when we read them just as they stand in the common text. Nor are we satisfied to close our remarks with any other words. Hence we quote them again, that the reader may repeat them, and dwell upon them, till filled with wonder and ravished with delight. Hear them, read them, and dwell upon them, ye progressing Christians; and mark the end of this glorious Christian progress—"For so an entrance shall be ministered unto you abundantly into the everlasting kingdom of our Lord and Saviour Jesus Christ." Amen, and Amen.

> *Thus* let the pilgrim's journey end,
> *Thus*, O my Saviour, brother, friend,
> Receive me to thy breast.

Onward! onward! ye progressing Christians; "Looking for that blessed hope, and the glorious appearing of the great God and our Saviour Jesus

Christ." And to this end, " Let us lay aside every weight, and the sin which doth so easily beset us, and let us run with patience the race that is set before us, looking unto Jesus, the author and finisher of our faith ; who, for the joy that was set before him, endured the cross, despising the shame, and is set down at the right hand of the throne of God."

And let all who thus journey, sing as they go,—

> " Who suffer with our Master here,
> We shall before his face appear ;
> And by his side sit down ;
> To patient faith the prize is sure ;
> And all that to the end endure
> The cross, shall wear the crown.
>
> " Thrice blessed, bliss-inspiring hope !
> It lifts the fainting spirits up ;
> It brings to life the dead ;
> Our conflicts here shall soon be past,
> And you and I ascend at last,
> Triumphant, with our head.
>
> " That great, mysterious Deity,
> We soon with open face shall see ;
> The beatific sight
> Shall fill the heavenly courts with praise,
> And wide diffuse the golden blaze
> Of everlasting light."

Just here, a thought arises, which we think demands a moment's notice. Will all those who finally reach heaven, have ministered to them the abundant entrance of which the Apostle here speaks ? We do not hesitate to answer this question in the negative ; for this abundant entrance is the *termination*, and the *reward*, of the progression here specified. But it is certain that many, through the abounding grace of God, will finally reach heaven, though they did not progress as here specified. Multitudes of children, for instance, who were never capable of this progression, are, nevertheless, saved in heaven through the atonement. And multitudes, we trust, after a life of sin, repent, fly to Jesus, and are finally saved, as it were, at the eleventh hour. Now these cannot be said to have made any progress, much less the progress here specified; hence, they cannot have ministered to them the abundant entrance of which the Apostle speaks, and which he promises to those who thus progress, and to those only. It is, in our judgment, folly to suppose, for instance, that the thief, who *repented and died upon the cross;* and Paul, who *fought a good fight, finished his course, and kept the faith;* shall have *the same entrance ministered unto them into the everlasting kingdom,* and *participate alike in the same glory.* No, they will most assuredly differ, even as one star differeth from another star in glory. The difference which distinguished them in this life, will equally distinguish them in that which is to come. Those who are distinguished by Christian progression here, and by corresponding moral power, will be equally distinguished by their glory hereafter. When John was permitted to look into heaven, he marked this distinction, and has made a faithful record of it in his book of Revelations. In the seventh chapter, he tells us of a certain number, who were nearest to the throne; and being struck with something peculiar in their appearance, as well as with the fact that they were nearest to the throne, he inquired, or "one of the elders" started the question: "What are these, which are arrayed in white robes? and whence came they?" To this inquiry the following answer was given. "These are they which came out of great tribulation, and have washed their robes, and made them white in the blood of the Lamb. Therefore are they before the throne of God, and serve him day and night in his temple; and he that sitteth on the throne shall dwell among them. They shall hunger no more, neither thirst any more; neither shall the sun light on them, nor any heat. For the Lamb which is in the midst of the throne shall feed them, and shall lead them unto living fountains of water: and God shall wipe away all tears from their eyes." And in the fourteenth chapter, he tells us of a certain number of exalted spirits who "sung as it were a new song before the throne, and before the four beasts, and the elders: and no man could learn that song but the hundred and forty and four thousand, which were redeemed from the earth. These are they which were not defiled with women; for they are virgins. These are they which follow the Lamb whithersoever he goeth. These were redeemed from among men, being the first-fruits unto God and the Lamb. And in their mouth was found no guile: for they are without fault before the throne of God."

Now, we do not pretend to point out the exact

difference between these and other happy spirits in heaven, it is sufficient for our present purpose to call attention to the fact, that there is a difference, a great difference, and also, to the fact, that the glory which distinguishes them in heaven, is connected with the peculiar piety and sufferings which distinguished them upon earth.—"They came up out of great tribulation," etc., etc. "Therefore are they before the throne," etc., etc. These are the ideas that Charles Wesley develops in the following beautiful hymn:—

> "Who are these array'd in white,
>   Brighter than the noon-day sun?
> FOREMOST OF THE SONS OF LIGHT:
>   NEAREST THE ETERNAL THRONE?
> THESE ARE THEY THAT BORE THE CROSS;
>   NOBLY FOR THEIR MASTER STOOD;
> SUFF'RERS IN HIS RIGHTEOUS CAUSE;
>   *Foll'wers* of the dying God.
> OUT OF GREAT DISTRESS THEY CAME:
>   Washed their robes, by faith, below,
> In the Blood of yonder Lamb,—
>   Blood that washes white as snow;
> THEREFORE ARE THEY NEXT THE THRONE;
>   Serve their Maker day and night;
> God resides among his own,
>   God doth in his saints delight."

The poet has seized the grand points of the argument as marked in the text; and to fix attention upon these points I have caused some of the words to be printed in capitals. *They nobly stood for their Master, they suffered in his righteous cause, they bore the cross, they came up out of* GREAT TRIBU-

LATION; *therefore, they are foremost of the sons of light, nearest the eternal throne, brighter than the noon-day sun!* "And they sung a new song before the throne, and before the four living creatures, and the elders; and no man could learn that song but the hundred and forty-four thousand." The particulars by which they were distingushed on earth, and those by which they are distinguished in heaven, and the fact that the latter are gifts of grace in view of the former, are so clearly marked by the inspired penman, and by the poet in the above verses, that further remarks are unnecessary. But if any doubts should still remain, the following declaration of the great Judge must forever remove them:—"Behold, I come quickly; and my reward is with me, to give every man according as his work shall be." Even in this world the gifts of grace are bestowed according to the improvement of those who are the recipients of them; and in the next world, the rewards of grace will be proportioned according to that improvement. To him that gained ten pounds the judge will say, "Well done, good servant, because thou hast been faithful in a very little, be thou governor over ten cities." And to him that gained five pounds, he will say, "Be thou also over five cities." This is clearly the teaching of the Bible with regard to the gifts of grace, both here and hereafter. Nothing, of course, is merited; "for what hast thou that thou didst not receive?" Yet, God bestows or withholds certain gifts according as we do, or do not, use those already bestowed.

And here, too, we see why some men are a power, while others are not :—" The manifestation of the Spirit is given to every man to profit withal ;" and to such as make a good use of the grace already given, the promise is, " he shall have more abundance ;" while from another " shall be taken away even that which he hath," in consequence of his unfaithfulness to the grace given. Hence the reason why the one is a power, and the other powerless, is alike obvious, rational, and scriptural. It is alike unscriptural, and irrational, to suppose that those who "dwell in ceiled houses, that lie upon beds of ivory, and stretch themselves upon their couches, and eat the lambs out of the flock, and the calves out of the midst of the stall; that chant to the sound of the viol, that drink wine in bowls, and anoint themselves with chief ointments ;" should be such a power as were the Wesleys and Whitefield, who flew from city to city, and from village to village, preaching the gospel. Or travelling from common to common, as did John Wesley and John Nelson in Cornwal, preaching Jesus to the neglected and perishing multitudes, and supporting themselves, occasionally, with blackberries which they plucked by the wayside, and at night sleeping on the floor of some humble cot, Nelson having Burkett's Notes for his pillow, while he gave Wesley his coat, and upon that coat the Fellow of Lincoln College, Oxford, reposed his weary head as he slept upon the floor of that cot in the wilderness. Blessed men :—

"That humble cot upon the wild,
That stone beneath the tree,
And souls to heaven's love reconciled,—
These are enough for thee."

And, remember, these holy men continued thus to labor, till, one by one, in a good old age, they yielded up the ghost, and were gathered to their fathers;—

"Their bodies with their charge laid down,
And ceased at once to work and live."

Such are they to whom "an entrance shall be ministered abundantly, into the everlasting kingdom of our Lord and Saviour, Jesus Christ." These are they who "lay up treasure in heaven, where moth and rust do not corrupt, and where thieves do not break through nor steal." These are they who "rest from their labors, and their works do follow them." These are they who, *having turned many to righteousness*, shall *shine as the brightness of the firmament, and as the stars forever and ever.* O let not the slothful Christian, if there be such a being, or the old sinner, though finally saved, suppose that they shall finally share in these glorious rewards of grace which only belong to the faithful servants who progress to the extent specified by the Apostle in the Scripture which we have been attempting to explain. Such expectations are unscriptural, and can never be realized. No, the Scriptures hold out no encouragement, no reward, to idleness or indolence. It is to the faithful, the progressing

Christian, that the "abundant entrance," the "exceeding and eternal weight of glory," is promised. Arise, then, ye careless ones, and "add to your faith, courage; and to courage, knowledge; and to knowledge, temperance; and to temperance, patience; and to patience, godliness; and to godliness, brotherly kindness; and to brotherly kindness, love." And "these things being in you," see that they *abound*, and that more and more; so that ye shall always be exceeding your former self; "growing up into Christ, your living head in all things." O ye children of God, arise in good earnest, and "press toward the mark for the prize."

> "Soldiers of Christ, arise,
>   And put your armor on,
> Strong in the strength which God supplies
>   Through his eternal Son;
> Strong in the Lord of Hosts,
>   And in his mighty power,
> Who in the strength of Jesus trusts,
>   Is more than conqueror.
>
> "Stand then in his great might,
>   With all his strength endued;
> But take, to arm you for the fight,
>   The panoply of God:
> That having all things done,
>   And all your conflicts past,
> Ye may o'ercome, through Christ alone,
>   And stand entire at last."

Such is Christian progression; and such is its glorious consummation. And to all his people God says, as he said to Daniel, "Go thou thy way till the end be: for thou shalt rest, and stand in thy lot at the end of the days." Amen, and Amen.

"Full of immortal hope,
 We urge the restless strife,
 And hasten to be swallow'd up
 Of everlasting life.

"Lord, let us put on thee
 In perfect holiness;
 And rise prepared thy face to see,
 Thy bright, unclouded face.

"Thy grace with glory crown,
 Who hast the earnest given;
 And then triumphantly come down,
 And take us up to heaven."

"Blessed are they that do his commandments, that they may have right to the tree of life, and may enter in through the gates into the city." Amen.

www.ingramcontent.com/pod-product-compliance
Lightning Source LLC
Chambersburg PA
CBHW021157230426
43667CB00006B/434